THE BOY WHO LIVED

DAVID HOLMES lived a young boy's dream. A competitive gymnast, he was thrust into the Hollywood spotlight having been cast as a junior stuntman on the 1998 sci-fi movie, *Lost in Space*. Two years later he landed the role as stunt double to Daniel Radcliffe in the Harry Potter films where he battled dragons, explored underwater worlds and racked up more broomstick miles than anyone else in the Wizarding World. Then in 2009, David's world changed when a horrific accident fractured his C6 and C7 vertebrae, leaving him paralysed from the chest down. In a period of emotional soul-searching, he came to an important realisation: *he was a survivor, not a victim.*

Since then, he has raised hundreds of thousands of pounds through the David Holmes Harry Potter Cricket Cup and is an ambassador for the Wings for Life Foundation and the Royal National Orthopaedic Hospital in Stanmore. Elsewhere, David has been a published essay writer in the *New York Times*, and has given speeches in front of members of the royal family at both Buckingham Palace and Saint James's palace. He produced a BAFTA-nominated documentary about his life entitled *The Boy Who Lived* and posed for a powerful portrait in which he stripped naked and set himself on fire. He lives in Essex.

THE BOY WHO LIVED

DAVID HOLMES

WITH

MATT ALLEN

Foreword by Daniel Radcliffe

**HODDER &
STOUGHTON**

First published in Great Britain in 2024 by Hodder & Stoughton Limited
An Hachette UK company

4

A CIP catalogue record for this title is available from the British Library

Hardback ISBN 9781399738811
ebook ISBN 9781399738835
Trade Paperback ISBN 9781399738828

Typeset in Plantin Light by Manipal Technologies Limited

Printed and bound in Great Britain by Clays Ltd, Elcograf S.p.A.

Hodder & Stoughton policy is to use papers that are natural, renewable
and recyclable products and made from wood grown in sustainable forests.
The logging and manufacturing processes are expected to conform to the
environmental regulations of the country of origin.

Hodder & Stoughton Limited
Carmelite House
50 Victoria Embankment
London EC4Y 0DZ

The authorised representative in the EEA is Hachette Ireland, 8 Castlecourt
Centre, Castleknock Road, Castleknock, Dublin 15, D15 YF6A, Ireland
(email: info@hbgi.ie).

www.hodder.co.uk

To my nephews and all the children in my life, dream big,
fly high and always hold onto hope

To my family, thank you for loving me to being

To my friends, thank you for joining me on life's adventures

To the NHS, care workers and all who dedicate their lives to
helping others live theirs, thank you

To my film family, stunt community, Potter fans and all those who
believe in magic

To all children and adults who navigate their lives with a disability,
don't ever believe you are less than others, you will always be more

To Tommy, thank you for everything, always with love

And finally, three little words

Follow this link for access to extra
photo, video and music content!

CONTENTS

FOREWORD

In one way or another, David Holmes has been one of the most important people in my life for the last twenty-four years. We met when I had just turned eleven, and he was seventeen. I had been cast to play Harry Potter, and Dave was going to be my stunt double. I was an only child who had, when I was younger, wanted an older brother, and in Dave I met the perfect candidate for that role. He was charismatic, knowledgeable, unbelievably talented, confident bordering on cocky and incredibly good fun. Over the next six films, as I turned from a kid into a teenager, he was a friend, confidante and guidance counsellor, offering me advice and perspective from his vantage point a few years further down the road.

David was a gymnast and a stuntman. He was someone whose identity was inextricably linked to his physicality. He was fearless, masterful and thrilling as a stunt performer, always seemingly totally in control, but always pushing himself to greater heights. Since his accident in 2009, I have watched him face a challenge the magnitude of which most of the rest of us couldn't begin to comprehend. He has had to rebuild his identity from scratch. He was a physical being suddenly forced to reckon with the question of who he was, without any of the gifts that had made him feel like himself. He faced this challenge with more grace, kindness and positivity than I could ever imagine doing.

I was lucky enough to make a documentary about Dave over the last few years and was incredibly grateful to be able to tell his story. But there is only so much you can fit into a 90-minute film, and there is a lot more to Dave's story. Some of what's included here was cut from the film for time, and some wasn't included in the film because, well, we simply couldn't for reasons you'll understand! But this is his book, and he gets to say what's in here. So . . . get ready to read a lot more about drugs, his private parts and his illegally fast driving than we let him mention in the documentary.

As I mentioned before, when we met I was eleven and Dave was seventeen. At that age, a six-year age gap feels enormous, you almost feel like different species. But as we've got older the meaning of that age gap has flattened until we're both just two men in our thirties, with more in common than ever, and more that separates us. Watching Dave in the years since the accident has been both painful – because of course, as a friend, you wish none of this had ever happened and that you could somehow undo time to make it so that everything was back the way it was – and also one of the privileges of my life: to be able to watch one of my best friends display so much courage, so much strength of character, so much empathy in the face of relentless adversity, has been humbling and awe-inspiring. I have been incredibly lucky to have Dave as a part of my life. Everyone who knows Dave feels lucky to have him in their lives and always will. He's a one-off, a rare human being and someone I'm proud and honoured to know.

DANIEL RADCLIFFE, 2024

THE BOY WHO LIVED

PILOT: YOU'RE ONLY LIVING WHEN YOU'RE
NEARLY DYING

CREATED BY DAVID HOLMES
WRITTEN BY DAVID HOLMES

RIPPLE PRODUCTIONS//

THE BOY WHO LIVED

OPEN ON:
101 WARNER BROS. STUDIOS, LEAVESDEN, ENGLAND

January 2009:
*In Leavesden's cavernous D Stage, we see a still image of
DAVID HOLMES – 25-year-old stunt performer and daredevil
double to the world-famous teenage actor DANIEL RADCLIFFE,
AKA HARRY POTTER. David is waiting to rehearse a dramatic
stunt for* Harry Potter and the Deathly Hallows, *the sev-
enth film in the multi-million-dollar franchise. In it,
he will fly backwards, as part of a showdown in Godric's
Hollow with Voldemort's pet serpent, Nagini. To achieve
this effect, David has been placed into a harness, which
is fixed to a wire that runs the length of the studio. At
the other end is a series of weights. When dropped, the
transference of energy will propel David through the air.
And if all goes well, he will collide – spectacularly, but
safely – with a wall of crash mats. It's a standard technique, and all the safety precautions have been taken. But
as with all stunt work, the risks are high, and accepted
as such.*

*All does not go well. As we wait for David's call to
action from industry renowned stunt director GREG POWELL,
he reveals the consequences of the dramatic events to come.*

DAVID:
[VOICEOVER] Here it is: The last second before my life
changed for ever. The last second I will stand for.
The last second I will feel everything. I've already
had my last cuddle, my last dance, my last use of a
shower or toilet unaided. Because one second after
this photo was taken, I will break my neck.

FADE OUT

GREG POWELL:
[SHOUTING] OK, David. Ready?

PROLOGUE

DAVID:
[SHOUTING] Yeah.

FADE IN

The still photo has come alive. David is preparing himself for the force of movement to come. He will feel pain – he knows that, but it's nothing he hasn't experienced, and overcome, before. During a ten-year career in the stunt game, his body has been marked with broken bones, fractured limbs, multiple concussions, and several bloody noses, plus a slight case of the bends. He is short, and small in stature – five foot two and slim – which has led a lot of people to underestimate him in the past. But David is also muscular and flexible and has learned to use these doubts as fuel. It energises him for death-defying feats like this one. His adrenaline surges. It's go-time.

The usual production crew is in attendance for a rehearsal of this kind. Among them is David's fellow stuntman and best mate, MARC MAILLEY. As they watch, David adjusts his feet and waits for the inevitable countdown.

GREG POWELL:
[SHOUTING] Three . . .
. . . Two . . .
. . . One . . .
ACTION!

The weights hit the floor with a percussive WHOOMPH. We hear the whizz of wires as David is launched into the air and across the room at high speed. But something is wrong. He's moving too fast. As his body connects with the wall of crash pads, spine first, he does so at a dangerous angle, his body folding into itself. David's nose smashes into his chest, severing his C6 and C7 vertebrae. He hits the floor with a painful thud. As he lies there, breathless, in agony, unable to talk, his nerve endings scorched, his muscles bucking and wrenching, there is the sense that something has gone terribly wrong.

3

Greg and Marc run to David's side. He isn't moving.

GREG:
[SHOUTING] David!
[THEN QUIETLY] *David . . .*

DAVID:
[MOANING]. . .

GREG:
[SQUEEZING DAVID'S HAND] Breathe.
[SLOWLY] Breathe.
David, can you squeeze my fingers? Tell me what you feel.

DAVID:
[MOANING]. . .
I can't feel anything.
Fuck. I've broken my neck.

David looks into Greg's eyes fearfully. He is struggling to breathe and can barely speak. His look says it all. This is bad. From behind him, people are running. Someone is shouting for an ambulance.

MARC:
Stay still, mate. Stay completely still.

[WHISPERING] Help's on the way.

David closes his eyes. Shit! Is he dead? Then they flicker again. Marc checks his breathing. He's blacked out. Thank God.

MARC:
Shit.

PROLOGUE

SHIT!
[LOOKING AROUND] Who's calling the fucking ambulance?

David's eyes open again. His face is twisted in pain. He's trying to communicate something to Marc, but the words are too quiet to hear. Marc leans in closer.

MARC:
Dude . . .
It's OK. Save your strength—

DAVID:
Don't. Call—

MARC:
[LEANING CLOSER]: Stay still, Dave—

DAVID:
Don't call . . .
. . . My mum . . .

MARC:
OK?

DAVID:
Don't . . .
. . . Worry her.

Marc and Greg look at one another in shock. A nurse from the studio rushes over. She's carrying a small bottle of oxygen. David's eyes flick to the left. He groans again.

MARC:
Mate . . . What?

DAVID:
[BETWEEN BREATHS] Camera.

Marc follows David's eyes. Across the studio is a cam-corder, a device he uses for every filming session. It's set on a tripod. A green light on the side is blinking, which means the camera has captured David's accident in full. The footage is normally used to check his performances, to see if anything can be improved in his latest stunt. This time, the camcorder contains his last ever stunt and a lifeline to his financial future.

DAVID:
[WHISPERING] Mate . . . Guard it with your fucking life.

The nurse fixes an oxygen mask to David's face, taking care not to move his neck. His eyes flicker shut. He's blacked out again. There is more shouting. Two paramedics sprint into the studio space. Greg and Marc stand back to let them in. They watch silently, their lives changed for ever.

FADE OUT.

INTRODUCTION

THE UNKNOWN STUNTMAN

Spoiler alert: This book has been written from a wheelchair. That's because your author is a quadriplegic, paralysed from the chest down due to the horrific accident described in that script, that scene, *that stunt* – the very last time I would walk, jump or fly as a stuntman. In January 2009, a wire gag* gone wrong resulted in me colliding with a crash mat at an incredible velocity, leaving me with fractured C6 and C7 vertebrae. My condition has since been diagnosed as being degenerative. That means my working limbs will fade in strength over time, and as well as losing the use of my arms, there's a very real chance that at some point in the future I'll need mechanical assistance to perform the God-given functions of breathing, speaking and eating.

So, fuck my life. *Right?*

Not a chance, because the Cliff Notes from my career make for equally powerful reading. Up until the accident, I had The Dream Job: between the ages of fourteen and twenty-five I worked as a professional stuntman, seven of those years as the lead stunt double to Daniel Radcliffe on the Harry Potter movies. As part of my contract, I became the world's first ever Quidditch player. I leaped from castles and combatted dragons; I navigated underwater worlds and racked up more broomstick miles than any other human. I even battled the dark wizard himself, Lord Voldemort – *He Who Must Not*

---

* Gag: an industry nickname for the word 'stunt'.

Be Named. That is, until everything was snatched away. Not that I am looking for sympathy. I knew what I was getting into from the very first day on a movie set where the mortal risks that faced a working stunt performer were bloody obvious to everybody involved. So if it's tragedy porn you are after, maybe go elsewhere.

I wasn't alone in that attitude either. My line of work was extreme and the stunt industry I'd joined was grounded in mortal risk. Among my peers in Wizarding World, there were all sorts of catchphrases and mantras that served as a reminder of the fine line between the successful execution of a gag and a life-changing accident where the performer crashed and burned – sometimes literally. Among them: *Never show pain, never complain. Take the whack.* And: *You're only living when you're nearly dying.* None of this was unusual, or even new. Alpha male and female stunt performers had been around ever since the game began and during the early iterations of movie-making at the start of the 20th century, some Hollywood actors performed their own gags. Audiences watched as the likes of Buster Keaton, Charlie Chaplin and Douglas Fairbanks hung from clock faces suspended several storeys up, stood frozen as tonnes of building collapsed around them, or slid down the sails of a pirate ship, cutlass in hand, a knife clamped between their teeth. The safety protocols in those days were sketchy. If an actor missed their mark by an inch or two, death waited for them on the other side, and audiences packed the cinemas to watch the action. The story behind the mind-blowing box office receipts was undeniable too: gags made proper bank.

Long before I'd signed my first contract as a child stunt 'man', the daredevil industry had been upgraded considerably and from 1910 or so, professional stunt performers, some of them former rodeo riders and circus showmen, were tasked with doing the dangerous work. With them came all sorts of cinematic advancements in tech and equipment. Performers, male and female, were thrown about by technical wires, hydraulic launch pads like air rams, and repurposed big top equipment like the Russian swing. Later, Computer Generated Imagery (CGI) transformed studio hangars stuffed with green screens, safety mats and wires into castle turrets, cliff edges, or the open ramps of a plane flying at high altitude. But realism was everything and some actors, like Tom Cruise, still insisted on performing their own stunts, the most famous of which took place in *Mission: Impossible – Dead Reckoning*, where he launched his motorbike from the side of a cliff before parachuting to the ground. Director Christopher McQuarrie later described it as the most dangerous stunt ever attempted, which wasn't surprising given the gag required 13,000 bike jumps and 500 hours of skydiving training.

Hollywood's worst-kept secret is that stunt work is the secret sauce – it brings films to life. Like the boulder escape during the opening minutes of *Raiders of the Lost Ark*, or the forest fight in *Crouching Tiger, Hidden Dragon*. Thrills and spills put bums on seats too, such as the chariot race in *Ben Hur*, the motorbike chase in *Terminator 2: Judgment Day*, and the rooftop helicopter scene in *The Matrix*. Violence is another crowd pleaser. There's the sword fight in *The Princess Bride*, and the harrowing opening scenes of *Saving Private Ryan*. Meanwhile, the James Bond films have always brimmed with action: who could forget the bungee jump in *GoldenEye*, the parkour sprint in *Casino Royale* and the parachute ski jump in *The Spy Who Loved Me*? Even the first Quidditch match in *Harry Potter and the Philosopher's Stone* was a memorable chapter in cinematic history. All these scenes added adrenaline to the stories they were telling. And all of them were coordinated and performed by people like me.

But these moments of Hollywood magic sometimes came at a cost, and way too many actors have been injured in accidents like the one that changed my life. Others have died. While filming *Top Gun*, the stuntman Art Scholl was killed when his plane spun out of control, causing him to crash into the Pacific Ocean. During the making of *For Your Eyes Only*, the performer Paolo Rigon lost his life when filming the scene in which James Bond skied down a bobsleigh track. He was dragged under the sled at high speed. Most recently, a motorbike rider died when she crashed through a plate-glass window during the filming of *Deadpool 2*.

Despite these tragedies, and the daily reminders regarding the dangers I was facing, I never felt fear when working as a stunt performer. Nerves, yes. A little anxiety, of course. But abject terror? *No way.* As far as I was concerned, the rewards far outweighed the risks, as they did for anyone engaged in an extreme sport or lifestyle. There was adrenaline. There was acclaim. There was respect. And the rush of nailing a big stunt and then seeing it on the big screen was enough to help me push past the fear. While working on the Harry Potter films, I was once blasted backwards by a spell from Severus Snape, the Half-Blood Prince, *and it looked great.* Later, I was swiped sideways through the air by the Whomping Willow, *and it made movie magic.* The money helped too. And every scar and broken bone put another story into the stuntman hall of fame.

Until, of course, the moment arrived when those breaks became life-threatening.

*

To the outside world, the average stuntman probably looks like a reckless lunatic. Somebody with very little concern for their personal safety, and who operates in a world of Hollywood glitz and glamour. They think: Ryan Gosling's portrayal of a stuntman in the 2024 movie *The Fall Guy*. (Or if they're a little older, the original *Fall Guy*: Colt Seavers, as played by Lee Majors.) Certainly, the myth is partly true. I've rubbed shoulders with some of the most famous actors in the world, visited movie premieres, and guzzled champagne and dropped pills in exclusive nightclubs, often with workmates. But from my experience, the stunt team on a movie set generally operated in much the same way as a Formula 1 pit lane crew. We were super professional; there was zero room for errors; and trust was everything because the risks were so high. Everyone's lives rested in the hands of the group and a tight bond was forged between us within an environment where the performers worked hard and partied even harder. Those moments of hedonistic glamour, while memorable, were far outweighed by the late nights on set, long hours in studios, and slogging shifts where I often limped home feeling battered and bruised.

Not that I moaned about it. Pain management was one of the many attributes a stunt performer needed to possess, as was the ability to keep any complaining to a minimum. During my Wizarding World debut on *Harry Potter and the Philosopher's Stone*, I was the unfortunate recipient of a crack to the ribs when filming a scene in which I dressed up as Harry in his Hogwarts uniform. The director, Chris Columbus, needed me to battle the Voldemort-controlled Quirinus Quirrell – the Defence Against the Dark Arts professor from the Hogwarts School of Witchcraft and Wizardry – in the Underground Chambers. During the script, the stone falls to the floor, and it was written that both combatants should leap for it. In the build-up, during a deleted shot, the stuntman playing Quirrell, Paul Herbert, was supposed to fly across the chamber on a weight-controlled line known as a wire, which was being manipulated by some technicians outside the stage. Through no fault of his own, he missed his mark and smashed into me, his knees driving hard into my midriff. I felt two ribs break in the collision.

Usually, I did my best to hide the pain. I was only seventeen years old at the time and still getting used to the type of war wounds that came with the job. This time, the pain in my midriff was too much to ignore.

'I think I've broken my ribs,' I panted.

A reassuring hand touched me on the back. 'Are you OK? Can you breathe?' said a voice.

I was winded, but able to gulp down some air. 'Yeah, I can—'

'Right, up you get then,' said the voice. 'You haven't punctured a lung, and you can't do anything about a broken rib anyway, so suck it up.'

I rose to my feet, slowly. It was as if someone had taken a baseball bat to my side.

'And David?' said the voice.

'*Yeah?*'

'Don't say anything to anyone. The last thing I want to be doing today is filling out a health and safety report. *There's a good lad.*'

I soon learned that unless an ambulance was required, this was the typical reaction to an on-set accident.

Over the course of my career, there weren't many stitches, but there were plenty of concussions, and every day brought a nasty bruise or two. One time I even picked up a slight case of the bends while working in an underwater tank. Whenever I was pole-axed, clothes-lined or body-slammed, there was very little sympathy from my peers, if any, but the same attitude applied to everyone working in the job. Being human pain magnets was what we did; it was our life, and we were paid handsomely for the hurt.

Despite these daily brushes with agony, I never stressed before jumping off a building, or when waiting for someone to knock me over with a fast-moving car. Fear management came to me naturally, but that's because I was confident in my ability to deliver, no matter the gag. A top stunt performer had to be athlete-level fit, which I was, and eager to work hard and thrive under pressure, which I did. Every morning, before filming began, I liked to train alone, either with weights or on a trampoline. There was a good reason for this dedication: if a stunt coordinator had any doubts about whether I was putting in the work, or noticed a few extra pounds around my belly, I'd have been given my P45 because there was no room for shirkers. This was particularly important given that Dan Radcliffe was a similar weight and build to me, even though I was several years older. If I were to gain a stone and Dan hadn't, my stunt double status would become untenable. This situation was much worse for female performers, because there was very little room for them to hide. If a stuntwoman had to fall down a flight of stairs, there was a chance she'd need to wear a skirt or a dress, and that made it impossible to disguise any protective padding. They usually went without. From what I saw, stuntwomen took harder hits than the guys.

Physicality was everything. I was strong and malleable, and I was also extremely aware of what my body could do, which gave me confidence and allowed me to apply risk management effectively, not only for myself but for others. Whenever a stunt was taking place, it would be the role of the other performers not directly involved to act as 'safety'. They would stand near to the edge of a Hogwarts wall to prevent someone from toppling over the edge, or be on hand with an extinguisher should a fire job go wrong and an actor be turned into a human inferno. During the making of the 2007 Nicolas Cage movie *National Treasure: Book of Secrets*, I even 'spotted' a camera operator as they had their eyes focused on the viewfinder while facing an oncoming flatbed truck. If the driver missed his mark and came too close, it was my job to yank the operator's belt and pull him away.

The pressure during these moments was always huge, not only because of the dangers involved – both to myself and to everyone around me – but because of the huge costs involved in setting up most action movie stunts, especially those that involved explosions, the hire of planes, speed boats or helicopters, and collapsing buildings. In some circumstances, one take could cost hundreds of thousands of pounds. Others required weeks of preparation. But the worst-case scenario was an expensive take that required days to reset if the first went wrong. Sometimes, when there was a huge production crew involved, in a hostile location such as a mountain or desert, and where the weather was brutally hot or cold, the pressure on a stunt performer to nail their job in one hit was immense. In those situations, the groans when it went wrong felt like a punch to the guts. The cheers when it went right were life-affirming. Luckily, I received more cheers than I did punches.

That's because I was able to hold my nerve when the stakes were high. I knew that if I were to put too much pressure on myself, I might experience self-doubt, which was the worst emotion a stuntman could face. In situations that were highly stressful, I might crumble and fail. Instead, every negative emotion had to be silenced. I once watched the stuntman Theo Kypri perform a dive away from a trampoline, his body arcing over a road as a horse-drawn carriage flew underneath him at full speed. If Theo had misjudged his landing by a tiny distance, a drop of 25 feet to a concrete floor would have killed him – that's if he'd not been crushed to death by a horse. But did he experience any second-guessing or insecurity in the moments before jumping? *Not a chance.*

I set myself up in much the same way. In 2005 I was called in to perform a stunt for a Mini Convertible commercial and the brief was typically gnarly. I had to take a running jump onto a small, square trampoline known as a trampette, before spring-boarding away in a spectacular leap through the air, my arms and legs cycling furiously as I did so. The landing zone was the driver's seat of the open-roofed car, and once in position I had to drive off nonchalantly. The target was incredibly small; everything had to be on point, because if I overshot my mark by a few inches, I might crash into the windscreen or impale myself on the gear stick. If I fell short, I'd likely lose my teeth in a faceplant with the steering wheel or bumper. Not considering the implications for a second, I nailed a succession of practice takes – but when the cameras were moved into position, everything changed.

As any stunt performer will attest, rehearsals are a piece of piss generally. There are very few people watching. There are no cameras or sound engineers; no runners or caterers; and no wardrobe assistants or make-up artists. The temperature is a lot cooler because there aren't any studio lights. Meanwhile, the ambient stress levels are a lot lower because the directors and bean counters aren't around to make comments. I can do rehearsals all day long, no problem at all. But once the moving parts of an expensive video shoot have been brought into play, the stakes are raised.

For the Mini Convertible advert, filming was scheduled to take place at night on a back street in south London, and the set was flooded with a massive bank of blazing spotlights. Dry ice swirled about the studio to create a moodier vibe and the car seemed to sparkle on camera. But during my first take proper I was almost blinded by the glare, and it was incredibly difficult to spot my landing zone – I only had an inch either side of the front seat and between the bottom of the steering wheel to plant my feet. Having adjusted, I looked around the studio, and sixty pairs of eyes were upon me, including the stunt coordinator who was paying me a lot of money for the work, and two back-up stuntmen, in place should I break my leg during a mistimed landing. With these added variables in place, it took fifteen attempts to get the shot right. I smashed my bollocks on the gear stick and cracked my knees against the dashboard. I winded myself on the back of a seat and flopped over the steering wheel. To get around the problem, I dropped a couple of small red LED landing lights into the footwell of the car. With just one adjustment, I was suddenly able to target the one-foot-square(ish) gap between the steering well and seat and drive away. I nailed the next take. And the next. Then I claimed my pay cheque and went home.

Stuntmen and women are a different breed: fear and stress wash off us, because to consider them as serious adversaries only ever invites disaster. (Though I'm evidence of the truth that bad luck can affect us all.) That's why I never cowed down to terror as a working performer, and why I won't cow down to it as a person having been paralysed from the chest down. In many ways, my life is scarier now than it was while I was flying broomsticks, battling Dark Wizards, and hanging on to the roof of fast-moving cars. After that day in January 2009, all sorts of anxieties kicked in. The anxiety of being abandoned. The anxiety of never meeting a life partner. The anxiety of being a stress to other people. And the anxiety of shitting myself on a long-haul flight, which was suddenly a very real possibility. I've worked hard to get past them all.

Today, I use those fears to push me on during rehabilitation and physical therapy, just as I did when lining up a stunt. Negative emotion has once again become the fuel for every new challenge. Because what's worse: *The fear of dying, or the fear of not living?* Don't get me wrong, there have been regrets. I feel sad at not completing my work as Dan Radcliffe's stunt double for the entire Harry Potter series, because seeing it through to the end had been my dream. The pair of us had met during the first film; he started off as my little brother and we became close mates towards the end of the franchise. But those feelings of regret are rare and fleeting because I've learned that the present is all I have control over, and everything else is just noise. Also, my injury, while shocking, was a known occupational hazard. I knew what I was getting into when I stepped forward for that rehearsal in Godric's Hollow. I wanted the adrenaline, the respect and the acclaim. *I wanted to make movie magic.*

So, don't feel sad for the accident that happened. Get inspired by the adventure I've lived – and still live today. And make sure to wiggle your toes from time to time, because it's a gift.

DAVID HOLMES, ESSEX, 2024

PART ONE
ACTION!

1

ON THE OTHER SIDE OF FEAR

As a little kid, I'd briefly experienced fear in a recurring and all too familiar nightmare: me in a supermarket, separated from my family, desperately looking for my mum's face in a crush of shoppers. Like all good horror stories, this one was based in truth, because at an age I can just about remember I'd briefly left Mum's side, just as she'd buggered off into another aisle with her shopping trolley, totally unaware that I'd been left behind. For a few moments I was lost, alone and vulnerable, and the event left me with a sense of dread. Every time the nightmare returned, I'd be transported back to that bloody supermarket, sprinting from checkout to checkout, desperately looking for some glimpse of Mum. As I slept, my lungs and guts felt constricted and my legs became heavier, like I was wading through quicksand. God, it was horrible, but even in the dream I knew not to yield to anxiety. As I ran through the supermarket, climbing the shelves to get a better of view of where Mum might be, I'd eventually see her as she frantically searched the store, calling out my name. Having been reunited, I'd wake up, knowing that safety wasn't far away, but only if I kept on looking for it.

Apart from this occasional nightmare, fear never really halted me when I was little, and the desire to ignore danger and crash through barriers was encouraged by my parents. Don't get me wrong, they weren't reckless or negligent. Far from it, in fact. Dad worked for British Telecom in a job that had him pinned to a computer; Mum worked nights at the local Sainsbury's and spent her days caring for – *irony alert* – disabled kids in the area, which was then a rough part of Essex, rife with unemployment and poverty. If you haven't guessed it yet, they were both hard-working and kind-hearted people who had the audacity to raise me with love and a sense of freedom. The result was a *Boy's Own* adventure, all of it inspired by action movies, Hollywood drama, and the story of Evel Knievel – a daredevil with balls so big he'd once launched himself across a row of single-decker buses on a motorcycle in a packed football stadium.

I always had the sense that anything was possible, *that the crazy could happen,* even in our back garden, and alongside my two brothers, Adam and Paul, I wreaked havoc. Whenever we were bored, and my parents' backs were turned, somebody would grab one of the garden darts they'd bought for us – oversized arrows that came with a razor-sharp plastic tip. The game we'd invented for ourselves, and one definitely not advertised on the box, was simple and potentially lethal. A dart was lobbed into the air as high as possible until it stabbed the lawn with a satisfying thud. In the meantime, everybody ran around in different directions yelling and pointing, wondering if the next few seconds might be their last. *Total chaos.* If one of us had been hit in the head, we'd have been killed instantly.

Our anarchic sense of adventure was ramped up even higher once we were given a trampoline for Christmas. Charged up with way too much energy, I liked to jump from my bedroom window and on to the trampoline below, before rebounding up and into a tree, or on top of the garden shed. I don't think Mum could have been too surprised that I'd turned out to be a ballsy kid, though. When she took me to the school gates for my very first day of classes, I slipped away from her grip and ran to a lamppost. Not wanting to go in, I shinned my way to the top and hung from the light, looking down at the confused parents, laughing as they gossiped and nervously ushered their children into the playground.

Like most families, TV was the great pacifier in our house. We were raised in the 1990s, a golden age of entertainment, and Saturday night usually kicked off with Adam, Paul and me gawping at Pamela Anderson on the hit show *Baywatch,* or an old episode of *Airwolf* or *The A-Team.* Mum and Dad often joined us with a takeaway, and we'd stuff our faces with prawn crackers and watch game shows. Then, when the light entertainment was done, the best part of the week arrived: *movie time.* At the end of our road was a newsagent that doubled up as a video rental shop. It didn't exactly carry the selection of a Blockbusters, but it had enough, and I used to love making the video choice for the weekend. There were only two rules. 1) If it was a grown-up film, we'd watch it on the Saturday. And 2) Family-friendly films were for Sunday nights. I couldn't wait to have my pick.

I grew up loving the movies. The very idea of Hollywood and the dream-making business felt like an otherworldly place, a fantasy land beyond my reach, but its power was undeniable, and I often lost myself for hours. Thrillers. Action blockbusters. Sci-fi. On the Holmes brothers' 'best films of all time' list was *3 Ninjas* – a 1992 story in which three kids were taught martial art skills by their grandpa, Mori Tanaka, played by Victor Wong. After every viewing, our front room was transformed into a karate dojo as we attempted to kick the crap out of one another. (Adam, the youngest, often finished up in the worst state. But I took my fair share of black eyes and busted lips.) We also loved the so-bad-it's-awesome *Fire, Ice and Dynamite* – an around-the-world race starring Roger Moore that was packed with batshit stunts, like the scene in which a group of crazy blokes skied down a rockface mountain, another one of them in a barrel. There was even a formative moment in the local cinema when I watched my dad, his eyes filling with tears, during the Kevin Costner film *Robin Hood: Prince of Thieves*. Right then, I knew how powerful storytelling could be.

Though I was essentially a happy kid, a sense of darkness came over me sometimes. I wasn't depressed, but every now and then I'd be struck by a feeling of deep sorrow. I was never able to put my finger on exactly what was bothering me, but the experience was always overwhelming. Often, I was reduced to tears at the thought that I was going to be hit by some insurmountable problem in my life, like the loss of a parent at an early age, or the death of a mate. Whenever the darkness came over me, I made a conscious decision to deal with my emotions there and then.

I'd think, *Instead of crying about it when it happens, get the crying done now.*

Then I'd go to the toilet to release my emotions. Sitting on the floor, my arms wrapped around my legs, my body shaking, I'd sob into my knees. I had no idea what the future had in store for me, but my outlook wasn't optimistic. When I later got into the film business, I discovered there was a word for the dramatisation of this exact event. Foreshadowing: *a narrative device in which the author hints at some heavy shit to come.* Maybe I should have paid more attention.

★

Given that I was a daredevil-in-waiting, and my two brothers were constantly crashing about the house, Mum decided to shove us into the local gymnastics club in Havering, presumably for a bit of peace and quiet. I was up for it. My trampoline stunts had shown that I was both brave and physically capable, and as with those weekend movie nights, I soon realised that gymnastics was an activity I could lose myself in. At school, I sometimes experienced anxiety, especially when meeting new people, but finding the courage to attempt difficult gymnastic skills helped me to overcome those stresses. I learned that while I wasn't the strongest or tallest of kids in my class, I was certainly the bravest. The discovery gave me an inner confidence.

Gymnastics became my passion, and though it was hard work, it rarely felt like a grind. Moving around the bars or propelling my body on the rings was a game. *It was fun.* And on the mat, I found a place to compete with just about anyone. Meanwhile, I learned how to overcome terror – such as the time I first had to launch myself on to a wooden horse – and I adapted quickly to managing physical discomfort. Sure, a lot of gymnastics training was playful and expressive, but there were some skills that involved agonising pain. Conditioning training was a gruelling experience, but as I lifted the weights and muscled up my body, I realised that hurt could be emotionally silenced and I was soon comfortable with contorting my body in unfamiliar ways. In doing so, I discovered that hard work and putting in the hours could pay off; that suffering was a process; and that directions from an experienced tutor needed to be followed if I was to execute a performance without serious injury.

Then my greatest teachable moment took place. I was six years old and learning how to pirouette on the parallel bars, but in one attempt I miscalculated the descent. My legs separated and both knees smashed into the hard wooden beams with a crack. A bone-crunched pain stabbed into my thighs, shins and stomach. I felt the tears brimming in my eyes. I was in agony.

My coach, Nick Inns, applied ice to the war wounds. Then he nodded to the bars.

'David: don't feel sorry for yourself,' he said. 'You can either go home, or you can get back up and do it again.'

'What do you mean?' I moaned. 'Everything hurts.'

Nick pulled me to my feet, my legs shaking. I was understandably hesitant after taking such a whack.

'Because if you don't do it now, you'll always be afraid of this move,' he said. 'But if you can try again? That fear will go away.'

I blinked back the tears, wiped the snot from my nose, and climbed back on. This time I nailed the pirouette, the dopamine rush hitting my nervous system like a painkiller, and in doing so I learned that it was possible to overcome any fear. I went home buzzing. As a young boy, it was the most memorable life lesson I can remember.

I felt like a man.

Nick was just about the best mentor I could have had at that time in my life. He wasn't older than sixteen or seventeen, and he'd enjoyed a competitive career of his own, though it hadn't resulted in any massive successes. That didn't stop him from sharing his expertise with enthusiasm. Nick worked hard to improve all the kids at Havering, and I looked up to him massively. Whenever he could, Nick used gymnastics to impart a series of life lessons, some of which helped me to survive as both a stuntman and, later, a disabled person. One of them involved the way in which an athlete should approach a new discipline for the first time. Nick told me I had to break the technique down into a series of smaller, more manageable parts, rather than allowing myself to become overwhelmed by the complexity of what I was attempting.

For example, when executing a new floor move, such as a backflip, I had to first focus on my jump to the mat. Then I'd look to the next move, by arcing my body backwards and tumbling over myself. Finally, I had to land squarely and stand. Once this had been done, Nick would remove the mat and support me through the same process by placing a steady hand at the base of my spine. Eventually, I would be adept enough to perform the move unsupported. When it came to doing stunts for the first time, Nick's advice often kept me steady too.

During one film, I was tasked with being knocked over by a fast-moving car. Rather than worrying about the consequences of getting it wrong, I rehearsed the gag in stages. First, I practised on a parked vehicle, taking two steps towards it, before jumping and rolling across the bonnet and landing on a strategically placed crash mat. After that I moved on to a slow-moving vehicle with a crash mat fixed to the front, and repeated the technique, committing it to muscle memory until I was comfortable with being smashed at increasing speeds. With every progression, I trained my mind and muscles to cope with the terrifying impact of a car travelling at 17 miles per hour. This might not sound like a particularly dangerous speed, but were I to blunder, I'd likely end up in hospital. Thanks to Nick's tutelage, the process of deconstructing an overwhelming challenge into smaller, more manageable sections was applied to every stunt I performed – high falls, explosions, even long dives underwater.

As a disabled man, I used this technique to stop me from becoming overwhelmed. I quickly learned that turning up somewhere new in a wheelchair, such as a hotel or restaurant, was a nightmare. There were all sorts of obstacles and fuckery that I hadn't considered as an able-bodied person, and so much of it screwed with my head. To overcome any meltdowns, I applied the same logical thinking as I had to a gymnastics manoeuvre or stunt roll. Rather than taking everything in slow movements, I prepared my mind by first checking out a location on Google Maps. I visited websites to assess the wheelchair ramps and disabled facilities on site. Once I was satisfied with the challenges ahead, I alerted the venue and notified them of any requirements I might have. Everything was broken down into smaller, manageable bits.

It was the only way to stop the everyday from doing my head in.

★

As the middle kid in the family, I loved showing off and was for-ever being told that I was playing up or acting stupid. My exuberant personality caused problems in the classroom, and once I'd made it to secondary school I was disciplined regularly. One time, a teacher tried to quieten me down by throwing an eraser in my direction, and the rubber missile struck me in the eye, leaving me with a proper shiner for a couple of days. Not that I could blame the bloke. He had thirty-odd kids to look out for, and I was ruining the class for everyone. Eventually, I went too far on a school trip to a canal boat and after I'd been shoved into the water by one of my classmates, I was sent to dry off. Feeling bored, I then climbed on top of the slow-moving barge, dressed in nothing but a skimpy towel, and when the boat passed under a motorway flyover, I ditched the towel, scaled the bridge and ran from one side of the road to the other, all while stark bollock naked. Dodging the passing traffic, car horns blaring, I jumped back down onto the boat as it emerged on the other side. When I was suspended from school for a week, it felt like a bonus.

I wasn't a total chaos magnet. I excelled during PE, and despite my size I had physicality and could do more push-ups than just about anyone else in the class. Team sports weren't my thing though. That's because I didn't like the idea of relying on other people to succeed, or of being at fault for a group failure. I wanted to win on *my* terms; I wanted to be accountable for *my* failures; and I loved activities that required a certain level of individuality. I was good at track and field, I was beyond handy on a trampoline, and because of my time at Havering, I was by far the best gymnast in the school, and so much fitter, stronger and body aware than my classmates. More than anything, though, I loved to perform. Whenever I was asked to put on a show, I came alive.

I'm sure if I was a kid now, I'd have been diagnosed with an atten-tion deficit disorder of some kind and probably prescribed a certain amount of medication or counselling. But during the 1990s the awareness of those issues wasn't as advanced as it is today, and I was written off as being a cocky pain in the arse. That was a shame because some aspects of my behaviour were related to circumstance and at four foot something, I was the smallest in my school, even during year 11.* That made me a target for bullies, and like most kids that were picked on, I learned that one of the best ways of disarming an aggressor was to make him or her laugh. I used this defence mechanism regularly, but the downside was that my attitude made me a disruptive presence in school. Therefore: suspension.

When in attendance, I was miserable a lot of the time, though I hid it well. Most mornings I'd wake up feeling a lurching churn of dread in the pit of my stomach. I didn't want to go to school and face another day of being verbally smashed about by the bigger lads. Some days, I was roughed up and stuffed into the class lockers, on others I was yanked to the floor by the straps of my backpack as I walked down the corridor. During rugby, I was often targeted for a showboating tackle by the better players, and the impact left me flattened in the mud. As if that wasn't enough, I was called names, and none of them were particularly original: Titch. Pipsqueak. Half-pint. Midget. And then finally, once *Austin Powers: The Spy Who Shagged Me* had become a box-office hit, Mini-Me, after the character played by the late actor Verne Troyer, who had cartilage-hair hypoplasia and was only two feet eight inches in height. The fact I was almost twice his size didn't seem to matter. The nickname was fired at me in class, across the playground and down the school corridors.

The abuse wounded me badly. Often, I'd go home to my room and cry, or play up in front of my parents, both of whom were

---

* At one point I was offered a course of growth hormones to help me to grow, but I didn't want to take them, fearful that they might hinder my progress in gymnastics. Seeing how the world's greatest footballer, Lionel Messi, responded to a similar course of treatment, that might have been a mistake.

short too. One evening I even took my fear and sadness out on Mum, blaming her for what felt like a rough genetic hand-me-down.

'It's your fault I'm getting bullied!' I yelled. 'You made me this way . . .'

I felt like shit afterwards.

I soon outgrew Havering Gymnastics Club. At the age of eleven, and after a competitive tour to Australia with Nick, I upgraded to the South Essex Gymnastics Club, which would later become famous for training the Team GB athletes Max Whitlock (who would win three Olympic gold medals), Annika Reeder (the winner of three Commonwealth Games golds in the 1990s and a British gymnast who competed in two consecutive Olympic Games in 1996 and 2000), and Danny Lawrence, another international athlete-in-waiting who would go on to become one of my best mates. Much of this success was down to the coach, Jeff Hewitt-Davis – a former British gymnastics champion, Olympian and stunt performer for the ITV firefighting drama *London's Burning*, plus some of the James Bond movies, and *Saving Private Ryan*. As far as I was concerned, Jeff was a hero. I could have listened to his stories for hours.

Training gave me peace. I didn't stand out as a target at South Essex because a lot of the kids in the club were short arses too, and the sport's most successful athletes were often small. One of the greatest gymnasts of all time, Kōhei Uchimura – who won gold medals in the 2012 and 2016 Olympic Games – was five foot four inches, which wasn't that much taller than me. Meanwhile, the attitude inside the club was one of positive mental action; there was very little bullying, and everyone was encouraging of progress and effort. Of course, there were moments when cruel jokes were thrown around, or some roughhousing went too far, but most of the time it was nothing more than a little bit of piss-taking and I enjoyed it. If there were occasions where I felt victimised or even a little bit scared, I leaned into my sense of humour again, just like I'd done at school, and I became known as someone who could take a lot of abuse without losing their rag.

I often trained at the gymnastics club four or five times a week, and Jeff taught me about the key attributes needed to be a successful athlete. He told me that bravery was a big part of the sport and I needed to push past the fear to master various jumps, landings and techniques. I also had to be body aware and understand exactly where I was going to land or move, often at high speeds. Most importantly, though, I had to enjoy pain because there were regular bangs and crashes and a fair amount of blood. But whenever I took a whack, I dusted myself down and had another go at whatever it was I'd been doing, whereas a lot of my mates would blub on the sidelines or call their mum for a lift home.

Not that it was easy. One time, I fucked up a *moy* on the parallel bars – a move in which I had to position myself in a handstand before swinging down and underneath. For a split second, I had to release my grip before catching the bar again in the middle. During one attempt, I lost concentration. I wasn't focused enough and as I swung down, I cracked my shins on the metal support beams. The pain was excruciating, like being beaten around the legs with an iron bar, and when I looked down, my flesh had been cleaved open. Through the bloody mess, I saw the exposed white of my shinbone. Rather than wailing about it, I was patched up with butterfly stitches and a field dressing and got back on the mat once the bleeding had stopped.

Stretching was a whole other story. Often, Jeff instructed me to sit in the splits position for several minutes at a time, until the flexing, twanging ache in my groin, hamstrings and lower back was almost unbearable. After a while I learned how to breathe through the hurt, and the sensation of my muscles stretching and grinding became an emotional endeavour. I liked knowing how far I could push myself; I wanted to feel the edges of what was possible. Every now and then, while I was positioned on the mat, my legs pointing in opposite directions, Jeff would press down on my hips to deepen the stretch. My body burned in agony, but once I'd moved beyond the physical and emotional distress, I'd feel a satisfying wave of endorphins. In those moments, I told myself pain was an indication that weakness was leaving my body, and if ever I wanted to quit, like during a never-ending session of muscle-ups on the rings, I'd hear Jeff shouting encouragement across the gym. 'If you're cheating, you're only cheating on yourself,' he'd yell.

Learning to negotiate extreme pain soon became a psychological asset and I used it to dissipate the emotional suffering at school, due to the wrath of those older, bigger bullies. I drew on the humiliation and used it to fire myself up. Whenever I needed to muster more motivation while curving around the parallel bars, I visualised the face of my latest tormentor leering at me from the other side. As my legs spiked upwards, I imagined my foot connecting with his jawbone in a violent collision. This mental image helped me to become more aggressive. If I'd been told to smash out thirty chin-ups, and the effort felt too much, I remembered back to a time when a kid at school had told me that I was too small or too weak to do anything. I saw their face dropping as I completed the task. Then I'd imagine them trembling under the pressure of being ordered to do the same thing.

When it came to competitive events, I wasn't the most consistent athlete, but I was brave. As I grew older, I travelled all over the country to compete in different gymnastics meets and while I did OK, my problem was that the other lads from the South Essex Gymnastics Club were winning trophies and I wasn't. There were times when I felt as if I were letting my parents down. Mum and

Dad were very supportive and seemed happy to pay for my travel costs, but the fact I couldn't find any regular success must have annoyed them a bit. Not that they ever showed it. They were glad I'd found a passion, and when I did well, such as the time I came first in the British Under-14s championships in the floor event (which was my favourite discipline, because tumbling was something I did everywhere – on the mat, in the garden and across the school playground), they were both chuffed.

Really, it wasn't about scoring points and winning trophies. The buzz I got from gymnastics came from the performance. I loved showing off. If I could entertain an audience, I was happy, and one day I earned my first kiss after nailing a series of backflips on a lunch break at school. I'd had a crush on this one girl for ages, from infants to the end of junior school, and in the last summer before leaving for secondary education, I decided to take the opportunity to impress her by throwing down a series of moves I'd learned in the gymnastics club. It worked, too. And as our lips locked, my brain fused the connection between risk and reward, and I realised that taking chances and putting my body on the line made me a hit with the opposite sex. This was useful knowledge because I'd never been shy. I projected myself to protect myself and delivering a show gave me pleasure. The realisation would set me up for a lifetime of heroics and hurt.

2

SMOKE AND MIRRORS

Other than Jeff's stories at the gymnastics club, I had no real clue about the life of a stuntman. *But I knew it looked bloody cool.* As kids, my brothers and I had obsessed over any *making of . . .* documentaries, specials that went behind the scenes on a Hollywood blockbuster. This was especially so if they revealed how the special effects were created or explained the death-defying feats that went into producing some of the industry's most famous stunts. We watched as the daredevil performer doubling Harrison Ford was pulled along by a truck on a dirt road in *Raiders of the Lost Ark*, his body lashed to its undercarriage by a bullwhip. We saw James Bond skiing through a town in *For Your Eyes Only*, knocking over wine glasses and scattering tourists enjoying their après ski in a Swiss mountain resort. And we stared, open-mouthed, as Arnold Schwarzenegger's Terminator launched his Harley-Davidson motorbike into a canal.

From the smouldering wreckage of planes, trains and automobiles emerged a weird cult hero – Robert 'Spanky' Spangler, a Hollywood stuntman, hellraiser, and former US green beret, who rose to fame after jumping the Rio Grande with a rocket-powered truck. Spanky claimed to have broken the world record for the longest distance jumped in a car (328 feet, apparently). If legend was to be believed, the man jumped rivers, he jumped dams, and he jumped suspension bridges. No bridge was too far, no inferno too towering, and no escape too great – in Spanky's mind, at least – but nine times out of ten, his stunts went horribly wrong, which amplified his top-billing status in our house. Whenever Spanky appeared in a video or documentary, I was glued. On one occasion, he jumped his car across a river, but the timing was all wrong, and when Spanky inevitably sank into the water, a dive team dragged his lifeless body to the bank. He was unconscious. *Oh no! Spanky's been killed!* Then, as he was stretchered away, Spanky rose from the dead and lifted his thumbs to the onlooking crowd. *Wait . . . He's alive!* Everyone went nuts and an important lesson was delivered to my fertile mind: *Defying death made you a fucking hero.*

Other than that, I had no idea what a stuntman *actually did*, or how they learned their craft in the first place – though from what I could tell, there wasn't much to it, other than trying not to die. In 1997, the internet was in its infancy. Even though Dad worked for BT, and we had a state-of-the-art dial-up connection, getting any relevant information on the life of a fall guy from Ask Jeeves was a pain in the arse. But when Jeff came into the South Essex Gymnastics Club and told us that he'd been asked to bring one or two of us to an audition as stunt kids for a Hollywood movie, called *Lost in Space*, I jumped at the chance, even though I had very little idea of what I was letting myself in for. *This was my chance to become the next Spanky Spangler.* I'd also gained some showbiz experience a year previously, when the ITV show *You Bet!* arrived at South Essex Gymnastics Club to film us training. Typically, I'd placed myself at the centre of things. I was interviewed by the TV presenter, Darren Day, and drew a laugh from a watching audience having declared I was 'knackered' by the work. It was my first taste of fame.

Having decided to try out for *Lost in Space*, I was fired into a magical new world, like Evel Knievel on a motorcycle. According to the notes, the movie was being billed as a cinematic remake of the

1960s cult TV show. It also arrived with a thrilling sell: *The Robinson family was going into space to fight for a chance for humanity. Now they are fighting to live long enough to find a way home.* According to my dad, who had watched the programme as a kid, this narrative was different to the original, in which the same family, who'd lived on a space colony, were thrown off course by a stowaway. Not that I was arsed. *Lost in Space* still promised to be an exciting ride, especially as the remake had roped in Matt LeBlanc as the character of Don West, then one of the most in-demand actors in the world following his time on the sitcom *Friends*. Alongside him was Gary Oldman, famous for his roles in *JFK*, *The Fifth Element* and *Nil by Mouth*, and the *Drugstore Cowboy* star, Heather Graham. As a thirteen-year-old, my mind buzzed at the opportunity.

The experience was game-changing. I walked through the doors at Shepperton Studios in Middlesex, and into a fantasy world constructed from scaffolding and flimsy canvas. I saw ominous, inhospitable alien planets. I spotted spaceships with flickering computer screens. Several Hollywood A-, B- and C-listers breezed past me; and the legendary stunt director Greg Powell treated me like *an actual bloody adult.* The bloke was a titan: he was well over six feet in height and broad-shouldered, with a head of curly ginger hair and a pair of Rubeus Hagrid-sized hands. In fact, Greg was so strong that he was able to lift me with one arm quite easily. This wasn't the most distinctive thing about him, though. I had actually caught a whiff of Greg's pungent Monte Cristo No.2 cigar before being introduced to him. This, I would later discover, was an extension of his physical form, and Greg would chomp through two a day, which, given they were around £40 a pop, made for quite an expensive habit. (While working on the second or third Harry Potter movie, Greg and I sat down and worked out how much he had blown on cigars during his career. He estimated it was a six-figure amount.) Greg also splashed himself with Jo Malone aftershave and rinsed his mouth out with TCP antiseptic in the morning. Put together, he emitted a distinctive aroma.

According to Greg, the *Lost in Space* production was looking for a stunt double to Jack Johnson, the actor charged with playing Will Robinson, one of the film's leads. Jack was younger than me by a few years. But when we were placed side by side in a line-up that day, a sense of excitement rippled through the studio. We had the same build and were pretty much identical in height. I had travelled over to the Shepperton with two mates from the South Essex Gymnastics Club, plus a few other hopefuls, and it was in that moment that I first witnessed the film industry's uglier side. After we had stood together, I was told the job was mine, as the other stunt-kids-in-waiting looked on, heartbroken. This was Hollywood Lesson #1: never expect anyone to pussyfoot around you on a film set.

Everything moved at warp speed from then on. Within forty-eight hours, my mum and I were travelling to the studios to sign a 'child double contract', a document that arrived with a simple brief. My job was to do the stuff deemed too painful or risky for Jack Johnson, and I was given a three-month contract for the summer. This worked out well for everyone given that a) I'd be off school for most of that time anyway, and b) I wouldn't need too much private tutoring, which was a legal requirement for anyone working as a child performer. Tucked away in the paperwork was the fee, and I was set to be paid £65 to £85 per day, depending on my workload, with fees for any stunts to be negotiated on top. This was an eye-watering amount of money for nearly everyone in 1997, but for a kid barely into his teens it felt like a lottery win. Mum was being paid too, as a chaperone. The family was chuffed.

I fell in love with the work on day one, and every day in the studio was a sensory overload. Everywhere smelled like Greg's cigars and plaster of Paris, the material used for making most film sets and props. Talk about smoke and mirrors: this was the movie business's very essence, and even walking into work felt like a cinematic event. To enter the studio, I had to use all my strength to push on two heavy, airlock-style doors that opened with a sucking noise. Once inside, a huge bank of scaffolding loomed over me, like a metallic T-rex, and it was hard to make out what the structure was at first, until I looked closely. *I was in the guts of the Jupiter II!* This was the Robinson family's spaceship in the year 2058 and tangled up in it were cameras, microphones and miles and miles of electrical cables. Skilled technicians, producers and boom operators buzzed about the place, and an excited thrum reverberated everywhere and fed back into the studio's nooks, crannies and corners. *Something special was being made.*

There was no time to hang about and gawp, and I was shoved into work almost immediately. Having been shown about the place by Greg, I was given my first Hollywood screen test. Alongside Paula, another athlete from the South Essex Gymnastics Club who had been brought into the production (and a future member of the Team GB squad), I was positioned onto a platform that hung a metre or so above a crash mat.

'Right, there's going to be a pyrotechnic explosion,' said Greg seriously. 'When you hear the bang, I want you to dive onto that mat. You OK with that?'

My adrenaline rocketed. *Of course I was OK with that.* This was the stuff of dreams – Spanky Spangler shit – and I felt like The Real Deal. Then I looked down at my clothes and realised I was still wearing my jeans and trainers, and hardly in character.

Greg moved away, crouching down on one knee in a spot where the cameras were set to be positioned once filming started for real. He then raised his hands and made a box shape with his fingers. This was the universal technique used for replicating a camera operator's point of view. Finally, he yelled a word that would later become my trigger to go full send. *Action!* There was a bang. Instinctively, I flung myself onto the mat, my body hitting the padded surface alongside Paula with a dull thud. Everything went quiet. My heart was banging and when I looked up, I noticed Greg puffing theatrically on his Monte Cristo. His face had split into a grin.

'Yeah, that'll do,' he said, chuckling.

I would soon recognise this phrase as acknowledgement of a job well done.

With my debut screen test nailed, I was taken to the costume department and squeezed into a claustrophobic rubber suit that had to be zipped and glued to my body to disguise the appearance of any fastenings. This was a replica of Will Robinson's costume, a condom-tight garment that I became uncomfortably familiar with over the next few months. Not only did the outfit leave next to nothing in the way of wriggle room, but the physical process of getting into it took around thirty minutes. Then I was told by a cheery wardrobe assistant that it was probably best if I didn't drink any water before arriving in costume, because if I needed to pee, it would take another thirty minutes to get out of it again. Not that I cared. As far as I was concerned, I was being given my own superhero outfit. My other costume was a looser-fitting, reflective set of military-style fatigues, matched with a sleek pair of sunglasses. My overall sense was that I was in for a cool experience.

This feeling was amplified further when I was taken into the creature effects department, which was being run by the legendary Jim Henson's Creature Shop, a company founded by the man responsible for creating *The Muppet Show* and helping to build the mythical *Star Wars* character Yoda. Their office resembled a sci-fi menagerie, and I was introduced to my first official co-star, the *Jupiter II*'s on-board robot, known imaginatively as 'Robot' – a hulking metal monstrosity that trundled along on a set of tank-style tracks. The creature was an intimidating brute. Robot had been armed with a fearsome set of steel claws and a bright-red orb that glowed aggressively in the centre of its steel head. Everything was powered by pistons and hydraulics that connected to a series of umbilical cord wires. At the end of them was a team of puppeteers with joysticks. The beast looked terrifying. And everyone working on it looked terrified.

I was then told that my first interaction with this bringer of destruction was to clamber onto its back and lock myself into a series of specially designed hand- and footholds. When I looked closely, I realised why it was so important for a highly paid actor like Jack Johnson to be doubled by a stunt person. Once the mechanical monster started moving and bucking, you had to keep your hands in exactly the right place if you wanted to avoid losing a finger in the crunching and grinding mechanics. But there were other occupational hazards to consider when working with Robot, who seemed to have a mind of its own, and during one of my first attempts at working with it, a valve exploded noisily, ejaculating a brightly coloured hydraulic valve fluid over the crew. Shortly afterwards, its back-up unexpectedly came alive during a programming glitch. There was chaos as it crashed around the set, several puppeteers and technicians frantically waggling their joysticks in a desperate attempt to bring it to heel. They were eventually able to power down the unit by yanking every plug within reach from its socket, the special effects equivalent of turning off a crashed computer and turning it back on again.

On that first day, I learned that stunts were called *gags* and my debut act on camera was an easy introduction to the world of a fall guy. Once dressed in full rubber, I was asked to repeat the reaction jump I'd nailed so enthusiastically during Greg's first screen test. There was one major difference in the set-up, however. During rehearsals, both Paula and I had been instructed to throw ourselves onto a soft, pillowy crash mat, but due to a readjusted camera angle there wasn't enough space for such luxuries.

'You're going to have to land on the floor,' said Greg, blowing a plume of cigar smoke my way. 'You all right with that?'

I looked at the concrete, and then at Paula. *Yeah, of course I was all right with it.* Our trigger was the sound of a deafening bang, and on cue we launched from our positions and landed in a roll across the floor. The impact was painful, but after several years of banging my bones against the gymnastics bars and rings, it was a sense of discomfort I'd been trained to shrug off, which Greg loved. My rubber suit had also absorbed some of the sting- ing impact. It was then announced that we'd executed the stunt in one take (which Greg also loved). But given we were now pro- fessional performers, it was important to repeat the work several times over, just to make doubly sure. Every explosion, jump and crash-landing gave me a surge of dopamine. It also racked up my take-home pay.

For three months I lived in a fantasy land where I learned the language, cues and accepted behaviours of a group of people that would soon come to feel like family. Phrases that would have sounded weird and otherworldly in a different context became a part of my everyday vernacular. To *check the gate* was to make sure that no hairs or dust particles had stuck to the thin piece of glass separating the camera lens from the celluloid film. (In 1997 the movie industry had yet to move into digital, but I believe the phrase has stuck around.) I discovered that the hair and make-up department was the best place to pick up snippets of Hollywood gossip and insider information. And even though I was a young teenager and eager to play Laser Tag with some of the senior crew members in the corridors, in the world of cin- ema I was treated no differently to the adults. I heard dirty jokes and tales of druggy misadventure and boozy debauchery going on else- where in the industry. Most of all, I realised that smoking looked good.

This was down to Matt LeBlanc, then one of the most famous men in the world. My first thought at meeting *The Real-Life Joey from Friends* was that the dark rings under his eyes might have been evidence of a life partied at 100 miles per hour. My second: *Bloody hell, this bloke puffs a lot of ciggies.* Matt seemed to burn through pack after pack, which only added to his *Rebel Without a Cause* vibe and my sense that he was undeniably cool. He was also incredibly friendly and kind, and eager to entertain. One day, Matt pulled out a lighter, rolled onto his back and ignited one of his farts, just to make me giggle. As a bright blue and orange flame spread around the arse crack of his jeans, my mind was blown that such a feat was even humanly possible and that one of the most famous actors on the planet was up for such immature behaviour.

The same couldn't be said of the more serious William Hurt, the actor best known for winning a BAFTA and Oscar for his role as Luis Molina in the 1985 film *Kiss of the Spiderwoman*. When I proudly showed off my brand-new Nike Air Max trainers and a pair of sunglasses – one of my first ever purchases as a working stuntman – William looked down at my feet and scowled.

'You do know these are made by children that are being forced to work in Chinese slave labour camps, don't you, David?'

I shook my head sadly. *I had no idea.* And I'd only bought them because they looked good. Receiving a scolding from such an established movie star felt like a slap across the chops.

Not everyone was so eager to kill my buzz, though. I later watched the MTV Movie Awards with Heather Graham, which helped me to move past the downer, because, like pretty much everyone else on set, I had massive crush on her. Heather was a magazine cover star, and when I mentioned this fact to one of the assistant directors, he informed me I should check out some of her previous work, because she'd appeared naked in *Drugstore Cowboy*. And never mind the fact I was only a thirteen-year-old kid and not yet old enough to watch that kind of stuff. Later, I plucked up the courage to ask out Lacey Chabert, the teenage actress playing Penny Robinson, who had been made famous by the US TV show *Party of Five*. (She said no.) And I also got to see Gary Oldman working up close, a talent many people considered to be the *greatest of all time*. Gary was always pleasant, but respectfully withdrawn, because he was so absorbed in his work. He also understood that the life of a Hollywood actor was a job, not a matter of life and death, and acted like the consummate professional. His ability to flip his creative, emotional state from benign to downright terrifying was something to behold.

Me: I felt like I'd smashed through the cinema screen and was living in a beautiful dream.

*

Every day was an adventure. I moved through spaceships with flickering computer screens and flashing consoles, and walked over alien landscapes where the trees weren't trees at all, but constructs of wood and rubber, and the spray-painted moss underfoot was a Technicolor plastic. At times the world fell apart, literally, and I remember being ushered from one stage when a set crumbled and collapsed around the watching cast, the director letting fly at his special effects department. I also learned new skills, one of which was the way a successful stunt double was supposed to work. It turned out that jumping from the back of an anarchic, freewheeling robot and hurling myself to the ground was only one part of the gig. As Jack Johnson's all-action doppelganger, I had to mirror his movements, and I spent hours studying how he walked, ran and jumped. I even learned to hold my shoulders in the same way.

The architect of much of my work-related chaos was Greg, a man widely regarded as one of the greatest stuntmen and action coordinators of his generation. If you've been to the movies in the past fifty years, there's a very good chance you've seen one of Greg's gags. Arguably the most famous in his portfolio was the nerve-shredding scene from the first *Mission: Impossible* film in which the lead character, Ethan Hunt, played by Tom Cruise, dropped into a security vault at the CIA's Langley HQ. Suspended from a wire, and entering a technologically protected environment in which a dropped bead of sweat could set off a series of sensors and alarms, the action was both intense and jaw-dropping. Meanwhile, on his Internet Movie Database page, some of Greg's listed skills include fighting, wirework, battle sequences and explosions. He went on to be nominated for a 2002 Emmy because of his stunts on the HBO mini-series *Band of Brothers*, and a Taurus Award for his work on *Fast & Furious 6* in 2014.

Greg was also a force of nature, having emerged in the 1970s, a less politically correct era, when the stunt industry was known for fighting and fucking. (I've heard that the film industry at that time was rife with sexism, racism and homophobia.) Much of his education had come from his dad, the infamous Nosher Powell, who was a stunting celebrity in his own right, having appeared in fourteen James Bond films, including *From Russia with Love*. (Nosher also had acting credits for the British comedy *Eat the Rich* in 1987, where he played the Home Secretary alongside cameo stars Paul McCartney, Dawn French and Rik Mayall.) Nosher was equally renowned as a heavyweight boxer in both the licensed and unlicensed game, and had once been sparring partner to Muhammad Ali. He'd also worked as bodyguard to Rat Pack singer Sammy Davis Jr, before becoming the doorman at several clubs. Later, Greg partly followed in his dad's footsteps by getting into the boxing game.

I soon considered Greg as my Hollywood father figure. He showed me how to perform and behave, in front of the cameras and behind them, which was an invaluable experience given it was my first time on a movie set. I learned about financial security and how to enjoy my money with flash cars, expensive watches and fine dining – once I was old enough. (But not the style of trainers that were possibly produced in Chinese sweatshops.) These lessons stuck because Greg was an incredible storyteller and I discovered that he'd been a seasoned traveller and could comfortably operate in notoriously tricky working environments, like Morocco and India. He was once chased by a mob of Hell's Angels while filming in Berlin, but he'd hung around long enough to see the Wall come tumbling down. Whenever we sat in the Shepperton canteen, Greg held court and told tales, and I was always enthralled. I wanted to live a life like his.

I also discovered that he demanded bravery, loyalty and respect, and if a team member didn't display those three qualities, they weren't likely to be invited back. He was also of the belief that a stunt performer should be happy to experience a fair amount of pain. If ever Greg felt that someone was trying to save themselves from the odd bump or bruise, he'd call them out publicly, and nobody was spared a beasting.

'Sometimes you've got to take a whack,' he would say over and over.

A few years later, while working on one of the Harry Potter films, Greg even scolded me in front of the entire crew because he believed I'd been holding back. I was performing a wire stunt with another performer, and we were supposed to violently collide on a line suspended over a series of crash mats. During our first take, I instinctively opened my body up before impact. It was as a way of protecting myself, and I knew it. As did Greg, who pointed this out to me on a monitor, as my peers and workmates looked on.

'Hold your shape, David!' he shouted angrily. '*Take the whack.* It'll look more effective.'

I didn't question it. Greg was the stunt world equivalent of Tony Soprano, and I wanted to please him. Annoyingly, he tended to be right a lot of the time too. So, when I eventually *took the whack*, holding my shape firm and pinging off the wire spectacularly, the effect was way more dramatic, just as he'd predicted. The rebound of the impact meant I travelled further than I expected, to the edge of the crash mat. On the other side was a concrete floor. The stuntwoman positioned nearby as safety prevented me from falling off the mat.

I learned a lot of lessons about the stunt trade during my few months on *Lost in Space*. Key to these was forgetting any hopes I might have had of my face making it into a film. During the making of one scene, Jack Johnson had overshot his permitted working hours, and I was called in to double for him for a few background shots. After we'd gone through the first take, I rushed over to the camera to see the results, feeling chuffed that I was going to be recognisable on the big screen, if only for a split second or two. But Greg was furious. He scowled, clamped down on his cigar and shouted to me from across the set.

'Come here, you!'

Greg was gesturing at me with one of his banana-sized digits.

'David, you're fucking up here,' he said, his face darkening as I ran over, my enthusiasm fading.

I looked up at him, confused. *What do you mean?*

'That ain't the job you're being paid for,' he said, pointing at the camera. 'Showing your face. Your job is to do the stunt work. Now get up there, do the scene and keep your mug out of it.'

I felt crestfallen. Greg was someone who I looked up to. I knew his status in the industry and I wanted him to rate my abilities, because I felt as if I'd found my calling. *I wanted to do another film.* When it came to the next take, I did everything I could to keep my face out of the shot. And when the director called 'Cut', I looked over to Greg, who was staring at me kindly.

'Good lad,' he said quietly.

It was the next best thing to a round of applause.

★

If I wasn't in make-up, costume or catering, I could be found in the stunt office in Shepperton Studios, a large space comprising a trampette and crash mats, stunt supplies and box rigs. The room had cheekily been nicknamed Porky's Gym in a nod to the frat comedy *National Lampoon's Animal House.* And I spent hours working with the other stunt performers, showing off, trying to prove myself as I performed backflips and somersaults. At one stage, I even threw myself from a 15-foot ledge on the side of the R-Stage and into a mountain of crash mats that had been cut into small squares. During the run up, I planted my feet and threw my body upwards, twisting into a double front somersault, before landing safely on my back. As I scrambled upwards, I heard Greg laughing at me in the background. I was making a positive impression.

The thought of being a serious gymnast faded away almost immediately. Whenever I returned to the South Essex Gymnastics Club, my work fell by the wayside. I wasn't interested in improving my competition technique or honing the skills required to win another trophy. I wanted to learn how to execute explosive jumps; I tried to do pratfalls; I pestered Jeff to teach me how to react to a thrown punch in a barroom brawl. My form on the mat became sloppy because I wasn't thinking about my performance technique. I was more bothered about how my shape would look onscreen as a plaster of Paris set collapsed around me. Not that anyone in the gym believed my stories from the summer. It took me ages to convince anyone that I'd been hanging out with Matt LeBlanc, or that I'd watched the MTV Movie Awards with Heather Graham. (And been knocked back by Lacey Chabert.) It was only once I'd developed the photos that the piss-taking stopped.

What I didn't know at the time – but would become acutely aware of later – was that I'd experienced a lucky break. The film industry was rife with nepotism and only a small number of stunt-men came from a working-class background. That's because to qualify for the job, a hopeful needed to pass a series of courses and the cost of completing them was eye-watering. I once heard a performer complain that their bill had been upwards of a hundred grand, and not a lot of people from my background could afford such an endeavour. Despite these obstacles, Greg was a champion for working-class actors and often fought to give someone their chance. If ever a stuntman was struggling, Greg worked his arse off to find them a job. Meanwhile, he was always putting his neck on the line for new talent, no matter their levels of experience. This generosity would later help to shape several impressive careers. It would help to shape mine too.

3

THE SCHOOL OF HARD KNOCKS

When *Lost in Space* had finished filming, my world jolted back to normality. I returned to school and the bullies, even though I'd been a bona fide movie star a few weeks previously. Then, a couple of years later, Greg invited me to work on the Harold Ramis-directed movie *Bedazzled*. The plot: *Hopeless dweeb Elliot Richards is granted seven wishes by the Devil to snare Alison, the girl of his dreams . . . In exchange for his soul.* My work was limited. In a scene that was eventually cut from the film, I was tasked with sitting in a packed classroom as the Devil, played by Liz Hurley, dropped a board rubber. My instructions were to leap forward once it had struck the floor, desperately scrabbling for it as a group of schoolkids piled on top of me, all of us vying for the Devil's attentions. It wasn't the most taxing of gigs, but it soon proved to be one of the most impactful. As I rested between takes, Greg came over with an invitation.

'Are you up for more work?' he said, chomping on yet another cigar. 'Because I'm starting on a new film. *Harry Potter and the Something Something*. And I might have a gig for you.'

'OK. *Yeah*,' I said, unaware of how my life was about to change for ever.

At the time, J.K. Rowling's bestselling Harry Potter books hadn't yet flashed across my radar. I knew what they were – everyone had been talking about them – but I was unaware of the lead character's adventures at Hogwarts, the lovable wizardry of

Albus Dumbledore, and the evil *uber villain* Voldemort – AKA *He Who Must Not Be Named, You Know Who* or *The Dark Lord*. But younger mates at the South Essex Gymnastics Club *had* read the first three titles in what would become a seven-book series – *The Philosopher's Stone, The Chamber of Secrets* and *The Prisoner of Azkaban*. And they'd bloody loved them. Given I hadn't yet bought into the story, my only thoughts were that I'd be working on a film adaptation of a kids' book, Greg was involved, and that it might represent another step towards my goal of becoming a fully fledged stuntman. Plus, I was getting 150 quid a day, a serious upgrade in pay.

My attitude shifted having picked up a copy of *The Philosopher's Stone*. Like a lot of fans, I was immediately dialled into J.K. Rowling's writing because it was clearly pitched at both children and grown-ups. I tore through the pages. The narrative brimmed with an adventurous spirit; there was magic (obviously); and I experienced a nostalgic call-back to some of the stories I'd read, and been read, as a little boy. By the end of the book, I was invested in Harry's adventures at the Hogwarts School of Witchcraft and Wizardry because everything felt so real. I connected with the supporting characters, Ron Weasley, Hermione Granger, Rubeus Hagrid and Professor Albus Dumbledore. Even Neville Longbottom. I bristled at the slippery antics of Draco Malfoy and Professor Severus Snape's eerie malevolence. I felt unsettled by the shadowy presence of Voldemort. Most of all I was intrigued by the lead character, a spirited kid, dogged by bullies, and on the verge of discovering a special talent, unseen by anyone else – even himself. Harry's narrative seemed to rhyme with my own, like it had with a lot of readers. Suddenly, Greg's offer felt even more appealing. But I had no clue that I was being lined up as the stunt double to a kid who was about to become one of the most famous on the planet.

My first day on set only amplified the idea that I was entering into something special. If J.K. Rowling's Wizarding World had felt vivid on the page, then it became supersized within Leavesden Studios – a series of cavernous, former Second World War aircraft hangars. The Great Hall, scene to so many sumptuous banquets in *The Philosopher's Stone* (particularly the Christmas Dinner, where the Hogwarts pupils were served with endless bowls of roast potatoes), had been brought to life in vibrant detail. Cauldrons bubbled, the flames around their base kicking up some serious heat. The flagstone floors felt lived-in and historic. And floating candles dangled from the ceilings on wires. These real candles were eventually replaced by CGI for health and safety reasons, thus preventing anyone standing below them from being burned should the candles fall from their positions.

I felt humbled. Everything was mind-blowing. Even the benches and tables looked amazing. They were also bloody heavy, as I would discover to my cost when one toppled over and landed on my foot. It seemed obvious that when it came to bringing J.K. Rowling's story to life, no detail was going to be spared by Warner Bros. – the studio that owned the Harry Potter franchise. The scoreboard that marked the awarding of points for each of the four Hogwarts houses – Gryffindor, Slytherin, Hufflepuff and Ravenclaw – *actually bloody worked*. (I'm pretty sure that over the course of the franchise, I'm the only person to have worn the uniforms from all four houses.) Each of the Hogwarts teaching staff had their own specially designed chair at the High Table (an extra-large one for Rubeus Hagrid, and a much smaller one for Professor Flitwick). And when I looked through the windows of the Great Hall, I realised the world beyond the school had been painted onto a huge plasterboard wall. I saw an idyllic countryside scene with rolling hills. A shimmering trail of silver strips, stuck to the painting, created the rippling effect of a nearby lake.

Around that time, I had my first meeting with Dan Radcliffe, the kid tasked with playing Harry Potter and someone who would become a great friend in the years to come. We had first been introduced while sitting in the make-up department, but once the cast and crew had gathered together a little while later for our first location shoot at Goathland Station on the North Yorkshire Moors, I fully understood the magnitude of what we had been thrust into, particularly the three main actors – Dan, plus Rupert Grint, who was playing Ron, and Hermione Granger's Emma Watson.

The scene being filmed featured the students as they arrived at Hogwarts for the first time, via train, where Rubeus Hagrid, played by the brilliant Robbie Coltrane, was to greet Harry and his new schoolmates at the platform. As we worked, I noticed a gang of paparazzi had set up their long lens cameras on a hill in the distance. Then somebody mentioned the rumoured tabloid reward for any snapper filing the first shot of *Harry Potter*'s young cast, together on set: the fee sounded more like a telephone number than a freelancer's pay cheque. What ensued was a comical game of cat and mouse as the photographers were chased across the valley by a team of security guards. All of them were under strict instructions not to touch the snoopers, but to instead wave umbrellas in front of their cameras and to protect the actors from having their pictures taken. As the ridiculous scene played out in front of us, Greg whistled the *Benny Hill Show* theme tune. The chaos was a taste of things to come for everyone involved.

*

My first day of proper work on *Harry Potter and the Philosopher's Stone* turned out to be a life-defining event. In the weeks before filming began for real, I was shown into an empty studio space in Leavesden, which would later be transformed into a sound stage, complete with blue and green screens, the venue for many hours of visual effects work. The place was freezing; it carried a dirty, industrial vibe. But having been introduced to some of the people who would make up the stunt crew, while showing off with a backflip or two, I was sent towards the special effects workshop where a six-wheeled Dodge pickup truck with a flatbed rear was parked. The vehicle was a beast. Fixed to its structure was a giant mechanical arm, and the daunting metal limb had been fitted with a wooden broom handle and bike seat. I instantly recognised a key piece of Hogwarts lore. *A Nimbus 2000!* The high-powered broomstick was gifted to Harry by Professor Albus Dumbledore via Professor McGonagall before his first ever Quidditch match, which, as every reader knew, was the Wizarding World equivalent of a high-stakes Premier League football fixture.

Having been rigged into a climbing harness and settled on the bicycle seat, I was told to hold on tight and adopt the riding position familiar to Grand National jockeys and Tour de France riders. With a lurch, the contraption lifted me around eight feet in the air. Someone called out that this was a screen test, and I should pretend to be riding a broomstick in the book's memorable Quidditch match where Gryffindor play Slytherin, a scene in which Harry's ride is hijacked by a malevolent magic force, later revealed to be Hogwarts' dark-hearted teacher Quirinus Quirrell. In J.K. Rowling's prose, Harry was barely able to hold on. But at this stage in the production, there was no need for any violent acrobatics; I only had to focus on the basics, and I soared gracefully over the crash mat, watching for a Snitch and ducking from the fast-moving Bludger being thrown towards me by the stunt boys. My first ride was a buzz, and presumably a much less terrifying experience than Greg's original idea for bringing the script to life. I later learned that he'd asked a skydiving stuntman to leap from a plane with a broomstick. His plan had been to toss a load of child stunt performers wearing parachutes from a plane, all of them doubling as junior wizards, but the idea fell through when someone pointed out that the work wasn't insurable. It was also impractical, given the actors' faces needed to be seen onscreen.

This was the first time anybody had ever ridden a Nimbus 2000, and while my screen test had apparently been impressive, I was told the broomstick would be required to move at high speeds if it was to look realistic on film. 'Flying doesn't look legit without wind,' remarked Greg. And his suggestion was put into action shortly afterwards, when I was taken outside to an old Second World War runway, where the Dodge was waiting for me yet again, its crane-broom still dangling ominously from the back like an oversized hunk of Meccano. I prayed that nothing snapped off or spun out of control while I conducted a screen test. *Because this time, the car would be moving.* Greg stood nearby. Alongside him was Chris Columbus, the director of *Harry Potter and the Philosopher's Stone* and the creative mind famous for writing *Gremlins* and *The Goonies* and directing *Home Alone.* In cinematic terms, Chris was a grandmaster.

'Right, up you get, David,' said Greg, nodding at the metal limb. 'Time to fly.'

I mounted the broomstick and settled into the bicycle seat once more. Then somebody grabbed my leg. When I looked down, I saw a crew member from the wardrobe department.

'Here, put this on, mate.'

They were holding a red wizard's cape, the style worn by Harry in his first Quidditch match. *Bloody hell, this was it.* Chris then clambered into the flatbed of the truck and sat behind a camera that had been installed ahead of me.

'OK, David, I want you to pretend you're looking for the Snitch as you fly,' he shouted, staring into the viewfinder.

No problem. I was primed.

The Dodge pulled away. The wind caught my cape dramatically, fluttering the fabric and ruffling my hair. I scanned the skyline, looking for imagined Slytherin players and a tell-tale flash of gold – the sign of an approaching Snitch – taking care not to gawp directly into the camera lens. It was a bloody cold day. At some point, the Dodge must have hit the 30 miles per hour mark, and the air buffeted my face, making my eyes water. But I wasn't distracted, not even as the cloak yanked painfully at my neck. Flying was a fantasy of mine. It didn't take a lot of imagination to believe I was really cruising through the air on a broomstick.

As I moved, Chris shouted excitedly, 'We're getting it! This is definitely going to work!'

Eventually, the Dodge completed its circuit of the runway, and as I looked up and wiped the tears from my eyes, I heard applause from the watching crew members. Greg pulled on his cigar and beamed. *I'd nailed it.* The celebration sent a rush of excitement through me, and the exhilaration was far greater than anything I'd experienced when competing in a gymnastics comp. Then Chris shot out of his seat and grabbed my hand.

'Great job, David,' he shouted. 'You were really in it. You looked awesome.'

Then he called out to Greg. 'This is our guy,' he said, pointing to me.

Our guy? I had no idea what he was talking about.

Greg smiled proudly. 'Well, that's that settled then,' he said. 'David, you're now the lead stunt double for Harry Potter.'

★

My casting made a lot of sense. Not only was I physically capable of nailing the stunt work required for *Harry Potter and the Philosopher's Stone* (notable tasks included: flying Harry's broomstick; saving Hermione from a troll; my gloved hand doubling for Lee Jordan – played by Luke Youngblood – as it struck the scoreboard during the Quidditch match; and battling Voldemort in the story's nerve-shredding finale), but I was also built a lot like Dan Radcliffe.

We were the same height, give or take an inch, and with the right haircut, a cape and a nerdy pair of glasses, I passed for Harry quite easily. From a distance, at least. Given I was the same size as a lot of the kids on set, I could step into stunt work for several other actors. The role also gave me the opportunity to do something I'd dreamed of since landing my job with *Lost in Space*. I was about to fulfil every schoolkid's fantasy by telling my teachers to stick it.

At that point, I was still in the second year of sixth form, and studying French, Business Studies and PE. But the thought of completing my exams and working a regular job filled me with dread, especially as I was getting a tidy basic wage as a stunt per-former on *Harry Potter and the Philosopher's Stone*. One hundred and fifty quid was a lot of money at the time. But contractually, any stunts I did commanded an extra fee on top of my basic wage, and I negotiated those deals myself (some gags would earn me several thousand pounds a day further along in my career). Meanwhile, I was seventeen and legally old enough to quit full-time education. When the time arrived to announce my decision, I didn't hold back.

'I'm going to jump off buildings and set myself on fire for a living,' I said boldly.

The school's career advisor tried to talk me out of it. They pointed out the fact that a lot of stunt performers were ravaged by injury, their careers cut short at a young age. That didn't bother me in the slightest. I was bulletproof. Superhuman. *The next Spanky Spangler*. I had the evidence-based belief to back it up too: whenever I'd taken a knock during gymnastics, the pain had ricocheted off me, and I always recovered quickly from injury. It would be just the same in my Hollywood career. I then detailed my projected earnings for the next ten years, after which there wasn't much anyone could say. I was set to earn more money than my career advisor and any of the teachers working at the school. After that, I had their blessing, and

I'm sure one or two staff members were relieved to see me go, given my attitude and disruptive nature.

My parents were supportive of this career choice. They knew I'd found my passion, and a productive way in which to channel my boundless energy plus any urges I'd had to be a performer. Mum first noticed my enthusiasm while working on the set of *Lost in Space*. She guessed that even if I didn't make it as the next Spanky Spangler, my unusual talents might lead me to an interesting, creative destination, such as Cirque de Soleil. My parents also trusted me to look after myself, and not once did anyone try to change my mind. Noticeably, nobody wanted to talk about the risks either. If ever I was being asked to do something that sounded scary to someone not versed in the stringent safety procedures of a movie set (like being strapped to a metal arm on the back of a fast-moving flatbed Dodge), I wouldn't tell my parents until the gag had been completed. I loved my mum and dad dearly. I didn't want to worry them.

Every day at work was a crash course in Hollywood's smoke and mirrors approach, and it was a film fan's dream. The art department was incredible, and in the early days of Harry Potter they really captured the vision and scope for Hogwarts. In between filming, I spent hours staring at the drawings and schematics for future sets or scenes; the storyboards were incredibly detailed and every frame seemed to be an adventure all of its own. Elsewhere in Leavesden, the creature effects department, run by Nick Dudman, was another place to lose myself in. I had first encountered these geniuses at Goathland Station, having spotted the massive animatronic 'Hagrid Head', as worn by the England rugby player Martin Bayfield. Whenever a shot was needed to emphasise Hagrid's massive bulk, Martin – who was six foot ten inches tall, and built like a brick outhouse – was called into action. Sometimes he even wore stilts inside his costume, which was no cakewalk given he weighed around 120 kilos. Seeing Martin sitting alongside Hagrid's animatronic bonce was an awesome and unnerving experience. Every facial expression he made was replicated on the latex features, as a team of special effects artists buzzed around him frantically.

Away from Leavesden, all sorts of adventures took place. Australia House, the impressive embassy building located on the Strand in London, was the location for the Gringotts Wizarding Bank on Diagon Alley – where goblin staff assisted wizards and witches as they exchanged their Muggle money for magical currency. I explored the whole building while working on set, wandering into places I probably shouldn't have. But I didn't care; I loved visiting the make-up department, especially when the film's small performers were being transformed into Gringotts goblins. They were inspiring. Some of the actors carried severe disabilities; they put themselves through a lot of pain to contribute to the art of film-making and just the process of being made up lasted around four hours. The derigging work that took place at the end of the day lasted another ninety minutes, and wearing the prosthetics was hot work. Plus, goblin prosthetics hindered the wearer's vision, so tumbles and collisions could happen. I was there in a stunt safety capacity because the small performers had to sit on chairs that were four feet in height, and it was my job to make sure they got up there safely. Not that it was all stress. There were several, probably untrue rumours that full-scale goblin orgies were taking place somewhere in Australia House. The detail everyone loved was that some cast members had insisted on wearing full prosthetic kit for the fun and games.

Well away from this madness, and directing the on-camera magic, was Chris Columbus, who was brilliant at orchestrating his young actors and team members. None of us ever felt patronised. We were talked to as equals. And Chris was excellent at getting into the mind of a child, shouting memorable catchphrases as a way of focusing the cast on any required emotional responses. When someone needed to look scared, Chris yelled out, 'Eyes wide: *terrified!*'

Meanwhile, every action was made to feel fun; I never noticed him getting flustered or angry, and Chris created a safe space in which the crew could work to the best of their ability. I often spotted him standing behind the bank of TV monitors, known as Video Village, laughing his head off as he watched the latest playback. Chris was so thoughtful that he even rewarded his driver, Harry Taylor, with a small part in *Harry Potter and the Chamber of Secrets* as a thank you for all his hard work. Harry was cast as the ticket inspector at King's Cross Station. Because of his work on those first two films, Chris really set a positive tone for the franchise.

The bad cop to his good was Chris Carreras: the first assistant director and a terrifying motherfucker. Chris was approachable, but nobody really talked to him at work given he carried a Snape-level aura of scariness on set and shouted better than anybody else I've worked with. That's because life as an assistant director was full-on, especially when working with a cast of kids. At times, Chris must have felt as if he was herding a horde of drunken ferrets, never more than when ordering dozens – sometimes hundreds – of pre-pubescent wizards into action. If anyone spoke during a take, Chris bollocked them. If one of us made a noise behind the camera, he went ballistic, even if it was miles away and unlikely to affect the sound. In the event of a blunder, the crew was first scolded and then reminded that every wasted roll of celluloid was expensive. Away from the studio, Chris was a lovely guy. But when it came to applying professional pressure, he knew how to crack the whip better than anybody. Without his presence, filming probably would have taken an extra two or three months to complete.

★

Throughout the first production, my role was as varied as you could imagine. Sometimes I lined up shots for Harry, and several other characters, whether that was running at full speed, jumping from ladders or dangling from out-of-control broomsticks. In *Harry Potter and the Philosopher's Stone*, I doubled for every member of the lead cast. I was Hermione in the bathroom stalls when a troll smashes its way in. I did the grunt work when Ron sacrifices himself by jumping on the back of an oversized chess piece so that Harry can retrieve the titular stone at the film's end. And when Dudley Dursley falls into the snake enclosure of a zoo, I was zipped into a fat suit and asked to tumble across the enclosure. I recently found an old photo of myself in the costume and wondered how it might have affected the actor, Harry Melling. Harry was a chubby kid back then, though he's in great shape now, but having someone step into a fat suit to replicate your build can't have been a great feeling. I hope he wasn't emotionally scarred by the experience and developed a healthy relationship with his body image.

Whenever I was asked to wear the glasses and double for Dan, I always felt inspired. The stunts were fun but taxing, and if someone suggested that a gag couldn't work, or that the physicality required for a certain task might have been beyond my capabilities, I took it as a personal challenge. At times, my determination was an asset. On other occasions, it resulted in some nasty cuts and bruises, most memorably when I was asked to perform a reference shot – a piece of footage where a performer's movements are recorded so they can be digitally replicated on film by the visual effects department. (Once the gag was captured, a VFX designer worked against a stunt actor's movements for accuracy and to build a more realistic CGI shot.) In cinematic terms, my reference shot made up the background work for one of *The Philosopher's Stone's* most memorable visuals: the moment Harry catches the Snitch in his mouth during his first Quidditch match.

Getting the footage was no easy matter. To move like a wizard hitting the deck, it was decided that I should tumble from a fast-moving skateboard, the necessary speed generated by towing me on a quadbike via a length of rope. Riding the bike was Greg, who revved his engines and pulled away, building up speed. I aimed the skateboard at a small brick wall positioned just in front of a row of crash mats, and the plan was for the board to hit the obstacle, the impact propelling me forward. If the work itself wasn't troublesome enough, it was freezing cold and I was wearing a motion capture suit – a Lycra all-in-one gimp outfit dotted with bright orange ping-pong balls. This weird onesie allowed my body shape to be tracked on computer. Obviously, I looked like an idiot, and because of the bone-chilling temperatures, not a lot was going on 'downstairs'. But that wasn't the worst of it. As Greg sped towards the mats, it was almost impossible to maintain a solid form on the board, the camera capturing my body's reactions from side on as I experienced a series of unintended pratfalls.

At times, I jammed into the wall, and physics did its work, my body driving into the crash mats. On other occasions, I lost my balance and hit the deck in a nasty stack. The most painful bump of all happened when a stone jammed up one of the wheels. The board was ripped away from beneath me at high speed and I slammed my feet into the concrete. The pain was excruciating. When I later complained to a crew member that I might have broken my foot, Greg overheard me and scowled.

'Don't worry about it,' he said. 'Take your bruises and move on.'

In the School of Hard Knocks, this was yet another invaluable lesson. Pain was the reward for a good day of work. And there was no room for cry-babies in the stunt department.

★

But I didn't want to be a cry-baby. I wanted to be a stuntman. And to get there, I had to prove myself every single day. I showed off whenever I could, somersaulting from portacabin roofs and climbing ladders and walls like a monkey, because I was determined to be judged on merit, rather than as someone who was there because they resembled the lead actor in shape and height. That probably made me a bit much for some of the older, grizzlier team members. The action movie scene was packed full of macho men, blokes who liked to smash themselves up on the job, laugh away their head injuries afterwards and then drink themselves silly in the nearest bar. Some (not all) of the attitudes towards race, women and sexuality were outdated back then; they would create a human resources nightmare today. In all the fighting and fucking talk, there wasn't much time for my teenage bullshit. I remember being told to calm down on one or two occasions.

'Don't come at me with your stories,' grumbled one bloke, after I'd engaged him with a little too much energy. He then pointed to the cavernous studio hangar behind. 'When you've smashed yourself up as much as me, you can start your boasting.'

But I idolised the characters I met. Not because of *who they were*, or *what they thought*, but because of *what they did*. The war stories I heard on set only reinforced the feeling that being a stunt performer was the greatest job in the world.

Greg was full of tales. And every day I learned more lessons about the fantasy world of Hollywood, one of which was that it wasn't smart to work with either kids or animals. This was ironic given both seemed to be running the first *Harry Potter* movie. I heard the story of how, in the 1980s, a stunt team was tasked with moving a stubborn camel that refused to budge from its standing position on set. Having had its reins pulled, its arse smacked and its hind end pushed by several burly men, the animal showed no signs of compliance. Then someone had the bright idea of stacking a bundle of hay underneath the beast and setting the lot alight. 'This'll shift it,' assumed the crew, who then watched in astonishment as the camel stood fast, unmoved, the flames tickling its belly.

Some stories held a personal connection for Greg. Like the time his brother, Gary, another Hollywood stuntman, launched a Russian tank from a ramp and through a St Petersburg wall for the James Bond movie *GoldenEye*. (He also performed a 360-degree barrel roll across the Thames in a speedboat.) According to legend, Gary had been suspended inside the vehicle with bungee cords, to protect his spine from shattering once the tank's tracks had landed and bounced off the concrete road. Over time, I heard it all: stories of people nearly dying for their art, and tall tales of stunt performers walking away from mangled, smouldering car wrecks with barely a scratch. My mind raced at the thought of nailing a similar gag. I wanted to be those stories. I wanted to be the guy at the heart of them. I wanted people to say, 'Fuck me, did you hear about the stunt David landed the other day? *It was incredible.*'

Under Greg's tutelage I was being gifted an opportunity, and I worshipped him for it. That's because he was a bloke who commanded respect from everyone he worked with, even the movie and stage icon Richard Harris, who played Albus Dumbledore. On the first Harry Potter movie, Richard crossed the set to shake Greg's hand. But Greg wasn't arrogant, or The Big I Am; he was generous with his knowledge and willing to show me the tricks and hacks required to make it. He even taught me how to flirt with women and to engage with studio-sized egos; he allowed me to present myself with confidence. As I grew in stature and nailed more and more stunts on *Harry Potter and the Philosopher's Stone*, Greg looked on like a proud parent. That felt great. He was the person I admired most of all in the business, and I couldn't push back on him. After jamming my toes in that skateboard accident, I never wanted to look weak in front of Greg again. Or scared or hurt, for that matter.

It helped that life as a working crash test dummy was fun. The bumps and cuts were often laughed off, and every day felt like playtime. At some stage during production, the crew decamped to London Zoo* for the scenes in which the Dursleys, plus Harry Potter

---

* In the book, the zoo was an unnamed establishment in Surrey.

(the black sheep of his adoptive family and a perennially unwelcome guest), take a day trip for Dudley's birthday. As they wander through the reptile house, Dudley – the school bully and Harry's nemesis – goads a Burmese python in its vivarium. Then he's transported into the pen by a little accidental magic. Given we were filming in the actual reptile house, and there were slithering beasts and highly venomous fangs everywhere, anyone with ophidiophobia endured a lot of sleepless nights. For the rest of us, it was a party.

One day, Greg was struck by a cruel idea. 'Here, take all this cash,' he said, stuffing some twenties into my hand. 'Go to a toy shop and buy as many rubber snakes as you can.'

Why?

'You'll see,' he said, laughing darkly.

When I returned, Greg disclosed his scheme. We were to plant the lifeless but very real-looking rubber snakes surreptitiously behind cameras and into chairs. Some of them would be discreetly placed in the wardrobe and hair-and-make-up departments. Others were to be dropped into the shadows at the reptile house. Unattended bags were considered legitimate targets too. Greg's hope was that any crew member stumbling across a rubber snake would naturally assume that it was an escaped resident, highly venomous, and to be avoided at all costs. Then they would freak out. He was right, too. For a couple of days, we heard shrieks and screams as our victims discovered yet another dummy reptile in their rucksack or under their boom microphone. The pair of us folded up laughing with every scare. That is, until the gag backfired.

One of the joys of working behind the scenes in a famous location like London Zoo was that the cast and crew pretty much had the run of the place. Later, during *Harry Potter and the Philosopher's Stone*, the Hogwarts infirmary (where Harry is cared for following his first, fateful run-in with Voldemort) was recreated in the famous Divinity School at the Bodleian Library in Oxford – one of the oldest libraries in the world. In one particularly knackering night shoot, I ended up falling asleep on one of the bookshelves at three in the morning. The access at London Zoo was just the same, and Greg and I often wandered along the back of the glass display cases that housed some of the world's most dangerous snakes, including the Mangshan pit viper, which was a particularly worrying presence, seeing as nobody had yet discovered a suitable anti-venom.

One day, having peered into the vivarium for a while, Greg pointed to a display case at the end of the row. There was no clue as to what was inside, other than a large sign stuck to the front with the ominous warning 'Do Not Disturb'. Given the environment, this seemed like solid advice, especially as some of the inhabitants had the tools to either poison or crush a person to death. When I looked, the paper covered the entire window.

'Go on, David, lift up that sign,' said Greg. 'See what's inside.'

I shook my head. 'But it says *Do Not Disturb* on the front.'

Greg sucked on his cigar and scowled. Even in London Zoo, he refused to be separated from his Monte Cristo No.2s.

'All right, I'll do it,' I sighed, nervously approaching the glass.

Big mistake. As I lifted the sign and peered in, there was an almighty bang, causing the vivarium front to tremble. The impact had been so loud, and so violent, that I assumed Greg had slapped his palm on the screen to give me a fright. Then I looked down and jumped back in shock. A king cobra was eyeballing me aggressively from behind the glass, its hood flared, the sign of an imminent strike. The snake must have spotted my movements as I'd lifted the paper, taken my approach as a threat, and attacked. Not that I took any time to consider the implications of what was happening. I turned and sprinted, Greg following behind me. As we ran, the pair of us laughed like drains.

4

HEALTH AND SAFETY!

On one of the very first days of filming, Greg pulled me over. He had been watching Dan, dressed in full wizarding kit, as he attempted to swing a Beater's bat at an imaginary Bludger.

'You're going to have to do a lot of work with this one,' he said, pointing as Wizarding World's hero-in-waiting took another clumsy swipe. And then another. *And another.* At one point, Dan tripped on his laces and looked set to topple over.

I understood Greg's concerns. Despite being eleven years old, Dan had all the coordination of a blindfolded kid slashing at a piñata. When it came to the dangerous stunt work on *The Philosopher's Stone*, I knew I'd be doing a lot of the heavy lifting as Harry, as would the younger Tolga Kenan, who was the child stunt performer also doubling for for Harry Potter. But there was still plenty of physicality to Dan's role. He was required to run, jump and reach for Snitches onscreen. It wasn't going to look very good if he had all the timing of a mountain troll. At that point in the production, I'd had very little to do with him; filming had only just begun, everyone was getting to know one another, and apart from being introduced to Dan as his stunt double – a concept he'd loved – we hadn't enjoyed a lot of interaction.

Everything changed later that day when we strapped Dan into his basic broomstick for the first time – a contraption similar to the beast I'd trialled with Chris Columbus a couple of weeks earlier. The good news for Dan was that he wasn't going to be speeding down a runway at

Leavesden Studios at 30 miles per hour, the wind buffeting his eyeballs and freezing his nipples off. Instead, the experience was studio-based and a lot more static. The rig had been set up at Alnwick Castle, near Newcastle, the physical home of Hogwarts, and having helped Dan onto the bicycle seat, I imparted some advice on how he should position his body and distribute his weight in the uncomfortable saddle. At the South Essex Gymnastics Club, I'd become regarded as a senior athlete, and was occasionally tasked with educating the younger kids on certain techniques or warm-up sessions. In those situations, I spoke to everyone as if they were equals, rather than people six or seven years younger than me. That was how my coaches had taught me, Greg too, and the approach had left a positive mark. I wanted to apply the same style when working with Dan.

'Right, I'm putting this harness on you,' I said, clipping the strapping around his hips. 'A mechanical arm is going to lift you off the floor, but there's a mat underneath in case you fall. Don't worry, mate: you're going to be nice and safe.'

Really, that's all a person wants to hear while perched on a mechanical broomstick that looks as though it might catapult them into the air at any given moment. Even though it was a comparatively steady version of the Nimbus 2000 I'd tested a few weeks earlier, riding a broomstick was still an intimidating thing to do, especially when performing in front of the cast and crew. But Dan took to it like a duck to water. (During the filming process, these rigs were upgraded and moved by several pneumatic pistons positioned underneath. Having been placed in front of blue or green screens so that CGI could be added after filming, a series of extending arms then moved the broomstick in almost any direction. The saddles were still perched on the end of pole arms with counterweights at one end, and for certain shots upwards of sixteen people were needed to manoeuvre them, adding to the sense that it was a precarious ride.)

That's not to say the tech was outdated, or poorly put together. Quite the opposite, in fact. I remember one scene in which Harry and Malfoy had to engage each other on broomsticks in the Quidditch match during *Harry Potter and the Chamber of Secrets*. To capture the shot, two identical rigs were set up, both comprising pole arms, but with slightly different broomsticks fixed on top. Away from these mechanical beasts, a special effects puppeteer worked with two small-scale replicas, and as they were moved, the real mechanics responded in kind. As with anything technological, these rigs would occasionally glitch, and any problems usually made themselves apparent when I was perched in the saddle. Sometimes a broomstick would shake so violently that I'd have to cling on for dear life, but as a professional crash test dummy, I told myself that if something was to go wrong, it was much better that it happened to me, a trained athlete who could control a fall, than one of the lead actors, who couldn't.

The most painful part of the whole process was the razor-thin bicycle seat. If you ever want to know what it feels like to ride a Nimbus 2000, just sit on a bike, take your feet off the pedals and put all your weight through your backside. Then stay in the same spot for several hours at a time. For a while I wore a pair of heavily padded cycling shorts to protect my family jewels, not that it did much good, and I often walked away from the set like a constipated Charlie Chaplin, such was the discomfort in my undercarriage. That all changed as the franchise continued, and by the sixth film any cast members tasked with flying a Nimbus broomstick were presented with a bespoke seat, moulded perfectly to the delicate curvature of their bum cheeks. But in the early days there were no such luxuries, sadly, and given that I was flying more wizard miles than anyone else on the crew, my bollocks were mangled beyond recognition.

I didn't see Dan again for a few weeks after his first ride on a broomstick, but it was decided that I should help him take his coordination skills to the next level. Greg had suggested the idea and one day Dan joined me in the crew's 'Stunt Stores' – a space positioned in the depths of the studio, away from the major sets, and built around two portacabins. One of these was an office, the second a gym, fitted with a running machine and stationary bike, plus all the weights and a pull-up bar. Lying about the place was a series of crash mats, some high wires, and all sorts of toys for the stunt crew to train on and jump from, among them a trampoline and a Russian swing. As far as Greg was concerned, playing around was to be encouraged. He hated the thought of his stunt team dossing about between scenes and scratching themselves silly. Instead, he wanted us to train harder, to push ourselves to the limit as we developed new skills and in such an environment there were always opportunities to learn. Sometimes a specialised stuntman might arrive to shoot a particular scene, such as an actor trained in the art of judo or fencing. As they moved, I studied them closely. As they recovered, I picked their brains on technique. I wanted to do everything I could to improve.

But I noticed that Dan was cut from the same cloth as me. Although he was a quiet and enigmatic kid – and very much like the Harry Potter character – he buzzed with energy and was eager to learn. Rather than lording it up as the headline act in a soon-to-be blockbuster movie, Dan acted like a sponge, and he made the most of his time away from the cameras by picking brains and soaking up knowledge. He loved chatting with crew members from various departments, just as I did. Together, we wandered happily from department to department, talking to the team in wardrobe, or special effects, where we all loved playing with the remote controls that orchestrated the facial movements on a fantastical beast.

Interestingly, Rupert Grint didn't show the same levels of curiosity and was an entirely different character to Dan. For starters, he wasn't into his keep fit, and all he had in his room for 'exercise' was a table tennis set-up and a PlayStation, which kept the young cast entertained for hours. That's not to say he couldn't do the physical work. I remember while making the first Harry Potter film, Rupert was asked to fall from a fan descender* that had been set to a height of 30 feet. He looked up at the intimidating drop and didn't even flinch. As he fell, the cable slowing his descent, it was obvious he had confidence in his ability to act in a more physical way, but it just wasn't his thing. Whenever someone asked him if he wanted to perform one of the less dangerous stunts, Rupert would shrug his shoulders. *Meh.* That was his vibe all over: laid back, funny and sweet as a nut.

I only doubled for Rupert once, during the scene in *The Philosopher's Stone* when Ron, Harry and Hermione entered the Chessboard Chamber, an obstacle guarding the titular stone. In a high-stakes game of human chess, Ron – straddling a black knight – sacrifices himself to the white queen, allowing his friends to advance safely. But in doing so, he is thrown backwards from his piece, a gag that required me to fly 6 feet through the air and onto a hard marble floor, all while avoiding the fire pits that lined the perimeter of the board. I managed to nail the gag in one take, which gave me a rush at the time. Then, when my pay cheque arrived, I realised I'd been paid a grand for just one attempt and regretted not taking a few more hits. Pain was profitable after all.

Rupert was blessed with an incredible sense of comic timing, and during the first two films both he and Dan would piss about constantly, which must have driven Chris Columbus mad. Every now and then, I shared the same view. During the flying car sequence at the beginning of *The Chamber of Secrets*, I was forced to spend too long wedged behind the pair of them in the back of the cramped

---

* A fan descender allows a person to experience freefall on a wire for a few seconds before a safety mechanism kicks in, slowing the user's descent for a safe touchdown.

Ford Anglia as it swung this way and that on a hydraulic gimbal, the pair of them cracking dad jokes and giggling. While they cocked about, I had to sit out of sight while holding an owl cage in place, the live bird inside pecking angrily at my fingers. The work was agony, and the humiliation was compounded whenever I was thrown about and both boys howled loudly at my muted groans.

Meanwhile, Dan's visits to the Stunt Stores became a daily event, and I embraced working as his personal trainer. Our sessions always began with a warm-up, and we grunted through a series of push-ups, sit-ups and burpees. Then the fun began, and I often encouraged him to look past his fears in a series of controlled jumps and twists from an increasingly challenging height. During our first training day together, I asked him to fall backwards from the top of a portacabin and into the inflatable crash mats positioned below.

'Go on,' I said, pointing to the ladder leading to the office's flat roof. 'Climb up there and jump off that.'

Dan looked at me like I was mad. The drop was around 10 feet.

'It's all right.' I laughed. 'You'll be fine.'

I was right, too. And when he tipped backwards from the portacabin and was sucked into the oversized crash mat, he leaped up with a huge grin, his fears crushed.

Throughout filming, Dan came to me a couple of times a week, and we would shut the stunt room doors and wreak havoc together. We jumped on trampolines and fought with prop swords. I taught him throws for judo, combinations for boxing and, most importantly, some gymnastics moves, such as somersaults, handstands and one or two acrobatic manoeuvres. For the most part, I wanted to check on his fitness, but I also wanted to study his general movement so I could then work out in what areas he needed to improve, whether that was in his running style or jumping skills. Everything we did was viewed through the lens of how it might look on camera; but, most importantly, the Stunt Stores became a place for us to play away from the film crew, where there was pressure and prying eyes.

I was always careful with Dan. There would be hell to pay if he were to injure himself. He was the lead actor in a multi-million-dollar movie, after all. Most of the time, though, I wanted him to be like a kid and have fun. That's why everything we did was based around play: it was important Dan had a safe space in which to learn and grow without it becoming a ball-ache. An example of this was the push-up game, a gnarly test of balance that involved two opponents facing each other in the plank position. The object of the competition was for one person to pull their opponent's hand from underneath their body, causing them to fall onto the mat, face first. The pair of us would roll about the place laughing as we played, and anyone passing by would have assumed that we were messing about. The truth was very different. As an exercise, the push-up game was great for building core muscles. Once we were done, Dan often returned to his make-up chair sweating, with bright-red hands and wrists, his biceps bulging and abs aching.

As he became stronger and more athletic, we worked on punch reactions and fight routines with various weapons. I then increased his gymnastic vocabulary by doing both forward and backward somersaults, on and off the trampoline. But I had another reason for training Dan: as his stunt double, I needed to understand the way he moved and how he reacted to a bang or a fall. Yeah, my job was to do the dangerous stuff so that he didn't have to. But I also needed to know what he was capable of, because whenever I doubled for Dan it was important I mirrored his style of movement. Forget the costume and glasses: *I had to move like Harry Potter*. That way, the editors could seamlessly blend the work of two people.

Through training, I was able to pick up on some of the subtle but defining nuances in his posture and physicality. For starters, I noticed that when Dan walked, he appeared a little flat-footed. It was the same when he ran too, and upon impact the front of Dan's toes seemed to slap the floor a bit harder – he never moved from heel to toe like a lot of people. I also realised that whenever he did a push-up, his left side dipped slightly lower than his right, and in training we worked on improving his weaknesses. Today, whenever he exercises with a personal trainer and performs pull-ups or plank holds, Dan has an almost perfect alignment.

Occasionally, accidents happened during filming, especially as Dan became more comfortable with doing some of the minor gags himself. (There were never any accidents in the Stunt Store, thankfully.) One of these took place at the 'flight shed', a massive hangar at Leavesden Studios at the bottom of the runway. This space was to house some of the greatest sets in the franchise's history, but in the first film the giant chessboard was built there. We also shot the scenes in which the ghost of Voldemort passed through Harry towards the end of *The Philosopher's Stone*, a moment that sends him tumbling to the floor. Dan was performing this move himself, and I had gifted him his own set of hip and back pads to mark the occasion, but during the set-up he'd taken the wrong position on stage and was a couple of steps ahead of where he was supposed to be. Worse, I hadn't noticed. As filming began and Voldemort's ghostly form passed through him, Dan fell back as planned, but rather than landing on his arse, he smacked his head on the wall behind.

It was a big hit. Someone shouted, 'Cut!' and a crowd gathered around Dan. When I looked down at him, his eyes were brimming with tears.

My stomach lurched. I was his stunt double. Not only was I responsible for taking the whacks on his behalf, but I also had to check his safety whenever he was doing any physical work. Instead, I'd become distracted. The previous day I had busted a rib or two in a wire gag that had gone wrong. A stuntman, Paul Herbert, had overshot his mark and crashed into me, his body colliding with my chest. At the time of Dan's accident, I had been nursing my own bruises. In doing so, I had taken my eye off the ball and another cock-up had taken place.

Chris Columbus looked at his watch. Child actors had strict rules about how long and how late they could work for, and it was close to wrapping-up time for Dan. But when it was decided we should stop for the day, he looked crestfallen. That's when I realised: Dan hadn't been crying from the pain. He was worried that he wouldn't get to complete his first ever gag.

Greg agreed. 'He's taken a bump,' he said, glaring at me. 'Let's not get him to do anything else.'

Then he pulled me to one side. 'He's your fucking actor,' he snarled. 'You're in charge of his fucking safety. What the fuck are you doing?'

'I fucked up—'

Greg hadn't finished. 'You should have been there.'

'I know.'

'You should have been more alert. You should have been telling him how to do it. You should have been showing him in rehearsal. Instead, you let other crew members set him on the floor. *And you didn't tell him.*'

I felt sick, and humbled. I had let Greg down, which I hated doing more than I also hated seeing Dan hurt because I cared for him. Rather than proving I was a safe pair of hands, I had lost focus for a split second and the consequences had nearly been disastrous. This, I told myself, was a sign I had to work much harder. Even though I was teaching Dan how to be a stronger, fitter and braver Harry Potter, I still had plenty to learn myself.

★

The Stunt Stores were the perfect place in which to improve. On some days, I practised jumping onto the studio trampoline, launching myself up, up, up, *as high as I could*, until one day, I'd learned how to grab hold of the girders that criss-crossed the ceiling. Hanging there for as long as I was able, my muscles turning to jelly, I then dropped, tumbling into the trampoline again before springing away into a clean landing. Other times, I'd work with members of the stunt crew as we rigged a series of wires and pulleys around the office. One of us would climb into a harness attached to the lines, as the others took hold of the wires. They then pulled, hard, yanking whoever was dangling from the contraption up into the air and over the portacabins, as if they were flying over Hogwarts or being blown backwards in an act of dark magic.

But the most intense piece of training I remember doing was to attach myself to a *dead man's wire*. This was a cable with very little flex. One end was fixed to a wall, the rest of it was attached to me, and it was my job to run as hard as I could, sprinting at full tilt, until . . .

Crack!

Having reached the end of my tether, the solid-state wire tightened sharply, snapping me backwards at high speed and with nothing in the way of deceleration.* On film, the physical reaction made it look as if I'd been shot dead or fatally electrocuted. *Hence the name.* But the act was incredibly painful and took a lot of balls to execute. At times, the experience of being whiplashed backwards through the air wasn't too dissimilar to being involved in a high-speed car accident. My internal organs slammed into my ribcage

---

* In the old Western movies, a similar practice was used on horses for whenever one needed to be 'shot' or fatally injured in a scene. One end of the dead man's wire was attached by hobbles to the front legs of the horses, the other to an immovable object. And when the beast galloped and hit the point of no return, it was dragged violently to the ground. This technique was bloody cruel and has thankfully now been banned.

with every propulsive move. I'd feel my jawbone extending forwards and I sometimes wore a mouthguard to protect my gnashers. At the other end of the line was Greg, who liked to stand there, his fist extended outwards to a fixed point that left a gap of an inch or so between his knuckles and my final extension.

'Run into my punch, as fast as you can,' he would shout.

I'd launch myself towards him, unthinking, into what I hoped would be a ghostly right hander. With centimetres to spare, the dead man's wire pulled taut and I'd explode backwards, as if knocked out by a Rocky Balboa upper cut, my intestines throbbing, my teeth grinding.

Bits of kit came and went, and we played with any new toys until they'd been mastered. For a while, we even had an air ram – a catapult that was used to throw a stunt performer, attached to a wire, through the air after a pyrotechnic explosion. Rigged full of hydraulic pressure, the device came with a footplate. When somebody stepped on it, a ramp flipped upwards, launching the user through the air at a fair height. When you stepped onto one, it was important to keep your legs straight because if you bent your knees your limbs would buckle during connection. The result was a mangle of legs because instead of flying forward, a loose-limbed jumper was instead rocketed upwards and they then landed on the ramp with a painful bang, triggering it once more and propelling the injured victim skywards. That air ram was a notorious breaker of bones for the unwary.

Elsewhere, I was taught the important ratio between flying distances and the amount of crash mats required to protect a person from injury. For every 10 feet travelled, a stunt performer required a foot of padding to land upon, or decelerate into, if they were to avoid suffering too much pain or a serious injury. Though looking at the flimsy material was often unnerving – the standard padding used for high-velocity collisions were no different to the type of kit I'd used in PE at school, or in the gymnastics club, and they came in three depths: 3 inches, 6 inches and 12 inches. None of them looked particularly safe, but they served their purpose and a lot of the time I was thankful to have them around.

The stunt office was also a crucible of film history. There were no streaming services in the days of the early Harry Potter movies. Blockbuster Video was king, and DVDs were considered the cutting edge of technology. But in one corner of the office was an old VHS and DVD combination player, and Greg loved gathering the core stunt team together so we could review our most recent work or study the gags and explosions from any newly released action movies. We re-watched classic stunts too, some of them performed by Greg or one of his mates, and he'd amassed a stockpile of films for us to look at together. I can distinctly remember studying the harrowing, bloody opening scenes of *Saving Private Ryan* and marvelling at the way the actors were being pulled this way and that by exploding mortars and turned into mincemeat by German machine-gun fire. Every now and then, Greg would pause a frame to point out a technique or some renowned stuntman. Other times we'd watch *Doctor Zhivago*, just because he reckoned it was one of the greatest films ever made.

Alongside Greg in what was a family dynasty of daredevils was his brother-in-law, Brad Farmer, who was becoming a core member of the Harry Potter stunt team and later scored credits on *Game of Thrones*, *Skyfall* and *The Dark Knight Rises*. Brad was hardcore. What he lacked in gymnastic expertise, he more than made up for with his balls of steel, and he never shied away from attempting stunts that some people might have considered as being too sketchy. He was also a fearless stunt driver and once travelled from southern Spain to London in a day by racing at full tilt. Brad and me quickly became firm mates and once I'd passed drinking age, he opened me up to a world of illicit wonder. I used to stay over at his house and smoke weed, and he later took me to Pacha in

Ibiza, where I gobbled my first ecstasy pill. Talk about a chemical romance: as I danced with The Beautiful People in one of the world's greatest nightclubs, my eyes were opened to a brand-new consciousness.

Also in the group was Greg's brother, Gary Powell, then in his late thirties and the younger of the siblings by ten years. Like Greg, he was a beast of a man, and like Greg his CV read like a *Best of Hollywood* ... list from *Empire* magazine. Gary had worked on some of the industry's greatest modern efforts, including *Braveheart*, *Mission: Impossible* and *Saving Private Ryan*. After I met him, he worked on *Casino Royale*, *The Bourne Ultimatum* and *Ready Player One*. This was a stuntman at the peak of his profession. And as with his brother, Gary believed that stunts were supposed to be scary, stunt performers were supposed to take whacks, and the job was about enjoying the hit, dusting yourself down, and getting the fuck on with it, even when you were in agony.

Together with Marc Cass, Lee Millham and Paul Herbert – plus Tolga Kenan – our group designed the Harry Potter stunts by trial and error. If a script called for Harry or Draco Malfoy to be pulled through the air, Greg would firstly figure out how the gag was going to work. Then I, or one of the others, acted as a triallist. This generally involved me climbing into a harness and suspending myself from a cable. From there, my safety was very much in the hands of a wire team, two rigging experts who jumped on and off a platform while hanging from the line in order to yank me one way or another. There was very little in the way of mathematical calculations going on; everything was figured out through repeated action. Ideally, you needed the ropes to be pulled by those with an understanding of aerial awareness and the different ways your body can fly at speed – people who had spent time in gymnastics clubs.

My very first time on the wire took place on *Lost in Space*. I was clipped into a flying harness – a belt-like device that was wrapped around my waist at a point that represented my centre of gravity. This allowed me to perform a series of somersaults and poses in mid-air, and I loved it. When I first flew across the studio, I was able to perform rolls and acrobatic spins as Greg and his team looked on approvingly. I soon grew accustomed to the job and used my experience from the gymnastics club to try new manoeuvres, having realised that wirework required me to break down a large, complicated task into a series of smaller, manageable stages. The first step was to get into the harness. Then I had to grow accustomed to being lifted into the air by two riggers as they pulled on a series of ropes. Finally, I had to hold myself in such a way that it looked as if I was flying, falling or hanging from an out-of-control broomstick.

When it came to the testing of new techniques, I sometimes felt that liberties were taken with me because I was small and eager to please. On a movie I won't name, and with a stunt performer I won't identify, I performed the type of gag that would bring a health and safety official out in stress hives. The instigator, who was an incredible performer but also an absolute headcase, had worked out a way of reverse engineering an air ram. Instead of the hydraulic platform firing a performer up in the air, it was raised in advance so that it could catch them as they fell, a safety wire slowing their descent on the way. That was the theory, anyway; no practical tests had been performed, and, to get there, this one stunt performer had decided that I was the perfect guinea pig for the job.

Having outlined the plan and pointed out – not too convincingly – that there was zero risk involved, the individual in question led me to a studio set positioned away from the main stages, presumably in case anyone of seniority was watching. They then attached me to the cable dangling from the ceiling at a height of around 10 metres.

'David, I'm going to hoist you all the way up.'

Right.

I gulped.

And then?

'And then you're going to freefall onto the air ram, which is going to catch you, decelerate, and bring you down to safety. Don't worry, the wire will slow you down.'

I didn't ask questions. I was a kid and desperate to be accepted by the stunt community. More terrifying than the fall was the idea that I might be rejected if I refused or, worse, branded a coward, which I'd learned was a death sentence in the daredevil game. The reputation would follow me everywhere, and I didn't want to be tarnished so early on in my career. Keeping my concerns to myself, I was strapped into a safety harness and winched slowly to the top. Then I waited for the drop.

'You happy?' shouted the stunt person, pulling a series of crash mats around the air ram.

No! I thought. 'Yes!' I shouted.

'Three . . .'

Fuck.

'Two . . .'

Fucking fuck.

'One . . .'

Fuck. Fuck. Fuck—

The brake holding me in place released with a click and I fell, my body levelling out into a flat position. I dropped like a stone, my adrenaline soaring, and then I felt the wire tugging at me reassuringly. My descent slowed, the harness strained, and as I prepared to connect with the extended air ram, I braced for disaster. But rather than hurling me up into the air again, the contraption lowered me slowly to the ground, as promised. I started laughing. I was a bit winded, but other than that, miraculously unharmed.

My colleague-turned-tormentor looked delighted too. 'Right, now we're going to try it again,' they said. 'But I'm going to set the ramp to decelerate a bit later.'

Why the fuck would you do that? I thought. 'All right, let's do it,' I said defiantly, as I was winched to the 10-metre-high mark once more.

But when I looked down, I noticed the stunt person was pulling the safety mats away. That's when I realised: *I was being toyed with.* The experiment had already been a success. There was no need to push me any further. But what had initially been set up as a challenge of logistics, physics and movement was now being twisted into something completely different. *A battle of nerves.* And in those situations, I never backed down, regardless of the risks.

My heart hammered. The Little Man Syndrome in me rose up. *There's no chance you're going to get to me, you fucking idiot,* I thought, angrily thinking back to those bullies at school. *You can push me as far as you want. But I'm not bottling it.*

The brake released me again, and I rotated perfectly, my body set in the classic Superman-in-flight position. Then I felt the tug of the wire and connected heavily with the ram, my abdominals taking the brunt of the impact. But this time, with the platform set to decelerate a split second later, and without the cushioning of a safety mat, my extended arms slammed into the concrete floor. The impact reverberated agonisingly through my palms and into my elbows. My shoulders and back vibrated; my hands, forehead and cheekbones suffered such a bang that they were later shadowed by heavy bruising. *But I hadn't chickened out.* And that was the most important thing of all.

These tests, when passed, helped to cement my rep in the business: as far as everyone around me was concerned, I could cut it. I certainly wasn't going to lose my nerve, or cry over a bruised rib or a black eye. But passing these screwed-up rites of passage also showed that I could handle the pressure, which in Hollywood was sometimes the toughest challenge of all. Plaster of Paris studio sets cost hundreds of thousands of pounds to design and build – sometimes even millions. They were manned by highly paid technicians and support staff, creatives and performers, all of them on huge wages. If a prop was designed to blow up, or a ludicrously expensive car was due to be concertinaed in a high-speed crash, one mistake could put a massive dent in the production budget. Certain stunts had to be executed in one take, or else.

As if that wasn't bad enough, there were often unexpected variables to contend with, factors that could throw a stunt performer off his or her game. Successfully testing a wire gag in advance of a costly scene was one thing. Performing it in front of an audience of judgemental filmmakers, plus banks of lights and cameras and pyrotechnic bangs, crashes and wallops, added an extra layer of tension. And that was before a visit to the wardrobe department. The physicality of stunt work was hard enough. But when wearing a superhero costume or a Hogwarts cape, it became a whole lot harder. Fortunately, the stress of it all bounced away from me, and when the stakes were highest, and a one-take stunt was required, I usually delivered, which kept the accountants happy. Likewise, when the pressure was off, and there was the time and budget to get things wrong, I was able to handle the pain until the gag had been nailed. In the aftermath, I ached for days, sometimes weeks. But the paycheque eased the hurt. The more takes I delivered, the more cash I earned, and that was a win in my book.

5

THE NASTILY EXHAUSTING WIZARDING TEST

Wherever I looked, I was surrounded by acting royalty, and the sun at the centre of this chaotic universe was Greg. I soon figured out why: he was the conduit to an old-school version of Hollywood where the stunt performers fell hard, *really hard*, and drank even harder, and everyone in the business respected them for it. Even Albus Dumbledore himself: Richard Harris, a proper dyed-in-the-wool Oscar-winning thespian, and a star in all sorts of blockbuster movies including *The Guns of Navarone* and *Gladiator*. By the time he arrived at *Harry Potter and the Philosopher's Stone*, Richard was around seventy years old, nearly blind and deaf as a post. He was also half-pissed a lot of the time, which meant that most of his lines were read from a cue card rather than memorised in advance.

But the bloke had gravitas and was held in high regard by everyone on the crew, and because of Greg, I saw quite a lot of him. Whenever they were working close by, a gravitational force seemed to magnetise them, Richard often pulling Greg away for a chinwag about the old times, where they'd laugh about the movies they'd worked on together, like *The Wild Geese*. Then one night, Greg asked me to escort Richard across a location set in Oxford to his car while he was wearing his full Albus Dumbledore outfit, complete with flowing robe, wizard's beard and hat. It was pissing down with rain, so Greg shoved a brolly into my hand.

'Keep him dry,' he said. 'And look after him for us. Make sure he doesn't trip up . . .'

I crossed the road with one of Britain's greatest ever actors, one hand holding the umbrella, the other supporting his arm, as we cautiously dodged the puddles and struggled to keep his cape away from the wet.

'Thank you, dear boy,' he said, smiling kindly as I helped him onto the back seat.

It was terrible to hear that he had died not so long afterwards, not only because he was such a nice man, but also because I only really learned of his impact on the acting scene once he'd passed. Richard was an icon of the stage as well as the big screen; he wrote and performed poetry; and he was a hellraiser for much of his life. *I had so many questions.* Coincidentally, I had worked with his son Jared on *Lost in Space*. Jared would go on to have a successful acting career himself, starring in *Mad Men*, *The Crown* and *Chernobyl*. I felt blessed to have been connected to such an incredible family, albeit in a loose way.

I soon got to understand the idiosyncrasies of the other actors working around me, and there was plenty to take in. Alan Rickman, for starters, refused to break character whenever he was in costume, which, given he was playing the doomy goth professor Severus Snape, was a bit unsettling. Luckily, he was a lovely bloke when not dressed up like Marilyn Manson. Of the younger cast, Dan and Rupert Grint were always messing around together, having a whale of a time, while Emma Watson, who was slightly younger than her male counterparts, was much more sensitive and serious, just like her character. She was also very keen on dancing, so I introduced her to a tutor, who visited her at the studio twice a week, where they worked on tap, modern, ballet and street dance.

There were occasions on location in Scotland where I'd sit with Robbie Coltrane in Hagrid's hut. Him in full costume, cracking jokes; me laughing my head off. Then I went too far and made a comment I might have picked up from one of the lad mags of the moment, like *Loaded* or *FHM*.

'We don't tell jokes like that,' said Robbie reproachfully. 'It's a bit misogynistic.'

Misogynistic. At the time, I didn't even know what the word meant, let alone the social implications of what I'd actually said. But I learned my lesson and resolved not to repeat the kind of comments I might have heard in the Stunt Stores. In my defence, I was naive, a seventeen-year-old kid still finding himself and defining his masculinity by doing backflips and chasing girls – I still had so much to learn. *About everything.* When Peter MacDonald, the second unit director, pressed me for my favourite Martin Scorsese film, I drew a blank. *Who the fuck was Martin Scorsese?* I shrugged, pleading my ignorance, and Peter looked shocked, presumably in disbelief that someone like me would have been allowed on a film set in the first place.

Of all the actors at work, Dame Maggie Smith – who played the fearsome Professor Minerva McGonagall – was the one I was most careful not to upset. She had a rep for being standoffish with just about everyone, though given she'd gone toe to toe with some of the greatest actors in the world, including Sir Laurence Olivier, my take was that she'd earned the right to be a little bit prickly. Still, despite her icy exterior, Dame Maggie struggled to intimidate one memorable disruptive extra as we filmed the scene in which her character morphed from a cat into Professor McGonagall's human form – all while Harry, Ron and Hermione looked on in shock. Around the room were several beasts in cages. Most prominent of these was a mandrill, an African monkey with a distinctive red and blue face. But it wasn't his appearance that was committing him to movie legend, it was his habits: the bloody thing wouldn't stop wanking. And despite repeated attempts to halt his rampant onanism, the mandrill refused to quit playing with himself. The kids were in hysterics, and while Dame Maggie probably saw the funny side, there was no way she was going to show it, not when there were children around. Some boundaries couldn't be crossed.

A sense of fun imbued everything we did, probably because the idea that we were making an era-defining movie hadn't yet been impressed upon us. Don't get me wrong: we guessed that *Harry Potter and the Philosopher's Stone* was going to be massive; we just didn't know how massive, and so we leaned into the anarchy whenever we could. Some days I joined with the special effects team, who had two battered-up old cars to play with, and we spent hours smashing them up even more. Across the studio, dozens of milk floats had inexplicably been abandoned in a strange graveyard of electric carts, and we often put them to good use transporting stunt equipment across the runways. Then we'd get bored and treat them like bumper cars. I suppose the high jinks would sound like a madness now, but it was 2000, an era where evidence-capturing smartphones and social media were both in their infancy, and film studios were still fun places to be. (Before the working environment turned super professional and super commercial.) It was a good time to be a teenage daredevil.

An incredible camaraderie had built among much of the crew and there were plenty of boozy nights in Newcastle's rowdy city centre. A buzzy, hedonistic vibe was only amplified by the crops of magic mushrooms sprouting in the grounds of Alnwick Castle. They were everywhere, and even though I was in the early stages of my psychonaut journey, I spent one or two evenings tripping balls in my hotel room, wondering what the hell was going on. I was also buzzing on what was an incredibly exciting adventure. It was soon announced that pre-production on the sequel, *Harry Potter and the Chamber of Secrets*, was set to begin a couple of weeks after the release of *The Philosopher's Stone* on 4 November 2001. The hype surrounding the new film was unreal. The Odeon cinema in Leicester Square, where the London premiere took place, was even restaged to resemble Hogwarts.

The world as I knew it was about to change for ever. The only downer was that I had been wrongly named in the film titles. To anyone paying close attention, my acting role as Slytherin Beater #1 had been mistakenly given to a kid called Scott, and my stunt credit was mistakenly given to a stand-in performer. For a while I was furious. By the time I'd started drinking myself silly in Magaluf on a two-week lads' holiday, knowing that pre-production on the second Harry Potter movie was about to begin, I couldn't have cared less.

★

The sense that I had stumbled into something special was cranked up when my first royalty cheque arrived. Having looked at the slip and noticed the zeros, my head spun. These were bonus payments distributed to the people involved, their size based on the overall success of a movie. Given *Harry Potter and the Philosopher's Stone* was on its way to making £649 million worldwide during the first theatrical release (becoming the second biggest film of the time behind *Titanic*), there was a little spare cash to go around. My first cheque came in at £65,000. When I went to my bank branch in Romford – barely out of school, standing five foot two tall and still baby-faced – the cashier gawped at me in shock.

'Are you sure?' she said.

'Yeah, I am. Put that money in my bank account, please.'

A second royalty cheque of £45,000 landed not long afterwards and my hunch about stunt acting being just about the best job in the world was confirmed. I'd also realised it was relatively hassle-free. After the film's release, Dan, Emma and

Rupert became world-famous movie stars, and possibly the most famous kids of their generation. TV interviews, newspapers and magazines: everyone wanted a piece of them, and they were presumably rolling in cash and love letters from fans. But while they were a hell of a lot richer than me, they were also a lot more recognisable, and fast becoming fresh meat for the paparazzi. The three of them were hounded wherever they went. But back in Romford, I had anonymity. Which was handy given I was close to drinking age and partying hard, all while surprising banking staff with the enormity of my pay cheques. Anonymity was great. But fame? *Sod that.*

When the money came, it disappeared quickly, because I loved spending. I was generous with it too. I wasn't greedy, I couldn't stand tight people, and the attitude had been hardwired into me as a kid when Mum gave me a fiver for lunch. Swerving the school canteen, I'd then spend the lot on ciggies (getting an older, much taller mate to approach the shopkeeper) before dishing them out to mates. This spirit extended into my working years. After earning £8,000 from *Lost in Space*, I bought the family a computer and treated my parents and brothers to a holiday to Florida. Nothing changed with the Harry Potter bonuses and I spoiled friends with holidays and nights out; I rented a flat with some of the lads and shouted everybody's monthly bills. I even looked after alumni from the gymnastics club. When I did treat myself, it was usually to buy a car, but I didn't go too crazy in the early days. My first was a green Citroën Saxo, which I bought off Mum, before upgrading to a silver Citroën Saxo VTS.

One night, I was speeding home from work and living up to the stereotype of an Essex boy racer. Rave music pulsed from the stereo as I handled the Saxo like a smashed-up Volvo on the Leavesden runway, taking all sorts of risks. Then, as I passed a car on a long bend, a fruit and veg truck reversed out of a driveway. For a spilt second, my life flashed before my eyes. Time seemed to slow down, but I was able to slam on the brakes and career into the side of the van, rather than striking it head on, which probably saved me, and anyone in the other vehicle, from instant death. The Saxo's bonnet crumpled up like an empty Coke can and the engine exploded through the dashboard and into the passenger seat next to me. Unbelievably, nobody was injured, not that it mattered to the courts. When I was booked for dangerous driving, the judge docked five points from my licence.

When Greg heard the news, he was unironically furious at my reckless behaviour. *He couldn't believe I'd taken such a risk.* Then he ordered me to buy a Smart Car. 'You're not driving a flash motor for a while, mate,' he growled.

I happily obliged, pimping out the boxy exterior of my nerdy Brabus with a body kit. Then I souped it up even more with a super-loud stereo system. Satisfied that I was taking his advice seriously, Greg then gave me something else to blow my money on.

'You've got to get on the Register,' he said, as work on the second Harry Potter film began.

The Register?

'Yeah. The British Stunt Register. If you ever want to be respected, and you want to have a continued career, you've got to get on it. Get qualified.'

I knew that becoming a stuntman was no easy gig. The British Stunt Register was an accredited list, like the actors' union Equity, and to secure regular work I needed to become a member, rather than relying solely on the gigs coming through Greg's contact book. But getting there was no cakewalk. That's because the British Stunt Register, which described itself as 'the longest established and largest association of stunt professionals working in the film and television industry, both in the UK and internationally', required a wannabe like me to achieve an elite level rating in six disciplines from the following five categories:

Group A: Fighting

I needed to learn Judo, Aikido, wrestling, boxing, or one of the following martial arts: Kung Fu, Karate, Jujitsu, Kendo, Taekwondo, or any form of kickboxing. Depending on the sport, I would have to reach *Cobra Kai* standards. And Thai Chi was definitely not acceptable.

Group B: Falling

Trampolining, and diving, with the participant to pass a test set by the British Stunt Register.

Group C: Riding and Driving

This was self-explanatory: I'd have to learn how to master a horse, car or motorbike. Given my recent scrape with the DVLA, I opted for equestrianism. Plus, the horse-riding course required me to walk, trot and canter while holding a sword or lance and a shield, *Game of Thrones*-style. That sounded like fun.

Group D: Agility and Strength

This section was in my wheelhouse: I had to either pass a course in gymnastics or become the next Bear Grylls and develop my mountaineering skills. I opted to stay at sea level.

Group E: Water

To complete this section, I needed to pass either a hardcore swimming test or a subaqua course.

It wasn't enough to simply sign up to the course either. Each participant had to prove that they were experienced in some element of performance, whether that be in acting, singing or street performance. I later heard of strippers working their way through the register, which made sense. All of us were selling parts of ourselves in one way or another, residual cheques (or twenty-quid notes shoved into bikinis) exchanged for our dignity, souls and pain: the very apex of capitalism.

Other than the effort and commitment required to reach the British Stunt Register's incredibly high standards (the course took four years to complete), anyone wanting to become a highly paid Hollywood performer had to fork out a fortune in training, coaches and gym memberships. To pass a high-diving course, for example, I had to pay £50 a lesson. (The cost would be closer to £200 these days.) The same went for horse riding. One upside was that, given my background, I wouldn't have to spend anything on gymnastics tuition, and I was still training at South Essex, free of charge. But even so I was staring down the barrel of a ball-tightening £100,000 bill, and I was beginning to understand why I hadn't yet seen a lot of lads like me in the stunt game. Whenever I looked around the set on *Lost in Space* or *Harry Potter and the Chamber of Secrets*, I noticed a lot of posh kids with loaded parents, or workers who were landing their roles through nepotism, and not many kids from the local estates.

There were also very few people from different ethnic backgrounds within the stunt industry. To this day the representation of race, sexuality and disability is skewed, and a shining example of how social economic conditions determine a person's ability to pay for the training. Currently, I'm the only disabled stunt performer listed on the British Stunt Register (and only as an honorary member), yet on films like *Saving Private Ryan* amputees were called in to perform stunts. Some of them were blasted into the air, their fake limbs blown off at the same time by the special effects department. It's safe to say a bloke from my background probably wouldn't have been able to pay the training fees for the British Stunt Register, not without the opportunity Greg had given me, and those *Harry Potter* royalty cheques. It required a massive financial leap of faith.

And I was an outsider.

★

Not wanting to waste time, or funds, I immediately pushed for my gymnastics and trampolining certificates. The first, in theory, should have been a piece of piss: Jeff Hewitt-Davis at the South Essex Gymnastics Club was an assessor for the British Stunt Register. It was his job to grade my ability, and in all there were over thirty elements to be nailed, including a standing back-flip, five double leg circles on the pommel horse, and a swing and back flyaway dismount on the rings. Jeff had taught me how to perform a lot of the techniques in the first place, watching as I'd mastered each one. But he was also a pro; there would be no waving me through, unchecked, and instead he decided to grind my balls to dust, like the saddle of a Nimbus 2000.

'If you do each move individually, you're going to pass, one hundred per cent . . .' he said.

I smiled. *Well, yeah.*

'. . . And we both know that's beneath you, so I'm going to judge you like a gymnastics competition.'

My heart sank. *So, he wanted to add an element of pressure?* Fair enough.

'Put all the discipline requirements together,' said Jeff. 'Make it a routine. I'll judge you on that.'

By the time Jeff had finished with me, I was physically rinsed. It was as if the Olympics, Commonwealth Games and British Gymnastics Championships had been collapsed into one brutal trial of strength. I passed, which was the good news, though I later learned that I'd narrowly missed out on a 100 per cent score, having bent my toes during a landing. According to Jeff, this one error had cost me a perfect score. I sucked up the mistake, knowing he was probably messing with me, and shifted my attention to the next course. *High diving.*

Given my gymnastics background, how hard could it be? Twisting and rotating through the air was my thing; I had aerial awareness; I knew how to move my body and hold a shape while dropping from a great height; and in the event of an error, I was slicing through water rather than thudding into a mat. *I could do this.* And I was right, too. *Partly.* When I first scaled the steps of an Olympic-height board – the intimidating 10-metre tower – a reassuring surge of adrenaline kicked in. *I was ready.* Springing upwards from a lower platform at 5 metres, I arced slowly, tucking my body into a roll, and for a split second I experienced weightlessness, like an astronaut floating through space. Then gravity plucked me from the sky. I extended my legs and arms fully as I descended, headfirst, the air rushing past my ears, a heavy roller-coaster lurch fluttering in my stomach. Finally, I knifed the water and plunged down, down, down, my body cocooned by percolating bubbles, and the dopamine hit was so big it wobbled me like an orgasm. Still buzzing, believing I'd stumbled onto a cheat code, I climbed the steps for another go, and then another, before moving up to the Big Boy's Board. *The 10-metre platform.*

Life has a funny way of humbling a person whenever they become too comfortable or cocky in a risky environment. A high diver entering the water from 10 metres up, at speeds of around 40 miles per hour, has very little margin for error. Misjudging a rotation, even by a split second, can off-centre the angle of entry by several degrees. That might not sound like a lot, but believe me, it's bloody painful when it happens. During my very next attempt, I bodied the surface, and the experience was like a faceplant on concrete. In another session, I over-rotated through a somersault and landed with a flat back. The breath was slammed out of me, and I spent several days coughing up globules of congealed blood. After a fast start, it took a year of bumps and bruises to complete the course, and if I wasn't flying around on a broomstick during the making of *Harry Potter and the Chamber of Secrets*, I was shivering at the bottom of a south London diving board in a pair of skimpy Speedos. To settle the vibe, I sometimes got stoned in the car park beforehand. There was nothing like taking the first plunge of the day while feeling as if my eagle was landing.

According to the British Stunt Register, I had to complete a series of dives from the 10-metre platform, Tom Daley-style, including: a forward dive from a straight or standing position; a forward dive from a running position; a back dive; a forward somersault; a reverse dive; a falling back somersault; a forward dive with a half twist; and a forward somersault dive with a half twist (also known as a *Barani*). Then I had to put my kit on and execute a fully clothed reverse somersault, a forward somersault and a falling back somersault. The effort to reach the required standards set by the British Stunt Register was gruelling, but I got there, and with some career-best bruises to show for my efforts. Not that I bitched about them afterwards. As Greg had taught me: a stuntman takes the whacks, then they crack on. *Ad bloody nauseam.*

★

I was a passive person. I only became aggressive when firing myself up, or if somebody had underestimated me. Throwing a punch or smashing somebody in the ribs with a roundhouse kick wasn't in my nature. That is, until I learned kickboxing, where cracking someone in the head, *while avoiding being cracked in the head,* was to be celebrated. Most of the time, these episodes of head-cracking took place with my mate Marc Mailley, another stuntman-in-waiting, who was a complete pit bull on the mat, despite being the same height as me and only a stone heavier. But that's because Marc had spent his school years punching back against the bullies rather than breaking them down with comedy, as I had. In sparring terms, we were an ugly mismatch.

Given his head start in physical violence, Marc smashed me up and knocked me over in training at an alarming rate, and of the thirteen concussions I've ever experienced in life so far, he must have dished out around 50 per cent of them. I remember in one bout, the pair of us jumped at the same time, Marc planting me on the chest with a high kick. My body swept out from underneath me, my back landed hard on the floor, and my head snapped back shortly afterwards. Even though I'd been wearing a head guard, the impact knocked me out cold. When I came to, I saw stars, but at no point did I want to quit. Instead, I remembered back to an old episode of *The Simpsons*, featuring the fictional daredevil Lance Murdock. In his quest for the perfect stunt, Murdock claimed to have broken every bone in his body. He once jumped a tank swimming with sharks, alligators, piranhas, electric eels . . . *and a lion.* When asked why he did it, he replied: 'Bones heal. Chicks dig scars. And the United States of America has the best doctor-to-daredevil ratio in the world.' My attitude wasn't too dissimilar. I carried the war wounds like a badge of honour, and every knockdown – and comeback – told me I could handle anything.

Out of all the disciplines I had to master, horse riding was undoubtedly the hardest because it required me to strengthen the muscles I wouldn't ordinarily have used for any other activity. *Where else would I need to squeeze my legs around a lump of solid muscle perched on 6-foot-tall legs?* For three hours at a time, I sat in the saddle, and my back, thighs, calves and hips burned with pain the following day. At first, I resented the sport. But with perseverance and commitment, I soon learned to love it, and after a while the connection between human and horse felt beautiful and moving. I have a strong memory of one hack during a cold wintry morning with a horse called Ted. Frost sparkled on the ground; my breath fogged on the icy air; and having dismounted, I noticed steam rising from Ted's back. His muscles shivered and flexed as I washed him down, and a weird, symbiotic link had formed – I felt privileged that he'd allowed me to jump on his back and race through the fields at full pelt.

Horse riding was also dangerous and a massive adrenaline rush. Hanging from the back of Ted, my arse tipped slightly out of the saddle, was simultaneously terrifying and exhilarating. Luckily, I had good coaches to steer me through the course, relatively unharmed. Caroline Dent was the mum of my good mate Kelly, and alongside her husband, John, had become a big deal in the equestrian world, having founded Littlebourne Farm in 1988, and with it a riding and training school. Kelly had become a renowned stunt trainer, horse master and stunt coordinator, and was highly thought of after teaching a long list of Hollywood A-listers, including Cate Blanchett, Kiera Knightley and Ed Norton. I was in safe hands.

But bloody hell, the test was a nightmare. Among the various elements needed to pass, I had to prove I could 'tack up' a horse efficiently, and lead it, in hand, while also showing consideration for the animal, myself, and the people around me. Mounting and dismounting to a required standard was a deal breaker, as was jumping a short course with fences. I needed to ride bareback in all three paces (walk, trot and canter). And, of course, there was the test that required me to wave a sword or lance, and possibly a jousting helmet. As if that wasn't enough, the British Stunt Register-approved examiner for my examination day was Greg, a man who was not known for giving anyone an easy ride.

I screwed up immediately, spectacularly falling while attempting to ride bareback. In the next stage of the exam, my horse dipped his head and pitched me forward as I jumped a fence. For a split second, I thought I was going to fall yet again, in a spectacular crash, but somehow I managed to hold on by clamping my thighs around the horse's neck. It wasn't pretty, but it was enough to spare me from an embarrassing failure. Finally, I was instructed to ride with several other entrants in formation, while holding a heavy shield and sword. (Thankfully, I was spared the jousting helmet.) At the close of play, Greg emerged to grade the field of applicants and was typically brutal, as he had been when breaking the hearts of those auditioning kids on the *Lost in Space* set.

I heard him walking down the line, dishing out his judgements.

Pass.

Fail.

Fail.

Finally, he arrived at me. '*Pass*,' he said.

My heart rate rocketed. I'd smashed the hardest part of the British Stunt Register's gruelling competency test.

Then Greg leaned in close. I smelled the funk of Jo Malone after-shave and stale Monte Cristo cigars. 'But only just, Dave,' he said. 'You managed to stay on the horse when it bumped you forward. *That saved you.*'

As I was painfully aware, there was always room for improvement when working with Greg.

6

THE DARK ARTS

When filming on *Harry Potter and the Chamber of Secrets* began, a race against time began too: it was important the kids' physical appearances remained true to the books, and given they were at the age when voices cracked, acne and facial hair broke out, and growth spurts tended to take place, Warner Bros. was eager to push ahead. As was the director, Chris Columbus, who had been signed on a two-film deal and wanted to return his family to LA. I think at that point everyone knew the movies were generational landmarks, *the Hogwarts Express had left the station*, but there was no atmospheric change behind the scenes. Greg still regaled his team with outrageous stories; Dame Maggie Smith was still standoffish; and the mandrill still misbehaved in XXX-rated ways. The supportive shield the crew had formed around the young cast had carried through, though, and after the hype and success of the first film there was the sense that Dan, Emma and Rupert should still be protected, and encouraged always to have fun. The vibe at Leavesden was as familial during the making of the second film as it was for the first.

This was important, because while filming *The Philosopher's Stone* through 2000, the fourth book in J.K. Rowling's series, *The Goblet of Fire*, had been released, and the franchise was fast turning into a phenomenon. Kids and families even queued outside bookshops to get an early pressing. When I picked up my copy, I rifled through the chapters with a totally different perspective to the audience, grabbing a pen and some Post-it notes and marking any scenes that might require a stunt. I can't think of too many people in the world who would have gone through the same routine. I was also watching Dan in a different way to everyone else. Every now and then, during filming or training, I'd cross my fingers, praying to the Hollywood gods that he wasn't going to grow by a foot or two. It was important that his stunt double remained a similar height and build, and the last thing I wanted was to fall off the Wizarding World gravy train because of my size.

Although he wasn't growing upwards, Dan was certainly getting stronger. Our gym sessions in the Stunt Stores continued, and he was suddenly able to smash out thirty push-ups at a time. He was performing handstands too. Meanwhile, Dan learned how to parry and thrust in a fencing duel in a style similar to the great Errol Flynn, and he brimmed with confidence when running, jumping and reacting to punches and explosions. Around that time, he told me that he wanted to push his physicality, earning his stripes with one or two bumps and bruises, which I respected. Dan even gave one or two interviews in the press where he explained that if things didn't work out with acting, he imagined making a career lane change at some point by becoming a stuntman. At the very least, he'd like to do some of his own gags, Tom Cruise-style (though nobody was expecting him to cling to the side of a plane or launch himself from a cliff on a motorbike). These days, whenever he performs a stunt of his own on an action movie, he'll proudly tell me of what went down. Given his ambitions, Dan looked up to me in much the same way that I looked up to Greg.

My work on the film started like the last. I wandered around the special effects department and looked over the storyboards. I tidied up the Stunt Stores and readied the equipment. Going by the script, there was a lot more action in the second film than in the first, and a couple of scenes stood out, among them a duel between Harry and Tom Felton's Malfoy in the Great Hall, and a high-stakes Quidditch match in which the same two characters tussled while flying around on their broomsticks. To get ready for another physical production schedule, I blew up some airbags and practised jumping from the studio roof. While this might have looked like a glorified play session, it was still the best way of staying in Greg's good books.

During breaks in filming, he would often plan something challenging or downright terrifying for me to do, such as the time he brought in a Russian swing. This was a device that resembled a playground swing but was fixed with a platform with enough space for two acrobats to stand. The idea was for the users to gain so much momentum as they swung back and forth that they were able to launch themselves into the air with a variety of somersaults or dives. I loved these random sessions. Aligning my commitment to passing the Stunt Register with a full-on filming schedule was tough work, but I never stopped soaking up new skills. Whenever an unfamiliar stunt person came on set, I liked to know what was packed into their pad bags – a giant duffel holdall (made by North Face ordinarily, because they were the brand of the moment) overflowing with various knee, elbow and hip pads or protective gear, such as tailored harnesses and fireproof underwear. Every time a new piece of kit was unveiled, I wanted to know what it was, what it did, and where I could get one.

Sometimes I might have been too curious, too enthusiastic. Maybe it was because of my attitude, or maybe it was a result of my size, but the type of bullying that had haunted me throughout school resurfaced. There were plenty of big blokes in the stunt industry. A lot of them were alpha male types. Aggression was part of their personality profile, and one team member, who I won't name, seemed to get his kicks from having a younger, smaller stunt performer to push around. I became the brunt of his bullying.

Given I was the youngest person on the payroll, and still in the early phase of my career, I was also verbally knocked about on set.

Old school wounds were reopened; I felt the stomach-churning nausea of helplessness and vulnerability once more. Eventually, the piss-taking and name-calling became physical and, at one point, I was pinned to the floor by a couple of team members. As I attempted to defend myself, a pair of hands yanked down my trousers, exposing my bare arse. Those moments were the worst. I went home from work feeling defeated and humiliated.

Sometimes, even Greg would jump in on the act. He could be forceful and a bit of a brute, and the stories of what he would do to stunt performers if they failed him could probably make for a book in itself. I'd heard that he once chased two blokes around the M25 at 100 miles per hour after they had enraged him on a film set. Eventually, I received an equally terrifying reprimand, and one afternoon, while his car was being serviced, I gave him a lift home. As I navigated my way towards his house along a quiet suburban street, everything went dark. Greg, who was sitting in the rear, had reached around the driver's seat and was clamping his hands tightly over my eyes.

'Greg, I can't fucking see,' I yelled, panicking slightly.

'It's OK,' he said calmly. 'Keep going straight . . .'

As I manoeuvred the car, Greg delivered a series of instructions. I followed them to the letter.

Indicate left.

Slow down.

Take the third exit on this roundabout . . . Now.

And so on. As far as Greg was concerned, this wasn't a reckless prank, it was a test of nerve. Driving blind meant I had to put my faith in someone else, all while doing something really fucking dangerous. It put me under pressure. *And pressure made diamonds.* But I remember thinking at the time how batshit crazy the test was, and a little hypocritical, given the way in which he'd lost his rag after I'd smashed my car into a fruit and veg truck.

That wasn't the half of it, though. Later on, during another drive home in my Mercedes SLK*, *my pride and joy*, I noticed a car racing up behind me in my wing mirror. Then my phone rang. *It was Greg.*

'Let's cut through all the traffic,' he said.

Then what?

'You'll see.'

I pushed past a short chain of cars and awaited my instructions. 'Are you ready?' said Greg.

Ready for what? My bum cheeks clenched a little tighter. Greg was right up on my bumper.

'Go faster,' he yelled.

I put my foot on the accelerator.

'More speed!' shouted Greg.

I surged along the fast lane of the empty motorway, my adrenaline spiking. The hairs on the back of my neck stood to attention.

'Faster!'

Fucking hell. When I looked down at the speedometer, I had hit 155 miles per hour and Greg was still on my tail. At times it looked as if there was only a Rizla paper between the two cars.

'Go on. Keep going,' said Greg. '*Keep going.*'

From time to time a car would appear ahead of me, but there was no letting up.

'Don't brake,' Greg shouted. 'Get round him. Go on. Go on. *Go on.*'

Eventually, Greg trailed away behind me, and I was able to pump the brakes. My heart rate slowed; a wave of relief and fear washed over me. *One of us could have been killed.* But the regret was fleeting and by the time I'd got home, I was already normalising the event as an act of stuntman bravado. I even told the story excitedly the next day in the

---

* This was a purchase after Greg had released me from smart car hell.

studio, because at the time both Greg and I were living in the stunt bubble, a space in which we were bulletproof and nothing bad ever happened. I'm not making excuses. I acted without thinking because I wanted to be brave for Greg – the man, the myth, the movie legend. No way was I going to bottle it in front of my Hollywood dad. However, since wrecking my spine, I've met too many people who have been smashed up in car accidents and motorway pile-ups, and I have a very different take on my behaviour now. Thank God no one was hurt.

★

Despite these episodes of mistreatment, I was hardly a victim throughout my career. Being small was part of my identity; it just so happened that people of my size tended to get picked on from time to time, especially in such a macho environment. It was part of the journey, a lot of people went through it, and I was no different to anyone else. Meanwhile, some of the pain had probably been self-inflicted – or at least, that's what I told myself. As my schoolteachers pointed out on several occasions, I was a disruptive influence and too mouthy for my own good. *I needed to be brought down to earth.* But while my discipline required a little tightening, the violence and psychological torment wasn't educational in any way, nor did it push me to become a better stuntman. My performances didn't improve because I feared the beatings; they improved because I was dedicated. Weirdly, though, I considered a lot of my tormentors to be mates. (But it certainly wasn't Stockholm syndrome.) I looked up to them as performers; some of them were world famous in the industry, and they gave me plenty of time to learn the trade. Most of the time they were nice to me. The torture was sporadic, rather than relentless.

Also, because of my age, energy and the fact I enjoyed being the centre of attention, I was occasionally a lightning rod for chaos. I loved flirting, and the status of my position within the Harry Potter franchise, plus my role as a stuntman, lent me a certain level of kudos in clubs and at parties, especially when the crew stayed in Newcastle. While working on location shoots at nearby Alnwick Castle, dozens of production staff made a temporary home in the city centre Malmaison, and there was often a party to stumble into. One night, I met two girls, who stayed over in my hotel room. The following morning, as they were about to pull away in a taxi, I tapped on the window.

'Do you want me to pay for the cab?' I shouted.

The girls shook their heads. *Everything was fine.* But I should have been more careful. At the time, BBC Radio Newcastle were running a phone-in segment called 'Potter Watch'. The station had learned, along with everyone else in the media, that filming was once again taking place at Alnwick Castle. The feature ran every day, and listeners were invited to call in with any sightings of Harry, Hagrid or Albus Dumbledore in the local coffee shop. What I hadn't banked on was that the public interest might extend to any members of the crew too. When some of us were travelling onto set in a car that afternoon, 'Potter Watch' came on air.

'Here we go,' moaned one of the lads. 'This nonsense.'

He soon stopped complaining when the latest slice of film-making gossip was broadcast to the city. The caller was a taxi driver. Apparently, that morning he had picked up two women who had spent the night partying with Dan Radcliffe's stunt double. Everyone turned to face me. My insides shrivelled up with embarrassment. I'd been busted.

'. . . He wines and dines two girls,' laughed the presenter, disbelievingly. 'Takes them back to his expensive hotel and doesn't pay for their cab fare home!'

I was rinsed. By the time I'd arrived on set, everyone had heard the newsflash. I took a bollocking from Greg and a bollocking from the head of Warner Bros. Though in the end, I wasn't sure which was more excruciating: the revelation of my evening's misadventures or the fact I'd been wrongly accused of stinginess.

Run-ins with the studio happened every now and then. My job required me to take chances with my personal safety and, at times, it was hard to find the 'off' switch. Often it was tricky to separate the daredevil persona from The Real Me, and that attitude sometimes spilled over into my life outside the studio. Occasionally, I felt the need to push the limits of what was acceptable. A couple of years later, while filming *Harry Potter and the Prisoner of Azkaban* in Glencoe, a village in Scotland, I was down to perform a stunt for the scene at Hagrid's Hut, in which Hermione and the two Harrys (one living in real time, the other a time-travelling version) attempted to save the hippogriff Buckbeak – a creature with the top half of an eagle and the back end of a horse – who had been sentenced to death after attacking Draco Malfoy.

In charge of the scene was the second unit director, Peter 'Mac' MacDonald – a lovely man famous for working on the hit buddy movie *Tango and Cash*, which starred Sylvester Stallone and Kurt Russell, and *Rambo III*. During the scene, it was my job to run down a flight of steps with Hermione's double, a task I had to execute on cue. For the perfect shot, Peter Mac wanted a break in the clouds and his camera crew were waiting patiently on top of a nearby hill for the right moment. As was typical with a lot of locational shoots, the work was slow, and a vibe known as *hurry up and wait* had kicked in. We had rushed to get there and rushed to get ready, and then . . . Nothing happened. To kill time, I stayed out of the way in Hagrid's Hut, where I gossiped with the crew. Suddenly, I heard a nearby walkie-talkie. Someone was shouting angrily. Then I heard my name through the static crunch.

'David. *David!* Go! Go! *Go!*'

Shit. It was Peter Mac.

I'd totally missed my cue, as had Hermione's stunt double, and the pair of us flew from Hagrid's Hut like greyhounds bursting from the traps. We sprinted down the steps to nail the shot, but because of our slight delay, the clouds had opened and then instantly closed again. Worse, it was late in the day and the light was fading. There was now little chance of capturing the shot in time and the entire second unit were forced to stay behind in Glencoe for the weekend, with filming resuming the following Monday. The dressing-downs came in thick and fast: first from Peter Mac, then from the assistant director, the late, great Jamie Christopher. This was followed up by various grumblings of discontent from teammates and crew members, who were now rearranging their weekend plans and feeling bloody annoyed about it. There were also extra hotel bills, day rate payments and catering costs to deal with, and all because I'd taken my eye off the ball for a few moments.

But that was only the beginning of my problems.

That night, in the hotel bar, I was punished for my fuck-up. The crew plied me with nasty-looking drinks, and I was the target of some heavy piss-taking, until Jamie Christopher gave me an order that would make up for my error.

'We want to go skinny-dipping,' he said. 'Get us into the hotel swimming pool.'

It was gone midnight. The pool had long been closed. 'But it's locked,' I said.

Jamie shook his head. 'Well, break in then.'

Given that everyone was stuck in Glencoe because of me, I had little choice but to scope out the area. Peering through the bolted doors, I noticed a skylight in the roof above the pool. Even better, it had a handle. I crept around the side of the building, shimmied up a drainpipe and scrambled across the roof. Once I'd reached the skylight, I was able to jemmy it open with one or two yanks. Then, peering down into the dimly lit pool, I lowered myself inside. As I dangled from the ceiling, it was difficult to get a read on the water below – the lighting was poor and I was hammered, but my guess was that it was a standard-sized swimming pool and not very deep. I did some maths. The drop from the ceiling was probably around 7 metres, but the depth of the water might only have been 6 or 7 feet. If I plunged into the pool, toes first, there was a chance I'd break my legs and maybe even drown. Instead, I took the sensible option. I swung out from the skylight, like a gymnast on the bars, rotated into a flat-back position, and body-slammed the water. The impact knocked the wind from my lungs, but I was able to climb out of the pool and unlock the doors.

With a lot of shouting and laughing, everyone stripped off their clothes and cannonballed into the deep end. The party was off the hook, like a scene from a 1980s frat-boy movie: boys were kissing girls; girls were kissing girls; boys were kissing boys. But after a while, I decided to sneak away. I was cold and knackered, and my back was throbbing after that painful landing in the water. Given I was now in the clear following my earlier screw-up, I padded up to my hotel room, ran a bath, rolled a joint and sucked in a deep and heavy draw.

I passed out seconds later.

Bang! Bang! Bang!

I jolted upright, not sure of where or who I was, but aware that somebody was pounding their fists against a door. *My door.* Hazily, I staggered forward. After turning the handle, I made two worrying discoveries. The first was that there was a red-faced hotel manager standing in the corridor. The second was that I'd forgotten to turn off the taps, and a lake of water was spreading from the bathroom.

'What are you fucking doing?' yelled the manager, pushing past me and turning off the taps. 'The plasterwork in the room down-stairs has caved in . . .'

Oh no. I was in serious trouble.

'. . . The poor bugger underneath you just got a nasty surprise. It's a miracle he wasn't killed.'

The fallout to my latest blunder was dramatic. When I woke the next morning, I was staring down the barrel of a £30,000 bill for the damages, though thankfully the incident was smoothed over by the film studio. This was lucky because I hardly could have argued had they refused to back me up: I was bang to rights after a negative spiral of poor decisions that had begun earlier that day. The ceiling in the room beneath mine had caved in because I'd got stoned and left the taps running. I'd got stoned and left the taps running because I'd wanted a hot bath after breaking into the hotel swimming pool and hurting my back. I'd broken into a swimming pool because the Harry Potter crew were furious at me. And they were furious at me because I'd messed up a shot after losing concentration. And my suffering wasn't yet over. When filming began again on Monday, my hand was used in what was referred to as a pick-up shot – a small clip that added to the story in some way, usually without involving any major actors. In the script, Harry was described as releasing Buckbeak as several angry crows pecked and jabbed at his hands. When looking for a stand-in, it was decided that I should volunteer that hand. Contractually, I had very little comeback. I was Dan's stunt double, it was on me to take the hits.

The birds clawed and nipped at my knuckles as everyone laughed.

*

There were other, less destructive moments of high jinks in which I was the only victim, though that didn't mean the fallout was any less painful or embarrassing. One incident happened during the making of *Harry Potter and the Chamber of Secrets* after I'd announced to the crew that I was dating a girl I'd met during my lads' holiday to Magaluf. She was from Scotland, and we'd arranged to meet in Newcastle while I was working. To show my affinity for the Scottish flag, I had the idea to dye my pubic hair blue for a joke. Given there was all sorts of trickery going on in the hair and make-up department, with their wizarding wigs and hirsute troll ears, I wondered if there was any blue hair dye lying around the place. Of course there was. One of the stylists, Zoe, gave me a pot of white goo and a spatula, plus a clear set of instructions: *Apply liberally to the bush before taking a bath.*

I couldn't figure it out. *The paste was white.* 'But I need blue.'

Zoe laughed. 'I know, but you'll have to bleach it first,' she said. 'Then you can apply this.'

She handed over a bottle filled with bright blue liquid.

Feeling chuffed at my scheme, and excited at what a woman from Scotland would make of the intimate, patriotic styling, I went home and took a bath, making sure to smear dollops of the bleaching paste around my crotch, hoping that it wouldn't burn too badly. Then I dropped into the tub. But when I looked down to check, my pubic hair was very much brown. Worse, it had detached from my groin and was floating on the surface of the water. Panicking, I splashed about to get a view of what was going on downstairs, only to see that I was now completely bald. *What the fuck was going on?* Was I ill? Or had I suffered an extreme allergic reaction to the bleach, in which case, what else was going to fall out? *Or off?*

I needed help. And there was only one person I could turn to in times of humbling crisis. *Greg.* He answered the phone gruffly.

'Shit, Greg,' I flapped. 'Shit. Shit. *Shit.* I don't know what I've done wrong, but something bad has happened . . .'

Greg could tell I was in a state. 'Calm down, Dave,' he said gently. 'What's going on?'

'I tried to dye my pubes blue,' I said, my words tumbling out at the speed of light. 'And now they've all fallen off. I need the number for anybody in—'

Greg coughed. Or choked. I'm not sure which. 'Say that again?' he said.

'All my pubes have gone, Greg,' I wailed. 'What have I done to myself? The hair and make-up girls have given me the wrong hair bleach . . .'

But there was no point in talking. Greg was roaring with laughter on the other end of the line. 'It's nine o'clock at night, Dave. You're not calling hair and make-up—'

'But my pubes,' I gasped.

'. . . Wash it off, get into work early and we'll deal with it tomorrow.'

I'd been humiliated. The following morning, I shamefacedly walked onto the set, as one by one my crewmates popped by the stunt office to check out the results of my botched restyling. Greg howled with laughter when I pulled down the top of my track-suit bottoms to reveal my junk, which now resembled a goblin from the Gringotts Wizarding Bank. The other stunt performers were next. And then finally Zoe from hair and make-up confessed to deliberately swapping my hair bleach for hair removal cream. I'd been well and truly stitched up, and my embarrassment was compounded when I checked the daily call sheet – a document that detailed the running order for the day's filming and the crew members that were taking part. Top of the list was my name. But it had been altered.

David 'Baldy' Holmes.

Then I remembered that call sheets were printed out the night before, which meant the entire crew had been in on the joke for at least twenty-four hours. I sucked up the embarrassment and dropped my pants to anyone who asked. Except for my Scottish date. I cancelled our meeting, fearing my new look might prove a massive turn-off.

★

While filming *The Chamber of Secrets*, I was dropped from great heights, slammed into inanimate objects, and chucked about the studio like a rag doll as the stunt department transferred the magic of J.K. Rowling's words onto the big screen. *Did it hurt?* Of course it did. (Running full pelt into the brick wall at the entrance of Plat-form 9¾, alongside stuntman Tony Christian, knocked the stuffing out of me.) *Did I care?* Not a chance. (Especially as you can now visit King's Cross Station and see kids repeating the same gag.) And I was thrown into action from the very opening of the movie, during the scene when Harry escapes the Dursleys' nuclear family home at Number 4 Privet Drive – *the very last place you would expect extraordinary things to happen.* Except lots of extraordinary things took place at Number 4 Privet Drive. And when Harry meets Dobby, a malevolent house elf, his antics disrupt an important dinner party, and a violet pudding is dropped on the floor, which, typically, Harry is blamed for.

Everything seems to be going pear-shaped, until Ron Weasley – plus his brothers, Fred and George – arrive to rescue Harry in a blue 1960 Ford Anglia 105E, a car that has the ability to fly. As the boys prepare for lift-off, Vernon Dursley, played by Richard Griffiths, grabs at Harry's legs to stop him from leaving. When the Weasley brothers take hold of his arms, a brutal tug-of-war begins. Given that Dan was still being spared this level of rough and tumble, and I was his double, it was my job to play the human rope. My limbs were yanked from their sockets in the scuffle. Greg, meanwhile, filled the role of Vernon and I remember thinking it was nice to see the boss leading by example – and taking the hits. During one take, he failed to rotate his body properly and tumbled from a window in a drop of around 18 feet. The landing looked painful, no doubt it would have tickled him a little bit, and when the scene was eventually wrapped, I watched as he lit up a Monte Cristo. Even though the wind had been banged out of him, nobody was going to see him grimacing in pain.

Sometimes, the bangs and crashes came with scars, and while that was all part of the job, nobody wanted to get hurt or see their mates smashed up in an accident. On one occasion, Tolga, who was still working as the child stunt double for Dan, was very nearly killed while performing a stunt for Harry during the flying car sequence.

In the movie, the passenger door swings open, taking Harry with it. Only a lunge for the handle saves him from a nasty fall.

The car had been set on a pneumatic pole and was being controlled by a special effects operator. The plan was for the vehicle to rotate, and as it did so, the door was supposed to open, causing Harry (or, in this case, Tolga) to fall out. The stunt had been rehearsed plenty of times, and the safety wire attached to Tolga was set at a specific height. The plan: when Tolga fell from the car, the wire would catch his body at a point that allowed him to reach out and grab the door handle. Meanwhile, it was my job to spot the camera operator positioned underneath, and I was ready to pull him away by the belt if the unthinkable were to happen. *Then the unthinkable happened.* Instead of the car simply rotating at the set height, the operator caused the pneumatic pole arm to swing downward and the Ford Anglia dropped much lower than expected. As it did so, Tolga fell and the vehicle moved past his head at high speed, the angular corner of the car door only missing his skull by an inch or two. Had it struck him, he would have been killed instantly.

Another on-set accident took place during a wire stunt later on in filming, in which the character of Gilderoy Lockhart, played by Kenneth Branagh, was yanked violently through the air during a duel with Severus Snape. The stage was set in Hogwarts Great Hall and Kenneth was replaced by the stuntman Rowley Irlam, who had a wire attached to his back. The technique for a stunt of this kind required a piston to be fired on the pneumatic ram, which then pulled dramatically on the wire, and anyone attached to it. This style of wirework was considered to be more effective than two blokes jumping off a platform and pulling on a rope, and the rehearsals went well. The pistons fired as they should; Rowley was snapped backwards and slid across a long table without falling to the floor. To make sure that nobody was hurt in the dry runs, a couple of crash mats were positioned at the back of the room, just in case.

When filming started for real, the mood changed – like it always did. Two hundred extras, most of them kids, were called into the scene, and a hush fell over the set as the ram, piston and Rowley were reset in their spots. Then the call for action went up. There was a bang as the piston fired and Rowley, dressed as the dandyish Lockhart, was pulled backwards and across the table. *But something went wrong.* The wire pulled too fast and too hard, and Rowley skittered uncontrollably across the surface and off the end, where he landed face-first on the flagstone floor in a sickening crunch of bone and concrete. The watching children shouted and screamed as the rest of the crew rushed to check on Rowley. The poor bloke was out cold. His face was badly mangled too. As he was carried away, I thanked the stars that it hadn't been me.

★

Alan Rickman was a movie powerhouse. He'd already played some memorable villains throughout his career, including Hans Gruber in the first *Die Hard* film, but as Severus Snape he'd managed to up the baddy stakes to another level. Whenever there were cameras around, he scowled, grimaced and pouted. J.K. Rowling had previously stated that Snape was based on a horrible teacher she'd once encountered at school, and Alan must have taken the idea and sprinted with it. When he was in costume, he was bloody terrifying.

Working with an actor of his stature was a dream, though, because like so many of the bigger names on the cast list, Alan was incredible to watch. He was even better to perform with, and my favourite close-up encounter with Snape took place in *The Chamber of Secrets*, during the scene where Draco Malfoy and Harry scrapped it out in a wizarding duel. In the first wand salvo, Malfoy sends Harry to the back of a 'duelling runway', his body somersaulting and cartwheeling mid-flight. Leaping to his feet, he fires a spell back, pushing Malfoy sideways, where he lands in the splits position at the feet of a glaring Snape. My role in all of this was to double for Tom Felton, who played Malfoy – a lovely bloke who was a bit older than the other kids. He had an air of polished confidence about him because he had already appeared alongside Jodie Foster in the 1999 movie *Anna and the King*.

To do the job, a length of wire was wrapped around my waist. The idea was to launch me into the air, where the unravelling line would create so much momentum that I'd spin horizontally over a distance of about 20 feet. But the gag was loaded with risk. My landing was bound to be painful, not only because a split-legged position was needed for the final shot, but also because the landing mat was nothing more than a wooden board with a layer of thin padding stretched across the top. Upon impact, I had to bounce across its surface on my arse, before being pushed back into the fight by Snape. (Not that the audience ever saw my face.) My family jewels were set to take a battering. There was also my flight path to consider. While being propelled through the air by a wire that might, or might not, land me in the correct spot, it was important to avoid crashing into Alan Rickman, who was well on his way to becoming a national treasure. To add an extra layer of danger, all this had to be done while wearing a cape. I was also surrounded by cauldrons and the smell of paraffin was overwhelming. It had to be like that, and we'd all taken the necessary precautions, but the truth is that stunts are inherently risky.

The scene turned out to be one of my favourites from the entire series. Dan and Tom square up to each other; the sneering Malfoy brings his wand to bear and attempts to unsettle Harry with some mind games. '*Scared, Potter?*' But Harry wasn't one for backing down, and neither was I. In the script, Malfoy was launched sideways, and when my turn came to throw myself across the room, I took up the correct position, my wand raised, my arms above my head, a length of wire pulled taut across my midriff. Then the countdown began.

OK! Ready. Roll cameras. Three . . .

I steadied myself and focused.

Two . . .

'Are you scared?' piped up a little kid behind me. It was a child extra brought in for the scene.

One!

There was no time to react. The wire tightened. I was sucked forcefully into the air at a height of around 10 feet, and span acrobatically, landing just short of Alan Rickman, my backside smacking into the barely-there padding. I bounced once, twice, and came to a stop as Severus Snape grabbed me by the scruff of the neck. It was hard to tell if he was acting, or genuinely pissed off. In landing so close, I had very nearly broken his foot. But while the shot had been close to perfect, all I could think about was that little kid and his snarky comment. He had tried to put me off at the worst possible moment. *The shithouse.* When I returned to my starting position for another take, I called him over.

'Oi. Don't say anything next time,' I said. 'Just stand there and do your job. Don't ask me about mine. *Please.*'

In the end, I made around eight attempts. My balls and backside throbbed painfully afterwards, but given my negotiated rate for a wizard somersault was around £1,000 per take, I didn't grumble too much. The work had also won me the respect of one of the greatest actors of his generation. The following day, as I sat in the canteen eating my lunch, Alan Rickman came over to say hello. He was out of costume and detached from his doomy onscreen personality.

'David, what you did yesterday . . .' he said. '. . . It was very good. *Ah-mazing.*'

I nodded a thank you.

'Are you OK? How does your body feel?'

I smiled. *I'm fine, cheers, Alan.* But it was a lie. I was battered and broken, and every muscle in my body ached. Then, remembering the stuntman code (*never in pain, never complain*),

I shrugged it off. The hurt was fleeting. But the pleasure of being recognised by somebody I'd admired for ages would last a lifetime.

*

An important footnote: I owe a lot to the late Alan Rickman. Prior to signing up for the Harry Potter movies, he had the foresight to spearhead a group of actors hoping to negotiate a payment clause. In it, everyone working on an Equity contract received royalties from each film, the pay depending on the number of days spent in front of the camera, whether they were Dame Maggie Smith or a scrappy stuntman from Romford. The maximum number of days was twenty-five, and I maxed out on every film, which meant I received the same amount of royalties as some of the biggest names in British cinema.

The cheques soon racked up, sending my bank balance into overdrive. Even today, I receive a fee every three months, thanks to Alan's campaigning. Currently, those cheques act as a safety net, and they have allowed me to buy electric wheelchairs, iPads and other equipment – not just for myself, but for other people more in need than me. And all because of that wonderful man. Alan laid a financial foundation for me that has since had an incredible knock-on effect for others. I love him for it.

7

EYE OF RABBIT, HEARTSTRING HUM, TURN THIS WATER INTO RUM

Behind the scenes, everything seemed to be *transfiguring* as pre-production began on *Harry Potter and the Prisoner of Azkaban*. That's because a changing of the guard was taking place behind the cameras: the new director, Alfonso Cuarón, was a very different character to Chris Columbus, and a very different artist, having previously taken charge of the 1998 remake of the Charles Dickens novel *Great Expectations* (starring Gwyneth Paltrow and Robert de Niro), and then the Spanish-language film *Y tu mamá también*, described as a sex, drugs and rock'n'roll coming-of-age story and pretty far out from the tone of J.K. Rowling's Wizarding World. As part of Alfonso's stylistic interpretation of the third book, he set about changing the look of Hogwarts, even redesigning the wands, which upset some of the more hardcore fans. But Alfonso was of a more serious mind than Chris, and he ushered in a less innocent vibe. (Interesting fact: when Alfonso arrived, he asked the three main cast members to write an essay on their character. Dan put one together, Emma's was ten pages long, but Rupert didn't bother. When asked why, he responded: 'Because that's what Ron would do.')

During our first meeting, Greg introduced us and delivered a simple instruction. 'Show him what you're capable of, David,' he said proudly.

Challenge accepted. I climbed a flight of stairs, backflipped from the top, and stuck the landing. When I turned to check Alfonso's reaction, the poor bloke seemed bewildered.

'You're a crazy man,' he said, walking away.

I sensed The New Guy didn't have time for any of my bullshit.

Thrown into this disorientating mix was a brand-new Albus Dumbledore, who was now being played by the amazing Sir Michael Gambon of *The Singing Detective* and *Gosford Park* fame. Like his predecessor, he was a stage and screen titan, though his work ethic stood in stark contrast to that of Richard Harris. Sir Michael was a pro, he remembered his lines, and didn't require any prompt cards. If anything, he felt like an even cooler version of Dumbledore. Whenever we went out for a break, we would chat cars and exchange stories, and share smokes from a packet of ciggies that were stashed away in the jumbled growth of his beard. I remember him being particularly proud of his Audi R8, which was newly released. When I saw him parking it in the studio car park for the first time, he patted the bonnet and laughed.

'An HSBC commercial paid for this one,' he said, beaming.

But I was changing too. Thanks to the intense training sessions required to enter the British Stunt Register, I was becoming physically tougher, more muscular, and increasingly adept at moving my body. The more I worked, the more invincible I felt, and there was a sense that I could overcome any knock or injury that came my way. *My attitude?* Yeah, I might snap a bone at work, shred some ligaments during a wire gag, or pass out after a fall like poor Rowley Irlam in the Great Hall, but everything would be OK. Nothing was going to dent me. My confidence soared, which then gave me the self-belief to try riskier, gnarlier gags. I jumped from greater heights; I took harder falls. I wanted to prove to my peers, especially the bullies, that my youth allowed me to do things that they couldn't. Whenever I heard a positive comment about my work, I puffed up with pride.

Because of my self-belief, I had very little fear that someone might come onto the scene and take my job, and, like Greg, I believed that people from all sorts of backgrounds should be given the chance to prove themselves, and that a moneyed upbringing wasn't necessarily the gateway to success. When Greg decided he wanted to remodel the Stunt Stores so that they resembled a Bedouin tent, he asked me to source some labourers to help finish the job. I immediately thought of my kickboxing sparring partner, Marc Mailley, who was working as a carpenter while training for the British Stunt Register. I'd been giving him a hand by paying for some of his lessons after we'd become friends at an Essex nightclub a year or so previously. Marc was then eighteen years old, only an inch or two taller than me, and had been entertaining two very attractive blonde girls. They were laughing and hanging off his every word. *He had an angle*, I thought.

But what was it?

My question was answered shortly afterwards when Marc moonwalked into the heart of a swaying dance floor. He had moves. The party suddenly seemed to orbit around his presence, so when I later bumped into him at the bar, I suggested an exchange of skills.

'Mate, you show me how to moonwalk,' I said. 'And I'll teach you how to do a backflip that'll blow the minds of everyone in this place.'

Having agreed, Marc and I met at the South Essex Gymnastics Club the very next day, where I put him through his paces and immediately realised he had some serious talent. When I asked him to try a backflip, breaking the move down into its several component parts, Marc picked up the technique almost immediately. I then showed him how to swing around the gymnastics bar, once again focusing him on the smaller components of the discipline rather than the greater whole. Within an hour's session, he was close to mastering that too. Marc had all the attributes of a gymnast: he was strong, supple, fearless, and able to listen to instruction.

'You're a wasted talent,' I said, once we'd finished. 'Forget putting together kitchens. There's a job for you in the stunt world.'

And so, when Greg asked me to bring in some help to fit his Saharan-themed workspace, I immediately thought of Marc, and I suspected Greg would soon be of the same opinion as me once he'd started working. I talked him up constantly. One day, as we messed around outside, I threw a grape at Marc. Its trajectory arced upwards for about 40 or 50 feet, and having tracked it all the way, he sprinted and jumped up to meet it in a half-turn, before catching the grape in his teeth. As he landed (on one foot), Marc had the agility to spring up and perform a backwards roll-out. Greg, who had been standing nearby, looked at me in surprise.

'That'll do,' he said quietly.

He marched over to Marc, and I watched them talking quietly. Greg was asking questions. Through a smog of cigar smoke I saw Marc nodding enthusiastically, while trying not to choke. When the pair broke away, both were grinning and laughing.

'Right, this one's now on the firm,' shouted Greg, to the assembled stunt workers standing nearby. 'David, you spotted him. You show him the ropes.'

In Marc, I'd found a hedonistic partner in crime, and on Saturday nights we were all about dancing for ages and chasing girls. At that point in my life, I loved getting stoned. My mind often raced at a million miles an hour, and its somnambulant thrum cuddled my insides, sharpened my senses in new ways, and stopped me from making a prick of myself during those quiet moments in a conversation when I couldn't help but show off or blurt out something provocative. With the devil's cabbage in my blood, I became instantly relaxed. Marc enjoyed the party vibe too and once our weekend parties were done, I'd crash on the floor at his mum and dad's house.

This was the beginning of a happy routine, where my career and my life found a psychedelic equilibrium, and, like most stuntmen,

I played in much the same way as I worked. *I took risks.* During the week, my days were spent working on the latest instalment of the world's biggest blockbuster franchise; in the evenings, I smashed my body to bits as I learned new skills for the British Stunt Register. When the weekends came and went in a blur, I gobbled down ecstasy pills and partied, living off very little sleep and doing my best to get laid. Handily, I owned just about the best pick-up line in the UK: *I was Harry Potter's stunt double.* Though, with a brain full of MDMA, conveying that fact often proved a real tongue-twister.

★

At work, I was the consummate pro, and after Dan's blow to the head during the making of *The Philosopher's Stone,* I became fastidious about the safety of those people working around me. I knew Dan's well-being was in my hands, pretty much always, and given he was keen to do some of his own stunts, the onus was on me to make sure he was well protected. I did this by ensuring he was fully trained for any scenes that required wirework, and I looked on proudly as he and Emma hung from a line while being struck by the Whomping Willow – a magical tree with a propensity for hardcore violence. I also toughened him up in the Stunt Stores. Dan was fast becoming a multifaceted action actor; he was able to deliver fight scenes, perform reaction jumps, and – even though he had dyspraxia and zero rhythm – become a bloody good dancer.

Our relationship was changing too. During the first couple of films, I was very much the older brother figure – somebody he looked up to because of my seniority, experience, and the fact I had a cool, daredevil job. When filming started on *The Prisoner of Azkaban* in February 2003, we were becoming close mates, a transition that began at my eighteenth birthday party a couple of years earlier, when Greg booked a table for twenty at London's Little Italy restaurant. Dan was invited, along with his parents, Alan and Marcia, and as I got pissed, and Dan sneaked in a couple of beers, there was a definite change. We weren't working acquaintances anymore. We were good friends, and Alan and Marcia had happily entrusted him to my care, even after I'd jumped on top of a table and threatened to strip off when the Tom Jones hit 'You Can Leave Your Hat On' was played at full blast.

Art and culture became our meeting place. Dan and I loved exchanging film recommendations, albums, books and ideas. He gave me reads by Hunter S. Thompson and Chuck Palahniuk (though he was also reading *Jane Eyre* as part of his schoolwork); I wasn't that much of a reader, so I usually passed on recommendations for comedy films, like *Old School* and 'zom-com' *Shaun of the Dead,* a film we were both magnetised to. Our music tastes were very different at the time, but we agreed that 'Up the Bracket', the first record by The Libertines, was an instant classic. When Dan later bought his first London home, I often went round there for the night, and we'd play music, talk art and share stories until the early hours of the morning.

Much of Dan's passion for learning came from his mum and dad, who loved consuming art and culture and often spoke to the cast and crew about new film and TV releases, old movies we should watch, and plays we had to see. But all three kids – Dan, Emma and Rupert – were intellectually advanced for their age, having been schooled on set. During *The Prisoner of Azkaban,* they were all around thirteen, and their tutors encouraged them to explore the wilder fringes of literature and journalism. I think the parents and the on-set tutors had recognised their position as teenage superstars, and that they were being forced to grow up at a rapid rate due to the attention placed upon them by the films' success. The culture they were consuming was chosen to reflect that maturing phase.

But they were still kids at heart. Alan acted as Dan's on-set chaperone for the first four films and was incredibly supportive of his development. While he recognised that Dan was still a kid, and finding his own way in life, he was also eager to instil a level of discipline and professionalism. If ever Alan suspected that Dan wasn't being fully present, he'd have a quiet word to remind him of his responsibilities.

I'm sure that, as a famous kid rapidly approaching young adulthood, these words would have smarted a bit, but Dan took on board everything Alan had to say and worked his arse off afterwards. At no point did he ever come off as a shirker, either: Dan pushed through pain and the kind of illnesses that some people would use as an excuse to stay in bed.

Dan, the actor, was learning from the very best. The cast in those first three Harry Potter movies was a who's who of talent from the screen and stage: Sir Michael Gambon. Alan Rickman. John Cleese. Robbie Coltrane. Jason Isaacs. Julie Walters. Richard Griffiths. Emma Thompson. Timothy Spall. David Thewlis. Just about the biggest names in British film-making had been brought on board, and the young cast looked up to them as mentors. Having been surrounded by cinema A-listers, Dan was soon taking his craft very seriously and he learned that closing himself down was a great way of harnessing a particular emotion or feeling. During *The Prisoner of Azkaban*'s production, Dan even kept his distance from me once or twice, and in those moments I learned not to approach him or mess with his mood. He had a process and I respected it.

Most of the time, if Dan required assistance in creating the right tone, this work was done with Alfonso, the director, or Alan. But if there was a challenging scene, or an event he was feeling nervous about, I'd crank up our work rate. I'm not sure if it helped or not. But my experience of competing in gymnastics events (while being bullied at school) was that if a person could handle a task while working under extreme pressure, that same task became a hell of a lot easier when the pressure was reduced.

He wasn't short of willing tutors, though. By the time filming began on the fifth film in the franchise, *Harry Potter and the Order of the Phoenix*, he had formed a solid connection with Gary Oldman, an actor who carried a *greatest of all time* aura about him. Gary was playing Harry Potter's godfather, Sirius Black, and had first joined the cast for *The Prisoner of Azkaban*. It didn't take long to realise that Gary's style was no-nonsense and zero frills. In the build-up to his scenes, there was very little in the way of *method*. Instead, he'd smoke a ciggy, drink a cuppa, chat with the crew, and wait for his call to action. Then he'd drop an acting masterclass, before returning to his brew, talking as if nothing much had happened. It was unbelievable to watch.

The greatest example of Gary's performance style took place on *The Order of the Phoenix*, where, in his final moments, he was killed in the Battle of the Department of Mysteries by his cousin, Bellatrix Lestrange, as played by Helena Bonham Carter. In the narrative, Harry was described as looking on, devastated. The teenage wizard had become very close to Sirius, who was the closest to a parent that he had ever known. With these notes, Dan's acting required some hefty emotion. From what I could tell, the actors involved, plus Alfonso and Alan, had been engaged in several discussions beforehand on how best to manage what was a potentially turbulent moment for him. Running through such a dark scene might have been emotionally unsettling for a kid not yet at drinking age and precautions had to be taken. I wasn't around for the meetings; Dan didn't share what was said either. But in the moments before filming began, an interesting moment unfolded: Gary took Dan to one side and started to build a dark intensity.

I was only there because Gary had been attached to a wire, and Dan was required to perform one or two dives across the set, but watching from the sidelines, I felt strangely privileged to have witnessed such a powerful spectacle. The actor famous for playing Sid Vicious, Lee Harvey Oswald and terrifying Drexl Spivey in *True Romance* was investing in Dan's talent. He was also sympathetic to both his age and the pressure he was under as a child star. This assistance helped Dan to deliver a moving performance. I'm not sure what was said, but by the time he'd stepped to his mark,

Dan had been brought to a state of mourning. He looked unsurprisingly rattled.

If there was one scene that underlined the acting power on the Harry Potter franchise, it was the moment in which Sirius Black, Severus Snape and Defence Against the Dark Arts professor Remus Lupin, played by David Thewlis, came together for the first time. Watching the three of them throwing down in *The Prisoner of Azkaban*'s climactic ending was an epic, one-off event, like a showdown between the best athletes of their era. No two takes were the same. The weighting on phrases and the pauses between lines varied from take to take. The looks shared between the three actors changed with every shot. Dan and Emma watched on in awe. We all did. It reminded me of those moments when, as a small kid, I'd gawped at gymnasts who were a lot older than me as they nailed routines of serious complexity on the pommel horse, or around the rings. It was a form of greatness that was hard to comprehend. And all of us were better off for seeing it.

Creatively, I was living in a dreamy bubble. There was something life-affirming about doing a good day's work among such a talented crew, especially if it had been a collaborative experience, as most scenes were. In those moments, I generally only had one thought.

Fucking hell, I'm really part of something special here.

★

Another film release, another box office smash: *Harry Potter and the Prisoner of Azkaban* was released in 2004 and immediately proved that the franchise was showing no signs of slowing down or boring its increasingly crazed fanbase. The film made over $795 million and the online clicks for Harry Potter-related news, plus the inevitable tabloid intrusion, ramped up even higher. Anyone attached to the series was given a sprinkling of stardust and I started to receive offers of my own, including a role in a lucrative advert for the latest line of Mini Convertibles and a stunt performer's position in the movie *The Last Legion* – a film set during the collapse of the Roman Empire, and starring Ben Kingsley (who the crew had to refer to as 'Sir' Ben Kingsley throughout) and Colin Firth.

This was the first movie I'd made that came from a contact away from Greg and his associates, and the change of scenery felt good. I was told I'd have to dye my hair blond because I was doubling for Thomas Sangster of *Love Actually* fame, and that I'd be working in Tunisia and Slovakia, both of which were a culture shock. Slovakia because it was so bloody cold. Tunisia because the seaside town of Hammamet – described as 'the Tunisian Saint Tropez' – was a sensory overload of Arabic sights (animal carcasses hanging in shop fronts), smells (unfamiliar spices) and sounds (parping car horns, bleating goats). I loved it. And when I saw the film set, which comprised a fully recreated cross-section of historical Rome, complete with amphitheatres, communal toilets and bath houses, I felt quite pleased to have scored some work off my own bat. I was landing premium roles away from my film dad; I was stepping out on my own. It felt like the grown-up move.

In the background, the Harry Potter franchise rolled on regardless. As with the other films, the attention on who would be doing what next and which person would be brought in to orchestrate the tone and storytelling of the next instalment was a hot topic. Several directors were in the frame, including Kenneth Branagh, Gilderoy Lockhart himself, who had been pitching to take the role for a couple of years. As had Mike Newell, whose range was so broad that he'd made the mafia flick *Donnie Brasco* and a massive rom-com in *Four Weddings and a Funeral*. Given the next book in the series, *Harry Potter and the Goblet of Fire*, was a coming-of-age narrative and featured plenty of teenage angst, the Yule Ball, and some excruciating dance lessons from Professor McGonagall, Mike was the unsurprising choice for the job. I liked him from the minute we were introduced: he was a bright and bouncy character, and very posh. Whenever I was on set, I'd hear him shouting congratulations to the actors as they finished a scene. He was very different to both Alfonso and Chris Columbus.

Thankfully, Dan hadn't experienced anything remotely resembling a growth spurt, which meant I was still in a job as his stunt double. My greatest fear was that he might grow to a height of six feet between movies, but genetically that didn't seem to be happening. Despite my troubles as a kid (and at work, with the occasional outbreak of bullying still taking place), I owned the fact that I was a short arse. I never felt embarrassed about my stature, and if anything I used it as motivation. Thanks to Little Man Syndrome, my size pushed me to greater dares because I was so keen to prove people wrong. Tolga was having no such luck, however. He was now too big for his original role and was doubling for older characters, and the last time he'd stand in for Dan was during the scene in which Harry nearly drowns during the Triwizard Cup.

I loved Tolga. He was a great bloke, and whip-smart (he was educated on set alongside Dan, Emma and Rupert, and smashed his GCSEs) and I'd happily shown him the ropes when he'd first joined the stunt team on *Harry Potter and the Philosopher's Stone*, having been spotted by Greg in a north London gymnastics club. It made sense to have both a child stunt double (Tolga) and an adult one (me) for the films, and given he was only twelve at the time, all the physical attributes were there. It wasn't as if I had a lot of experience myself at the time, but after *Lost in Space* I possessed just enough that I could give him a few hints on how to navigate a film set, and the pitfalls that might catch someone out, were they not to know where to go and how to behave. Tolga had soon clicked into the role, performing arguably one of the greatest 'pratfalls' committed to screen when in the closing stages of his debut appearance in film he tombstoned backwards while doubling as Neville Longbottom after Hermione strikes him with the Full Body Bind Curse. I don't know how he did it, but Tolga's shoulders locked, his spine went rigid, and his legs seemed to be pumped full of concrete. Then he fell backwards, his body set in a straight line, landing on the deck like a toppled wardrobe.

When filming on *The Goblet of Fire* began in 2004, Dan pushed to do even more stunts than before, and he was more than capable. Thanks to our training together, his specialist skillsets had expanded. He was also keen to perform a gag in the script where Harry had to slide down a wet rooftop, feet first, while sneaking past a Hungarian Horntail dragon. The manoeuvre was loaded with risk because it required the stunt performer to keep their feet pitched just above the surface of the roof, all while they hurtled towards a crash mat at the bottom. If their heels or toes touched the surface, even for a split second, the results would be disastrous. I once saw a fully grown adult crashing down a drop slide in an indoor adventure playground. As his trainers snagged on the plastic surface, his backside concertinaed into his heels, which caused both his shinbones to rupture through his lower legs in a grisly compound fracture. To avoid an equally unpleasant replay, I spent weeks improving Dan's core strength with sit-ups, lower leg crunches and V-ups so he could manage the physicality of keeping his feet away from trouble in such a high-speed gag.

All of us were growing into young adults, some of us faster than others. Given the nature of the narrative in *The Goblet of Fire*, and the on-trend hairstyle of the early 2000s, Harry had been given a shaggy, grown-out feather cut that was one part Liam Gallagher, another part Julian Casablancas of the indie rock band The Strokes. When it was announced that Dan was growing shoulder-length hair, Greg took one look at me and laughed.

'Well, it looks like you're doing the same thing,' he said.

What I didn't know at the time was that the groundwork for a particularly challenging gag had also been laid, like a booby trap, in the middle of the movie. Within the plot, J.K. Rowling's Triwizard Cup was set to take place – a series of trials contested by the three wizarding schools of Hogwarts, Beauxbatons and Durmstrang. When

I'd first read the book in 2000, around the time of my diving lessons, I'd been drawn to a scene in which Harry rescued both Ron and Gabrielle Delacour, a member of the Beauxbatons team, from the Black Lake. To do so, he swallowed a clump of Gillyweed – a mystical, slimy water plant that allowed the user to breathe underwater. After finishing the book, I'd made pages of notes on what I thought the scene might look like.

When the Black Lake scene was realised in script form a few years later, it sounded like a stunt epic. There would be a full-sized filming tank, scuba crews, and a specialised diver in play. 'Bloody hell, that's going to take a lot of work for some poor fucker,' I said, rifling through the pages.

Greg obviously agreed. 'You better get your PADI course done, Dave,' he said, the next time I spoke to him.

He was referring to the well-known scuba diving course. Then the penny dropped. *I was that poor fucker.*

The downer was fleeting. I loved being underwater. Having been trained, I held my breath for fun in the multi-million-pound filming facility at Leavesden Studios, where the Black Lake was recreated, but the work wasn't without risk. Decompression sickness, or *the bends,* is a horrific condition in which nitrogen bubbles form in a diver's blood, were they to rise to the surface too quickly after spending time at depth. The condition causes severe joint pain, dizziness, extreme fatigue and brain fog. My PADI course had taught me the bends had to be avoided at all costs. In an environment such as the Leavesden tank, which was 6 metres deep, the chances of getting ill were high. Though the bends normally occur in deep water, they generally take hold in the first 10 metres of a dive. I had to be careful.

My job, alongside Tolga, was to 'build' the scene with a second unit team as a preview, before filming began for real. To do so, I had to swim around as Harry (without the use of Gillyweed, sadly), all while taking gulps of air from a scuba canister that had been left on the floor of the tank and, afterwards, decompressing in a diving bell positioned nearby. Having topped up my lungs, we built the sequence in a succession of shots that sometimes lasted for up to two minutes. In the final film, I acted as Harry in several of the wider shots, moving up and down in the pool while wearing a full Triwizard Cup outfit, which comprised shorts and a singlet, and a wand strapped to my right calf – in a style similar to most divers operating at sea, though in their case they were using a specialist knife. The filming lasted for four months, and at times my body felt smashed. Then one day, when driving home after a full shift of bouncing around the pool, my elbows suddenly locked up. Fatigue hit me like a punch to the face. Then the edges of my vision started to blur and darken. I was blacking out. *I'd got a slight case of the bends.* Pulling over, I turned to Marc, who was in the passenger seat.

'You're going to have to drive,' I said, fighting hard not to faint.

We swapped sides and I drifted into a deep, heavy sleep. Once I'd made it to bed, I didn't wake up until five o'clock the next morning.

Forget the Wim Hof Method: it later turned out that getting in and out of a dive tank and completing long breath holds, day after day, wasn't exactly great for a person's health. I'd always been proud of my attendance record in the studio, and I'd never taken a sick day – that is, until I picked up a brutal chest infection after performing a series of loop-the-loops in the tank, my flippers kicking in a butterfly stroke, my arms fixed behind me. The shot was taxing. I had to make a tidy circle in the water by diving down for a full 6 metres, touching the bottom and arcing upwards. Once I'd broken the surface, I had to repeat the manoeuvre, but on one occasion my timing went askew. Lancing upwards, kicking smoothly, I suddenly realised I was all out of puff. I reached out and felt my hands breaking the waterline.

'Thank God,' I thought. 'I'm there.'

But I wasn't.

Sucking in a huge gulp of oxygen, my lungs filled with water. I'd been a split second too early, and once I'd thrashed my way to the edges of the pool I spewed violently over the side.

The crew rushed over to check on me, as my body rattled in a spluttering coughing fit.

'I can handle it,' I said, smiling. 'It's just a day's work . . . *Isn't it?*'

But it wasn't. The blunder cost me dearly and my lungs were soon inflamed, wheezy and gurgling with a bright green, gloopy phlegm. At the end of the filming day, as I packed up for home, somebody cheerily pointed out that I'd turned a deathly shade of blue. I didn't get out of bed for a few days.

★

Sometimes, great stunts were left on the cutting room floor, which was always frustrating, especially if a lot of effort and pain had gone into making them. During *Harry Potter and the Chamber of Secrets*, I sat in the passenger seat of the flying 1960 Ford Anglia 105E as it tore through the Forbidden Forest, AKA Black Park – 618 acres of woodland located near to Pinewood Studios. We were filming Harry, Ron and Fang's escape from the flesh-eating Acromantula, Aragog, and his army of spiders, and it was my job to double for Harry alongside the driver, Paul Herbert, as he tore through the trees at top speed, our path illuminated by a series of incredibly bright lights attached to a crane above.

The view was amazing, but eerie. It was a windy night, the leaves crashed and swayed overhead, and a blanket of dry ice carpeted the woodland floor. But the route was treacherous, blocked by trees and logs. Handily, a safe highway was marked by tiny little red lights. They dotted the tree trunks ahead and were invisible to anyone watching in the cinema, but there was enough illumination for Paul to see his way through. Which was handy because there were some incredibly tight squeezes, and though we were driving a car from

the 1960s, it had been souped up to 21st-century stunt requirements. A V6 engine fitted inside gave the Anglia some serious poke
and the rear tyres had been fitted with rally car-style grips. Every
time we swerved through a small gap between two trees, I sucked in
a deep breath and braced for impact.

But it never came.

When I later learned that the scene had been cut from the final
edit, I was furious. *Fucking hell, it felt like I risked my life for that*, I
thought.

Then I remembered I was at the whim of an editor. It was their
job to pick the best shot, the best line, the best close-up. It didn't
matter whether I'd nailed a gag in one take or smashed my nose on
the dashboard of a flying car. Nothing could get in the way of the
story, and rightly so.

That didn't make any of these cuts easier to take, though. One of
my favourite stunts ever saw me pitched alongside Ralph Fiennes,
Lord Voldemort himself, during the graveyard scene in *The Goblet of
Fire* where Harry is gripped by a statue as The Dark Lord is resur-
rected, the story taking a much grittier tone. When Harry is released
and faces *You Know Who*, he is forced to the ground with a flick of
the hand and ordered to bow, writhing as he does so. But in a take
not seen in the final cut, Harry is then flung through the air – an
effect captured by firing me up into the sky while attached to a wire.
To act as Harry in those moments was incredible. Ralph Fiennes
was terrifying. I'd heard from the other cast members that he was a
lovely bloke, but he was another method actor, like Alan Rickman,
and whenever I was in his orbit he was standoffish, harsh, and a person to be feared. Just like Voldemort. He flicked his costume as he
walked; there was a flamboyancy to his wandcraft; and he moved his
head unnaturally, like a person would if they were half-snake.

Not surprisingly, he scared the absolute shit out of me, and the
scene, had it remained, would have probably given me nightmares.

8

GROWING PAINS

Like a senior pupil at Hogwarts, I was rapidly approaching the peak of my powers, and after four years of training I eventually qualified for the British Stunt Register. My reputation soon spread beyond the Harry Potter cast and crew, thanks, in part, to *The Last Legion*. At one point I'd been dangled from the roof of Tabarka's Genoese castle, by the cast member Kevin McKidd. A metal 'arm' bolted to the floor and threaded inside his costume had kept us both safely pinned to the building, but there was no doubt that were it to break free from its fixings, I'd have been smashed to pieces on the rocks 100 metres below. Throughout 2007, I was in demand and commissioned to work on a list of other jobs, among them *Harry Potter and the Order of the Phoenix*, a kids' fantasy movie called *The Golden Compass*, and the latest TV show from the comedic actors Harry Enfield and Paul Whitehouse, entitled *Ruddy Hell! It's Harry and Paul*. Times were good.

The comedy roles were a laugh. My brief for *Ruddy Hell! It's Harry and Paul* was to play stunt double to Madonna. (The Queen of Pop wasn't *in* the show; a likeness of her was being spoofed in the filming.) As production started, I was instructed to back-flip around a stately home dining room in full Madonna costume, before turning around and 'kicking' Harry Enfield in the bollocks. As with these events, I wasn't *supposed* to land the blow; the way the cameras had been positioned would create the impression that my wild swing had connected with his private parts. In the costume department, a wardrobe assistant handed me a pair of riding boots as part of my outfit, but they were too big. Predictably, when I then aimed a realistic-looking swipe at Harry's crotch during the first take, I misjudged the size of my footwear and clipped the tip of his penis. The poor bloke doubled over with a groan.

In a bizarre twist of fate, I was reunited with Harry several years later at the premiere of the final Harry Potter film, *The Deathly Hallows Part 2*. Having noticed him chatting to Helena Bonham Carter, I went over to say hello. Then, after a little small talk, I wondered if he remembered my terrible misjudgement.

'Bloody hell, yes!' he said, laughing.

Slowly, Harry put two and two together. 'So, what happened to you, then?' he said, gesturing to my wheelchair.

He nodded sympathetically as I told the story, explaining how I'd been injured when a wire stunt had gone horribly wrong.

Then a wry smile creased Harry's face. 'Karma's a bitch, isn't it?' he said cheekily, taking an opportunity to break what was becoming a doomy vibe.

I laughed. Gags like that tended to make me feel a lot more comfortable about my situation. I hated it when people tiptoed around me, or my injury.

With my reputation soaring as a stunt performer, the pay cheques began to rocket accordingly. By the time I'd been called up to work on *Harry Potter and the Half-Blood Prince* in September 2007, I was on a basic day rate of £462, just for turning up at the studio. Fees for my stunts were still being negotiated on an as-and-when basis, but under Greg's tutelage, I'd learned to drive a hard bargain. During the making of *The Prisoner of Azkaban*, I was asked to portray Harry falling from his broomstick, a gag that involved me tumbling from a 65-foot-tall platform. A large airbag was placed at the bottom and my drop was controlled by a fan descender. I spent the whole day falling and landing, *falling and landing*, and raked in over £11,000. With the Harry Potter franchise doing so well in the theatres, plus the profits from a still-healthy rental market, there were quite a lot of royalty cheques coming in too. For a bloke in his early twenties, I was making a lot of cash.

Despite the occasional episodes of bullying that tended to kick off whenever certain performers were brought in to work, I did feel very much a part of the family, particularly while working alongside Greg. I trusted him, and he trusted me. Our working relationship was even more paternal than before (though I loved my real dad very much), and because of our bond, I was happy to help him whenever I could. That feeling extended to the studio, where he often asked me to do things he wouldn't trust to the other stunt performers. Though I'm sure he took advantage of this from time to time, I was happy to oblige because I felt part of the Powell family. One Halloween, he even asked me to spook his daughter, who was having a sleepover party at the house. Several teenage girls had crashed in the front room and were telling horror stories and watching scary movies in their pyjamas. Greg wanted to give them all a proper fright.

I arrived after dark and met him outside the house.

'Put this on,' he said, handing over a bright orange pumpkin outfit.

On the face of it, this didn't sound too terrifying. But then Greg told me to run around the garden and scare the shit out of everyone in the house. Having jumped over the garden wall, I sprinted towards the living room and smashed into the patio doors, pounding my palms against the glass. Then I sprinted back into the darkness, the screams of several teenage girls ricocheting around the house behind me. As far as I was concerned, it was a job well done. But when Greg called me the next day for a debrief, he sounded very upset. Apparently, one of the girls had been so disturbed by the event that her mum had been called to take her home.

I had reached the point in my career I'd long aspired to. People believed in me. I was doing the big stunts, and the industry was talking about my work in much the same way that I'd talked about other performers and their gags. Like Simon Crane, who had ziplined from one plane to another during the Sly Stallone movie *Cliffhanger*. Or Gary Powell, having watched him drive that tank through a wall in St Petersburg, his body suspended in the vehicle by a series of bungee cords to prevent his spine from splintering. Some of my gags on Harry Potter, particularly those memorable Quidditch matches, had become imprinted onto movie legend and my ego expanded as a result. I got a little cockier. I considered myself immune from pain or injury. I drove like a prick in my Mercedes SLK. I also partied like a loon and burned the candle at both ends by gobbling down ecstasy pills every weekend. I'd always been super confident, but my personality had gone into overdrive. As far as I was concerned, I'd made it.

You've done it now, I thought. *The thing that you wanted to achieve since you were fourteen. Now it's time for you to really bed in.*

Whatever was going on in my personal life, I always behaved like the consummate pro in the studio. I was determined to better myself, and to add to my rep as a serious stuntman, but that's because I'd realised the end was in sight for the original Harry Potter franchise. In July 2007, shortly before filming on *The Half-Blood Prince* got underway, J.K. Rowling published *Harry Potter and the Deathly Hallows* – the final adventure for The Boy Who Lived. When Warner Bros. announced they were adapting the story into two climatic movies, I realised there were only three more films to go. *Three more years as Harry.* Given I'd been involved with the franchise from the very first day, and that my role as stunt double to Dan Radcliffe felt like an extended part of my identity, I became even more determined to see the story through to the very end. I'd really fallen in love with the character, the crew and my film family, particularly Dan.

All of us had to go out on a high together. Anything else would have been a waste.

★

When pre-production began on *Harry Potter and the Half-Blood Prince*, my battered copy of the hardback became stuffed full of Post-it stickies yet again, the text marked with highlighter pen and scribbled commentary and gag ideas. The narrative was as gripping as ever. In the previous film, Harry had witnessed the death of his Uncle Sirius, and seen Albus Dumbledore and Lord Voldemort engaged in an epic battle. If that wasn't enough drama, he was also ambushed in the Department of Mysteries by the malevolent Death Eaters. Given the magnitude of the story, the scripts were handed around under a veil of secrecy to protect them from the snooping eyes of the press. Every printed copy was watermarked. That way, if there was a leak, the studio could identify the source and punish them accordingly. Unbelievably, one member of the production team still managed to lose their copy somewhere on London's bustling public transport network, and when a newspaper then called Warner Bros., announcing they had the plot and dialogue for arguably the most anticipated cinematic release of the forthcoming year, a deal was struck for its return.

Wandering scripts aside, a ring of steel had been coiled tightly around the production. This was partly due to an unexpected incident during the making of *The Prisoner of Azkaban*, when a joyrider gatecrashed a night shoot on the Thames South Bank, which had been sealed off from Lambeth Bridge to Elephant and Castle. The scene in question landed in the first few minutes of the film and featured the Knight Bus – a Cadbury's-coloured triple-decker London bus ('Emergency transport for the stranded witch, or wizard') that picked up Harry as he travelled to The Leaky Cauldron pub. The actual bus was a feat of engineering that required a huge amount of weight fixed on the bottom deck to (hopefully) stop all three tiers from toppling over as it careered through the city, unseen by Muggles. It was for this reason that it was me rather than Dan doing the tumbling and faceplanting for the cameras inside the bus. But whenever there was a break in filming, I'd take a nap on one of the beds bolted to the bottom floor.

Then one night, as I dozed, Greg's voice came over the radio.

'OK, everybody, eyes open. We've got a joyrider on the set.'

A joyrider?

'Yeah, some fucker has got through the cordon and is racing about,' he growled. 'Let's lock him in. I want it tighter than a turtle's pecker. Then we'll get the police involved.'

Everyone was summoned to a car and instructed to obstruct the only available through-road by parking across it. But as the team moved into position, the driver, who was speeding in a stolen Range Rover, mounted the pavement and squeezed through the tiniest of gaps between our convoy and a row of houses.

'Fucking hell,' laughed Greg. 'Can we get this bloke's number afterwards? We should put him on the firm.'

Suddenly, there was a shout and a loud crash. When I turned, the Range Rover was rolling across the road. The driver had made it past the set's perimeters, but in doing so he'd clipped the curve of a roundabout in an almighty stack. He was hospitalised and arrested, though I have no idea whether Greg gave him a job later down the line.

Helming the now locked-down director's chair for *Harry Potter and the Half-Blood Prince* was the brilliant David Yates, who had previously made his name for the acclaimed political drama *State of Play*, which, when watched now, resembles a petri dish for the Next Big Things in British film and TV. Among the cast were James

McAvoy, John Simm, David Morrissey, Kelly Macdonald, Benedict Wong and Tom Burke. And while David might have seemed an edgy choice for a fantasy franchise like Harry Potter – he'd only directed a couple of under-the-radar movies before – his work on the dark-hearted *State of Play* made him a good fit for a series of films that were becoming grittier in tone, and its villains more Machiavellian in spirit. I loved working with him, and any pressure he might have felt about stepping into a multi-million-dollar production seemed to bounce away. Whenever I did a scene, or one of the actors delivered their lines, he always took them aside and gave notes in a soft, quiet tone. There was no screaming or shouting from behind the cameras and lights. He was a director who cared for his actors, and anyone else who might have been working around the set.

David had a diverse cast to play with, some of them freakier than others, and the weirder employees were tucked away in the famous animal department, a vast menagerie that lived in one corner of the studio complex. The place was the size of a zoo and contained all sorts of fantastic beasts. There were birds, monkeys and bats. For a little while a golden eagle was given pride of place. To keep the owls exercised, the keepers wheeled out a series of giant fans, turning them on so the owls could float gently in the air currents. One day, I even tried a 'dog takedown' for fun, and two resident German shepherds from the nearby police training school were unleashed and instructed to drag me to the floor. This terrifying display took place on one of the Leavesden runways and I was given a head start as a handler yelled a series of instructions.

'Run straight with your arms out!'

My mind raced. *Run with my arms out: why the fuck should I do that?*

Having been kitted in a heavy-duty bite suit, my movement was already cumbersome enough. *Wasn't that going to slow me down even more?*

An answer followed soon after. 'And don't turn around. You need them to grab your arms. If you look over your shoulder, they might accidentally rip your face off.'

I heard the skittering sound of paws on concrete. *Fuck, they were fast.* The sound of slathering, panting killer dogs wasn't too far behind. Seconds later, I felt their breath on my neck. Then, with a yank, the first one latched onto my forearm, the other grabbed my bicep and I was dragged to the floor. As I wriggled and kicked, they both licked and slobbered my cheeks, their tails wagging furiously.

The canine actors were incredibly well trained, and I had learned this at first hand when filming the scene in *Harry Potter and the Chamber of Secrets* where the trusty flying 1960 Ford Anglia 105E arrives in the Forbidden Forest to save Harry, Ron and Hagrid's dog, Fang, from an army of giant spiders. During the shot, the car arrives with a dramatic jump from a woodland slope, landing in a J-turn in front of Harry (me) and Ron (Tony Christian), plus Widget, the Neapolitan mastiff who was playing Fang. To add an extra shot of adrenaline, the car was supposed to be driverless, and the driver's seat had been torn out. Underneath the dashboard was the stunt driver, Paul Herbert, who was controlling the vehicle, his view displayed on a monitor that relayed the feed from a small camera stuck to the top of the car. During one attempt, Paul got bloody close with his turn, missing us by a few inches. I flinched. Tony flinched. But Widget didn't bat a droopy eyelid.

What I learned from visiting the animal department was that the furrier members of the Harry Potter cast were incredibly well looked after. Most of the animals 'acted' up until the ages of six or seven, when they were then retired, presumably to a five-star life-style. They had rights, too, their welfare overseen by the American Humane Society, who ensured fair treatment for every performer, whether they were stick insect, rodent or bird of prey. There were even rules about how long an animal could work for, with a stipulated number of breaks per shift. I had to laugh. The same couldn't be said of the stunt industry. I later heard a story regarding the performers employed on the HBO fantasy drama *Games of Thrones* where a lot of the work involved them hacking and slashing through mud in bogs, fields and wasteland. In one series, trench foot and tick bites laden with Lyme disease had become a worrying occupational hazard. Even though I was picking up a tidy salary, it felt disconcerting to learn that I might have had fewer employment protections than a wanking mandrill.

Meanwhile, the human cast for *The Half-Blood Prince* was also growing in stature, and welcomed into the fold was the late Helen McCrory (Narcissa Malfoy), a cackling raconteur who brought laughter and warmth to the party. Arguably, though, the most impactful on-set changes for me involved the upgrade in broomsticks. Finally, after years of chafing, crotch ache and embarrassing rashes, the razor-blade-thin bike seats of the Nimbus 2000 in the early movies, and then the Firebolt, had been replaced by high-end customised saddles that moulded snugly to some of the most famous arse cheeks in cinema – and mine. Even the fitting process was luxurious. I first had to visit the props department, where I lay down on a bed and a gun filled with plaster cast was applied to my rear. The gloopy liquid felt uncomfortably warm on my skin, a bit like when a heated car seat gets a little too toasty, and as the mould hardened, I was given clear instructions to avoid the loo. Not that I cared. Any short-term discomfort in my bowels was offset by the realisation that my balls would be receiving five-star treatment from then on.

Despite these advancements in broomstick technology, the overall experience of dealing with magical air travel was still fraught with risk. Alastor 'Mad-Eye' Moody, an Order of the Phoenix member played by Brendan Gleeson, flew about on a broomstick that resembled an American chopper-style motorbike and, when filmed, balanced atop a gimbal. (As did all the broomsticks.) Later, in a particularly dramatic scene when a mob of Death Eaters swooped menacingly through a gloomy-looking London, a shot was captured along the River Thames. The radical pure-blood fanatics soared across the Millennium Bridge, causing it to buckle, warp and plunge into the churning waters below. In the script, their assault was set to take place in the middle of the day, which meant the bridge needed to be packed with stunt performers dressed as tourists. To represent the dramatic flailing of a person falling from a collapsing London landmark, Marc had to wear roller skates and flap around in place for as long as possible, his legs kicking, his arms whirling like a drunk riding a mechanical bull.

Throughout filming, I smashed myself up, broke my body to bits, and came up smiling. Partly, this was bravado. Even if I had cracked a rib or broken a finger, I'd have shrugged it off, because while I was past the point where I had to prove myself to everyone around me, I was still hardwired to the industry's macho spirit. Also, I had to work hard to convince myself that I possessed an invincible status. To act otherwise invited the thought that pain might be real and something bad might happen – eventually. But self-confidence was a force field and I used it to deflect mortal danger. Besides, I wasn't one for malingering, I was having too much fun on set. Meanwhile, given the alpha male culture in play, anyone who was incapacitated, for whatever reason, was often cajoled back into work with some friendly words of advice: *Take two paid weeks off, then come back in and continue your recovery here.* After contracting that nasty chest infection during *The Goblet of Fire*, I was given a course of antibiotics and told to rest. Four days later, Greg was checking in on me.

'Getting better?'

I fibbed. *Yeah.*

'You, sure?'

I fibbed again. *Yeah!*

'If that's the case, get back into work tomorrow,' he said. 'You're needed in the tank. Can you do your breath holds?'

I decided to tell another whopper. *Sure.* I wanted to work.

'Are you testing it?'

And another. *Of course!*

I wheezed my way back into the studio, hoping nobody noticed my hacking cough and gurgling chest.

When it came to toughing it out, I only had to look to Greg for inspiration. By the time filming for *The Half-Blood Prince* had begun, he was in his mid-fifties, an age where some people felt trepidatious about their ability to absorb the body blows or rebound from injury. The truth about that time of life is that circumstance has usually delivered some warning sign, either directly or via a friend or family member; a reminder that no one is impervious to physical disaster. *All of us move into a sniper's alley of misfortune.* But by the looks of things, Greg was displaying the same enthusiasm for delivering stunts as he had as a younger man. I even remember him racing down the Thames in a speedboat during the making of *The Half-Blood Prince*. He rocketed past the Houses of Parliament at the sort of velocity that ordinarily would have attracted the attention of the police had we not been given permission, a camera gimble attached to the front of the vessel as he arced across the water from left to right. The bloke was a beast.

Though there had been upgrades in kit and equipment across the film-making business in general, the stunt industry was still relying on wire workers to pull the levers and manage the weights for gags where people were physically lifted, spun, or hurled through the air. Greg pleaded for change on several occasions. All sorts of arguments took place behind the scenes about who was responsible for manning the wires. I know Greg didn't want us working in that way and he argued as much, but nothing seemed to change. I reassured myself that if I were to take a tumble, somebody would catch me. *Because that's what we did.* And if the worst came to the worst, and something went wrong, I would be fine. *Because I was impervious to pain.* I wasn't yet walking through the sniper's alley.

★

As the franchise continued, so did the pressure on Dan. As his friend, I was very aware that he needed a proper break. We all did. Harry Potter was just about the biggest thing on the planet at the time, maybe even bigger than Beyoncé, and the franchise and its branding was splashed across magazines, T-shirts and even lunchboxes. Dan's bespectacled face was just about everywhere, and there was a feeling that anything that could resemble a normal teenage experience would be good for him. He had often listened enthusiastically as I shared stories of drunken lads' holidays and nights out abroad with mates, especially whenever we got together with his wardrobe dresser and close friend, Will. I wanted Dan to experience a bit of wildness, away from the prying eyes of the world's media – or the studio, who were doing their best to kill the party buzz on set. The high jinks that had marked the early Potter films were now a distant memory. I remember after a water pistol fight had got out of hand and a fire extinguisher was unloaded into the front seat of someone's car, a memo went around that everyone should behave themselves in accordance with the biggest movie series on the planet. Talk about a downer. Nobody wanted The Golden Goose to get a bloody nose. Or a wet car seat.

One day, as filming on *The Half-Blood Prince* came to a close, I snuck outside for a cheeky cigarette with Dan. Then I made a suggestion. 'We should go up to the Lake District,' I said.

He looked confused. 'The Lake District? *Why?*'

'Well, it's beautiful for starters,' I said. 'But it's also secluded. People will probably leave you alone. We can get a nice cottage somewhere, party, and have a good time without anybody bothering us.'

Shortly afterwards, Dan, Marc and I were driving along the M1, the boot stuffed with Marc's fishing gear. During a moment of motorway tedium, I put my foot on the accelerator, and as Dan fiddled about with the stereo, the speedometer hit 130 miles per hour. Then I pumped the brakes, realising that if the worst were to happen, I'd be responsible for destroying one of the most successful film franchises in Hollywood history. Once we arrived at the Lakes, we spent the days ambling through the beautiful countryside and the nights getting wasted in a local pub before returning to the cottage we'd rented. Usually, we played indoor cricket into the early hours of the morning. It was exactly what Dan needed.

He wasn't alone in feeling the pressure. The lead kids involved in Harry Potter were arguably the most famous teenagers in the world at that point, and I know Emma Watson was experiencing some of the uglier aspects of growing up as a young woman in the spotlight. On the day of her sixteenth birthday, one or two of the tabloids ran suggestive headlines regarding her age. (This was before the Me Too movement and young women growing up in the limelight, like Emma and teenage soprano Charlotte Church, were having their sixteenth birthdays celebrated by certain quarters of the press in salacious or innuendo-heavy terms.) God knows how much it must have affected her back then. Growing up as a teenager is hard enough, without every aspect of your life being picked up by a pack of seedy journalists. The production team, plus everyone around Emma, did a pretty good job of creating a supportive environment, but undoubtedly, when it came to the press, she received the rawest of deals among the cast. I really hope she felt safe around me when we worked together. I made sure to be protective of all the cast – not just in a stunt and safety aspect, but also in the way I interacted with them as young adults.

By the time filming began on *Harry Potter and the Deathly Hallows Part 1*, Dan was coming into his own as an actor. Working alongside the likes of Gary Oldman and Alan Rickman had undoubtedly helped him, and he was more professional and present in the role. That gravitas allowed him to branch out and in 2007 he appeared in the West End play *Equus* – the tale of a child shrink who treats a man with a horse obsession. Dan played the character of Alan Strang, a role that required him to act stark bollock naked at one point, which caused a fair amount of controversy, given he was only seventeen years old at the time. The scene wasn't exactly gratuitous, but thanks to the work I'd been doing with him in the Stunt Stores, he at least looked the part while the public decided whether it was appropriate or not. When I went to see the play in London, and later Broadway, I was fully immersed in Dan's performance. He was a star, and totally unfazed when shouldering established theatre actors like Richard Griffiths, who also played Vernon Dursley. Dan's expanding acting range made me incredibly proud.

I also noticed in the later films that whenever Harry traded blows with Draco Malfoy, who was still being played by Tom Felton, their scenes carried as much heft as those moments when the likes of Gary Oldman, Alan Rickman and David Thewlis had come together. Tom, like Dan, was really growing as an actor. When he'd first started on Harry Potter there had been a bit more maturity and swagger, mainly because of his previous experience and some impressive roles. He also had range. Sometimes an actor will put a lot of their personality into a character, to such an extent that, at times, it doesn't feel as if they're really acting – it's more like they're playing an extension of their personality. That wasn't the case with Tom. Draco Malfoy was a horrible little shit. The man behind the character was an all-round top bloke and great fun to be around.

Growing up with actors of this calibre was exciting. Bringing amazing stories alive fired me up, too. But I was also aware that there was a life beyond the Harry Potter franchise, and I wanted to explore more of it. Yes, I'd already branched out with movies like *The Last Legion*, and I'd recently doubled Elijah Wood in the 2005 football hooligan movie *Green Street*, making me the only stunt performer to have worked with Harry Potter and Frodo Baggins. But I wanted to go bigger and bolder. My size meant that I was always going to be paired with smaller actors, or kids, when it came to doubling work, but there was nothing to hold back my ambition. My final stunt on *Harry Potter and the Half-Blood Prince* had also felt like a major leap forward, which was ironic given it was a physical leap *backwards*. Doubling for Dan in a wire gag at the film's close, as Harry confronts Severus Snape following the death of Albus Dumbledore, I was surrounded by the likes of Alan Rickman, Tom Felton and Helena Bonham Carter. The moment was all power, Harry storming towards the then Defence Against the Dark Arts professor, firing a spell, only to be hurled back by the magic of Bellatrix Lestrange. The gag was achieved by me being yanked in a wire stunt, and I landed painfully into an area of mud and grass in what was a pretty big whack.

There was so much I remember about that scene. I had to trade blows with Alan Rickman, which was always a buzz, and to get the timing right for the cameras, I had the opportunity to deliver Harry's famous line: 'Fight back, you coward . . . *Fight back!*' It was a rotten night, freezing cold and – thanks to a wind and rain machine – blowing a bloody gale. To keep ourselves warm between takes, Dan and I huddled in front of a heater that had been set up in a small tent, him escaping the worst of it thanks to a waterproof Burberry trench coat that had been gifted to him a few years earlier; me wearing a full Gore-Tex outfit. It didn't help that Harry's look for the scene was a burgundy T-shirt with a blue pullover on top plus a pair of jeans and some Converse sneakers. The damp cloth-ing clung to my body, though it was still thick enough to disguise the stunt harness underneath as I cowered from Snape, Alan Rick-man looming over me, snarling and uttering those famous words:

You dare use my own spells against me, Potter?

And then . . .

Yes, I'm the Half-Blood Prince.

In the background, Hagrid's Hut burned to the ground after being torched by Bellatrix's dark magic.

As all this went on, my physicality was at the mercy of two men jumping from a tower in the background, their body weight pulling me backwards by wire. My explosive tumble through the air was on point. *I flew.* My hard landing was realistic and believable. *I was bodied.* And my performance, surrounded by some of the greatest actors in British cinema, felt next level. *I loved every second.*

Had I known it would be the last time I'd ever perform as Harry Potter, I'd have made a little more of the magic.

PART TWO
CUT!

9

THE LAST TIME FOR EVERYTHING

My life up until that day in January 2009 had been full of firsts. The first time for flying a broomstick; the first time for sidestepping a dragon; and the first time for being scolded by an enraged Severus Snape in the Great Hall at Hogwarts. *But it turns out there's a last time for everything, too.* The last time for driving a car, unassisted. The last time for reaching down to pet the dog. And the last time for opening a water bottle, making the morning coffee, or going to the toilet without somebody having to shove their hand halfway up my arse.

Hindsight's always 20:20, set in Technicolor and backed with surround sound, but 28 January 2009 was a day that now seems stacked up with last times, some of them more impactful than others. From the minute I rolled out of bed at five in the morning for a day of work, hating the alarm, my routine was a well-drilled process fixed in speed, efficiency and functionality. Within twenty minutes I had dressed in my trousers, T-shirt, fluffy Kenzo coat and Timberland boots – all of them laid out in the bathroom the night before. I'd kissed the dog, a Yorkshire terrier puppy called Rosie. My Mercedes warmed on the drive, the seats toasting in the wintry cold, as I waited for Marc to arrive. By 05:20, we were on our way to Leavesden for another day of bumps and bruises, pad bags stuffed into the boot. Marc snored, open-mouthed, as I drove.

If these events sound inconsequential and uneventful, *maybe even a little meh*, that's because they were. But after my injury, they became fantastical actions, movements I'd always taken for granted (and now wish I hadn't), and as time passes, each one seems more unlikely to have actually happened. Did I really smoke three ciggies on the journey, sparking them up unaided, with one hand? *Yes. Because I had working function in both arms then.* Was that really me warming up my body for the day with a series of pull-ups, sit-ups and push-ups in the Stunt Stores? *Unbelievably, yes it was – because Greg always wanted me to be physically ready when we started work.* And was that me steaming up the bathroom, lying down on a towel, and having a final, glorious, unassisted wank, all by myself – the last pain-free orgasm I'd ever experience? *I'm not ashamed to say that, yeah, 100 per cent it was. Guilty as charged.* I liked to start the day feeling relaxed.

And what I'd give to go back there now.

In 2023, while making the documentary *The Boy Who Lived* with Dan Radcliffe, we stood in a space where the Stunt Stores had once been. This was a corner of the studio where the water tank had been set up, as well as the location for my final ever stunt. Then the director, Dan Hartley, asked me how it felt to be back there again.

I looked across the studio, the sadness churning up inside. I felt haunted, and everything about my new life was too real. I swear I could see ghostly wet footprints trailed out ahead of me in the bathroom, *my footprints*, like tracks from the past, marked on the concrete. For ten seconds or so, it was as if I were floating above the scene, looking down on myself in a wheelchair, and I wanted something normal to anchor me to earth once more – like a camera running out of hard drive space. Tears made for great TV, I knew, but no way was I going to break down in front of Dan, or the camera crew. In the aftermath of my accident, I'd made a point of never showing my emotions to others, because I didn't want them to feel my pain. Whereas, when I was alone, I was happy to cry and release it all, usually in the shower where nobody could hear me sobbing and the water could wash away my tears. Afterwards, I used music to turn myself around, or told a joke to the next person I saw.

As the film crew moved about me, I grasped for something to lift the mood. 'I think I had my last wank up there,' I said, smiling cheekily.

Radcliffe laughed. 'For fuck's sake, Dave,' he said.

Instantly, I returned to my body.

As we carried on with the filming, we were informed that the entrance to the stage had been locked. We were unable to visit the scene of my accident, but just seeing those ghostly footsteps, and the last door handle I would ever open independently, was enough pain for me that day. But the memories of my final working shift on Harry Potter were still painfully vivid; I could relive that morning in January 2009 – and I had done thousands of times since, in post-traumatic episodes. The memories often came to me in granular detail.

At the time, the stage had been just the bare bones. A stunt rehearsal had been scheduled for around ten in the morning and the area had been set up with crash mats, wire rig and a skeleton crew, which, handily, included a paramedic. We were rehearsing the stunt that was written to take place in Godric's Hollow, during the climactic *Harry Potter and the Deathly Hallows Part 1*. The scene: a showdown between Harry and Lord Voldemort's slithering serpent and familiar, Nagini. In the script, Harry was described as defending an attack strike from the snake and this evasive move required him to fly backwards through the air. The gag would be achieved by attaching one stuntman to a contraption comprising a series of weights, pulleys and wires and – *spoiler alert* – the fall guy, in this case, was me. As ever, the weights were set to be dropped, physics was expected to work its own brand of magic, and, if all went well, I'd be yanked backwards before slamming safely into a wall of crash mats positioned behind me.

After painstakingly going through the health and safety report for what happens next, it seems to me that there are certain aspects unaccounted for. But I can't live a life of what-ifs and whys. That only leads to a downward spiral, so I do my best to park those thoughts.

What is certain is that there was a suggestion, after seeing the video of me doing it the day before, that the shot wasn't quite right. Not yet. The general view was that the launch required more speed, greater velocity, and a sharper effect. A decision was made that the weight bag pulling me should be dropped into a slack line to make the takeoff snap.

No doubt about it, I was set to take a big hit on the padded wall, and it was going to smart. I'd also have to rotate my body fully, mid-air, to avoid striking the crash mats at a potentially dangerous angle. All these things I could handle.

'OK, it's violent,' I said. 'But I'll be all right.'

Famous last words.

I was clipped into a harness, its strapping clasped around the middle of my back. As I readied myself, Marc came over. He looked worried. 'Mate, you took a hell of a whiplash yesterday . . .' he said.

I nodded. I'd spent the previous day being pulled about on the wires during another stunt. In the car journey home, I'd mentioned my back was very sore.

'. . . Why don't I do this one?' he continued.

No way. 'Mate, it's a Harry stunt,' I said determinedly. 'It's my job to do it.'

Marc knew not to argue. I'd made up my mind, and Little Man Syndrome meant there was no turning back. Besides, Greg, my Hollywood dad, was looking on. He had the power over me. No way was I going to let him down by backing out.

I set my eyes on a plug socket on the other side of the room as a point of reference. It helped me focus and I knew to keep my eyes on it at all times. I knew from years of being a gymnast that my rotation would be directed by my eyes and head. Concentrating on the socket would hopefully prevent me from rotating into the wall.

'I'm ready,' I shouted, after the wire had been attached to a fixing point on my harness.

Then I planted my feet. 'Let's go flying.'

In the background, Greg counted me down.

Three . . . Two . . . One . . .

ACTION!

The weight dropped into the line, causing the wires and pulleys to spin wildly. The line tightened. I felt its lurch and force, but something was wrong. *I was moving too fast.* I tried to yell, but there was no time. My body was yanked back and within a split second I'd collided violently with the crash mats. Despite trying to correct my angle of rotation during the flight, because of the forces involved I had been thrown across the room like a dart, neck first, my arms above my head. Upon impact, my chest folded into my nose. There was a loud crack. It sounded like a tree branch snapping. *It was my fucking spine.* Then everything went black.

When I came to, seconds later, I was in serious trouble. My nerves burned, but I couldn't feel my legs. Around me, I saw people shouting. They were yelling for help. A studio nurse loomed over me. She was checking my vitals and calmly fixing an oxygen mask to my face. Marc was shouting for an ambulance. Then, as I lay slumped at the base of the crash mat wall, Greg leaned down.

I was winded and could barely breathe, let alone speak. 'Greg . . . I can't . . .'

Greg's eyes flickered with fear. 'David. *Just breathe.* Don't talk.'

My mind raced at a million miles per hour. *This is bad.*

'It's going to be OK,' he said slowly. Both of us recognised the lie.

It really wasn't. Something was terribly wrong. That sound. *That crack.* My whole skeleton was buzzing like a pranged funny bone. It was as if my mind and soul had been severed from my body.

Finally, I gathered enough oxygen to gasp out a sentence. 'I've broken my neck, Greg.'

'David, can you feel my fingers?' he said, reaching out a giant hand and gripping my palm.

But I couldn't. There was nothing. No sensation. And life as I knew it was done.

The last time for everything.

'Stay still,' said another voice. 'Stay completely still . . .'

I wanted to scream, but it was impossible. My pain and distress were manifested in punctuated grunts and groans.

I noticed more people crowding around me. Another nurse. Then another. I recognised people I knew who worked for the studio's health and safety team. Some of the producers too. Then my vision blurred and darkened. Everything went black. I hoped that slipping back into unconsciousness would kill the pain, and the fear, but there was little chance of that. When I came back, my entire body was burning again, and as I looked up, I saw Marc. He seemed more terrified than me. *The poor fucker had just witnessed something terrible.*

'An ambulance is coming, mate,' he said fearfully. 'Hold on.'

'Don't call my mum,' I croaked, but it must have been hard to hear me in all the chaos, because Marc leaned in to listen. *What?*

'Don't call my mum,' I said again.

Marc looked confused. *Why?* But it was an incredibly important request. I wanted to protect my parents from whatever was happening. I wanted to spare them from my pain. If there was a slight chance that my injury was minor, and that I was wrong about breaking my neck, I didn't want to freak them out unnecessarily. I loved Mum and Dad dearly, and it worried them that I had chosen such a dangerous profession, particularly Mum. I remember going to see her early on in my career and she'd checked in on how my day had gone, like most parents would.

'Oh, we did a fire test, and a wire test,' I'd said casually. As if setting myself ablaze and being suspended 50 feet from a studio ceiling was an everyday occurrence. *Well, it was for me.*

Mum had sipped on her tea, doing her best to look nonchalant. 'I'm not going to ask you anymore,' she said anxiously.

The last thing I wanted was for her to stress. 'It's too much,' I said to Marc eventually. 'It's too much . . . *For her.*'

He nodded. But I needed him to do one more thing. *My video camera.* It was placed on the floor and set to record, as it always was whenever I rehearsed a stunt. I liked to have a visual reference so that a director or producer could get an idea of what we were hoping to achieve during a scene, or gag. The clips also helped me to analyse my own performance, to see if there was any way in which I could physically improve. Though I was in a precarious situation, the shock and adrenaline had sharpened my survival instincts. I was still switched on enough to know that the camera might be a lifeline if, God help me, I could replay the accident one day. There would be a chance of calculating the rate of speed I'd travelled at, plus the load on the other end of the wire as it had propelled me backwards.

'Take it. Guard it with your fucking life,' I whispered.

'OK, mate,' said Marc. He knew exactly what I was thinking.

Then I blacked out again.

★

When I came to, I heard the squeak of trainers, the rattle of a hospital gurney, and the whooshing, pulsing roar of blood in my ears.

Above me, the strip lighting of the hospital corridor rushed past, like I was living in an episode of *Casualty*. My body thrummed all over, and from the chest down I felt swaddled and constricted, like I'd been buried in sand. I could move both arms, but not my fingers. I was in a bad place.

The events of the past hour came back to me in fragments. They were like shards of broken glass – impossible to glue together again as a whole, but parts of the wreckage were still visible. I'd been loaded into an ambulance and the journey to Watford General Hospital was a nightmare. Because of the nature of my injury, the driver could only travel at 5 miles per hour, and every speed bump had been avoided to protect my unstable spinal cord. It's funny, the things that have stuck with me from that moment: I'd heard a rattling of metal and realised I was still wearing my stunt harness. Then somebody put me on gas and air, which seemed to cool the burning in my veins, but it couldn't calm that sense that something was very, very wrong with my body. I felt disconnected from it, though weirdly I was very aware of my bones. They seemed alien and hollow.

Having arrived at the hospital, I'd experienced my first episode of priapism – or, as they're also known, uncontrollable boners – a condition that was known to follow extreme physical trauma of the kind I'd experienced. The shock of my injury had sent blood to all the wrong places – my desiccated spine was causing my nerves to fire erratically – and the first one sprouted while I was about to enter an MRI machine. Marc had accompanied me into the scanning room for support, along with eight members of the A&E department, and was cracking jokes to lift the mood. My stunt harness was cut away, as were my clothes, and the sight of my neck, cracked into an S shape, must have been traumatic for Marc to see. I was his best mate; I had brought him into the business – a business that suddenly had some very tangible consequences, should things go wrong. The ethos of the stunt industry was to perform dangerous feats with safety in mind, but that concept had suddenly been stripped bare. I had been stripped bare too, lying there vulnerable and stark bollock naked. Then it became clear to everyone that my manhood was standing to attention.

'Fucking hell, Dave,' whispered Marc. 'You should be proper proud. You've got these hot nurses around you and your dick looks like a baby's arm holding an apple.'

I slipped back into unconsciousness, laughing and crying.

★

Marc called my parents. He had to. There was a very real chance that I might die, and if the worst happened it was important that Mum and Dad were at my side. In the meantime, the MRI scan had revealed that my spinal cord was dislocated between the C6 and C7 vertebrae and I needed to be transferred to a specialist spinal unit at Stanmore Hospital so I could be operated on. The good news was that the ward was only five miles away from where I was lying, pinned; the bad was that I would have to take another ambulance ride, this time with a police escort, at 5 miles per hour. I cursed my luck. If Stanmore had been located a little further away, I'd have landed myself a helicopter ride, like they did in all the great stunt-man injury stories.

I had to go under the knife, in an intrusive operation known as *a fixation* – a procedure in which a person was cut open at the front of the body. In my case, a huge incision was made in the neck area and my dislocated spine was realigned by a surgeon. Various bits of supportive metalwork were inserted around the two vertebrae and then fused with bone shavings carved away from my hip. I later learned that operations of this kind required a fair amount of elbow grease and muscle to bring a person's spinal cord back into alignment.

They were also time-sensitive: the quicker a patient's body was reset, the greater their chances of recovery, and there had been one or two delays. One of them being that the studio wasn't required to keep basic medical details, such as the registered doctors, of anyone working in the stunt department – where life-and-death risks were taken daily. The hospital hadn't known whether I'd been allergic to any painkillers or medications, even general anaesthetics. For the first few hours, I'd had to hold it together on nothing more than gas and air. The delay in being operated on likely meant that too much damage had taken place – the bruising around my spinal cord would have worsened. Any hopes of recovering the function in my body's lower half were likely gone.

After the operation, I faded in and out of unconsciousness for days while lying flat on my back in the intensive care unit at Stanmore. The only time I was moved was when a nurse had to help me evacuate my bowels – a demoralising, dehumanising and extremely painful experience, both physically and emotionally. Drips hung from my body. A feeding tube had been inserted up my nose and my face was covered with an oxygen mask. I was in a morphine haze, but I spent any waking moments reassuring myself that everything was going to be OK. That I was going to fix *it*, or that someone was going to fix *me*. When Greg and Marc visited my bedside for the very first time, I told them the same thing.

'Don't worry, lads,' I said, holding on to hope. 'I'll be back to work once all this is sorted.'

Greg was holding on to hope too. His Big Man façade wouldn't allow him to see anything other than a vaguely positive outcome.

'Yeah, we'll have you working again in some capacity,' he said. 'There's a job whenever you want it. Just concentrate on getting better for now . . .'

But I was kidding myself, as was Greg, and in the aftermath of the fixation I endured all sorts of tests and none of them were encouraging. Some days, as I lay there, unable to do anything but stare at the ceiling and contemplate what the fuck was going to become of my life, a nurse poked at my body in what was called an ASIA Test. These were conducted around seventy-two hours after a spinal cord injury had taken place and were used to determine which parts of the body were still functioning. In my case, there seemed to be very little worth celebrating.

'Sharp or blunt?' the nurse said, over and over, pushing at my skin with an object that was pointed at one end and curved the other.

I felt nothing.

Again, she pushed on my flesh. 'Sharp or blunt?'

I watched the nurse's hands moving, prodding and poking, but my nerve endings refused to spark. Every jab told her a little more about the extent of my injury; every unresponsive gesture told me just how screwed I was going to be.

At times, I felt the occasional glimmer of hope. I had been so in tune with my body as a kid-gymnast and then as a stuntman that I'd performed feats of athleticism and coordination that were considered beyond the abilities of most people. That style of work required an intuitive understanding of how my muscles, ligaments and joints might react if I twisted a certain way, or if I landed in a certain position, and during those moments my nerves acted like antennae. I desperately tried to tune into them once more, in a vain attempt to wiggle my toes or to twist my ankles. Every now and then, somebody would tickle my feet, in the hope they might respond and that everything would be OK again.

Weirdly, that even happened a couple of times, and my feet occasionally twitched in response to a light brushing motion across the skin. My toes jerked, some part of the foot spasmed, and for a few moments I felt a surge of optimism. Then a nurse explained that it was an uncontrollable reaction in the aftermath of trauma, and not indicative of a recovering body, but I still endured the tests for hours. Visiting friends and family touched my feet and legs hopefully; they asked if I could sense anything.

Do you feel it here?

What part of your leg am I touching?

What about now?

They could have been jabbing me with a hot poker for all I knew. I'd been disconnected from all sensation. My body was a phantom.

During these moments, my parents often sat by my side. The studio had put them up in a nearby hotel, which I remember feeling grateful for at the time, even though it was a bog-standard business centre. *They should have been in a fucking five-star.* Dad squeezed my hand tightly but, as with the ASIA Test and the tickling, I couldn't feel a thing. Then he prayed. He had always been religious, as had my mum, and I'd often been jealous of the way they leaned into faith as a way of centring themselves, especially during moments of worry or crisis. Staying still and reflecting, or praying, hadn't been my thing, and before the accident my method for finding inner peace was purely physical. I'd looked inwards by training, stretching, breathing and pushing. I had run faster, jumped higher and worked harder. As a kid, I'd transformed the stress of being bullied into an emotional fuel that I then poured into my gymnastics sessions. As a stuntman, I used fear as stored energy, pushing it into my preparations for the next risky gag.

The closest I'd ever got to meditating was when performing breath holds underwater, or during a conditioning session in front of the TV, where I'd set my body into the splits position. I sometimes held my form for up to three minutes, my eyes watering, and I'd enjoyed the pain as I flitted at the edges of unbearable physical hurt. My hope had been to locate the perfect balancing point between manageable discomfort and muscle-bucking strain. Once there, I'd tolerate the sensation for as long as possible, noting my times and any improvements. I had been training myself to become comfortable with being bloody *un*comfortable, which would then allow me to focus and deal with my emotions internally.

Sometimes the splits weren't enough; I'd gone further. Almost every night as a working professional, I performed a physical test before going to bed. At the time I was living in a small bungalow, and I'd return home from filming at around eight in the evening, where I'd spend a couple of hours tuning out, eating dinner and playing video games. Then, when it was time for bed, I'd uncurl myself from the sofa, prop myself into the handstand position and walk through the building upside down, the blood rushing to my head. I'd move from the living room to the kitchen, and then through the hallway, like it was a home-made obstacle course. The bungalow had a loft conversion bedroom and bathroom, and I'd push upstairs, opening the doors with my foot. Then I'd turn around and head for bed, only standing upright once I'd reached my destination.

And all the while I asked questions of myself.

Am I still as capable as I want to be?

Is the stuntman strength still there?

Am I as on the ball as I was last year, or the year before?

If the answer to any of those questions was *No*, or if I fell out of my handstand at any point, I'd make sure to train doubly hard the next day.

Now I couldn't even do that. Finding an inner peace through physicality was suddenly a pipe dream; everything had been stripped away and my sense of masculinity had gone. The emotional spiral began. *Without my body, how was I going to define myself?* I looked across at Dad, watching as he prayed, my sense of optimism fading.

'Dad . . . I don't feel like a man,' I said quietly.

Dad looked at me. 'What do you mean?'

'I feel like a toddler,' I said. 'Like it's all been taken away from me and I'm just this vulnerable, lost child.'

Dad's eyes brimmed with tears. I realised he was breaking inside, but he held strong and smiled gently. He had his faith to prop him up. I only had cigarette breaks and handstands for comfort, and neither of those were going to happen any time soon.

But even Dad was tested from time to time. Shortly after my operation, a woman arrived on our ward, paralysed from the neck down following a serious accident. Her husband later came to visit and at some point he had talked with my parents, their conversation landing on the topic of faith. That's when things turned ugly. The man had a different religion and wanted to take the moral high ground. He then claimed that his god was superior to theirs, before making a cruel suggestion.

'Your son's ended up like that because you're a Christian,' he'd said coldly.

My dad's a very lovely and passive man, but when he returned to my bedside and told me what had happened, I could see the anger and pain in his face. He had attempted to connect with another person in their shared trauma, but his gesture had been rejected because his beliefs were different. I couldn't get my head around it. Yes, I believed in a higher power. That the universe was one part of a giant whirling clock, and we should all be grateful for the experience and enjoy the passing of time. But religion, or spirituality, only worked if it encouraged people to be kind to one another, or to stay true to a positive moral compass. To argue that one faith was better than another? To say: 'My God is better than your God'? *All in an environment where everyone was suffering?* Well, that was just fucked-up.

10

THE QUIET PLACE

Reality kicked in several days after my fixation was done. I was in agony and pumped full of morphine. The visitors and well-wishers on the ward had gone home; the hospital was silent; I was able to sleep. But with very little to disturb me, other than the beeping, whirring machines nearby and the occasional sound of a clattering medical trolley rolling past, a succession of doomy thoughts had arrived to fill the quiet. My inner voice, once a supportive, cajoling companion during the build-up to a stunt, began to catastrophise. I was on a downward emotional spiral.

I suppose this was the natural end point to what had been a sobering chain of events throughout the day. That afternoon, someone had turned on my laptop, which was fitted with an internal DVD player, and together we'd watched the latest Jason Statham movie, *Death Race*. It was bloody terrible, but at least it was an action film, and I'd enjoyed picking apart the bangs, crashes and violence through the lens of a stunt performance. Later, as I drifted off to sleep, I wondered how some of the more impressive gags had been executed. I thought back to my own work from the past decade and remembered the buzz of smashing up a car and the thrill of reaction-diving away from a powerful explosion. Then it struck me: *I was never going to work as a daredevil again.* All I had as a reminder of my previous life in Hollywood was the pain now burning through my body.

I looked up at the ceiling and cried. 'This ain't coming back, mate,' I said to myself quietly. '*This ain't coming back.*'

During my earlier conversations with Greg and Marc, I'd been lying to myself, and I now knew it. The claims I'd made of making a return to the business were all bollocks, and the grief sucked me under, like the currents of a fast-moving tide. I realised my dream of seeing out the Harry Potter series with Dan was done. I would never again get to work with the likes of Alan Rickman or Gary Oldman. From now on, the adrenaline rush of nailing a dangerous stunt under pressure was something I could only imagine. My sobs became louder. The tears dripped down my cheeks. I felt them running across my ears and around my neck, and they were soon soaking the fabric of my pillow. Then somewhere ahead of me, I heard a voice.

'Hey . . . You all right over there?'

Although I couldn't see anything in the dark, I knew who was talking. It was a bloke called Will Pike. He was in the bed opposite mine, and I'd heard him chatting with his family during the day. Given I was still flat out on my back and unable to raise my head, I had no idea what he looked like, but I knew that he was as fucked as me, and that he could probably empathise with my emotional pain. *He would understand.* I wanted to tell him that I was broken. That my world had caved in. Instead, I remembered the stuntman rules and shrugged away my emotions. *Never show pain; never complain.*

'Yeah, I'm all right,' I lied.

But Will knew that I was bullshitting. 'It's David . . . Right?'

Yeah.

'You're not alone here, David,' he said. 'If you need something, I can press a button . . . Get you a nurse.'

Fucking hell. So, this was my new existence in a nutshell. I was vulnerable and exposed and, with not-working hands, unable to reach over and press the 'Call' button next to my bed.

'Thanks, mate,' I said.

'Or we can talk. It's not like either of us are going anywhere at the moment . . .'

I was struck by a weird sense of gratitude. Will was also suffering from a huge amount of emotional and physical pain. I'd overheard him retelling the circumstances that had led him to Stanmore Hospital and the story was heartbreaking. Will's injury had taken place in Mumbai, at the end of a two-week holiday to Goa with his then partner, Kelly. At the time, he had been a filmmaker. One night, as the two of them were getting ready for dinner, they'd heard explosions and gunfire, and when Will had looked out of the window, he'd seen gun smoke in the street below. But what the couple hadn't known at the time – though it was becoming horribly obvious to the outside world – was that Mumbai was under attack from the Lashkar-e-Taiba group in a series of co-ordinated terrorist assaults. The campaign would eventually last four days, during which time 175 people were killed and over 300 more injured. Before long, shooters were patrolling the corridor outside Will and Kelly's room. They were looking to execute any American and British tourists.

With no easy way of escaping, the couple constructed a make-shift escape rope from towels, bed sheets and curtains. Though the line wasn't exactly safe, they had been left with no other option than to give it a go, and Will offered to test the line by climbing down first. As he dangled precariously from the window, one of the knots gave way and he fell four storeys before landing on a concrete walkway. During the fall, Will suffered an injury to his spinal cord, a crushed elbow and one snapped wrist, plus a fractured pelvis and broken vertebrae. A bone protruded gruesomely from his left arm. Lying prone on the ground, unable to move, Will was soon spotted by an approaching emergency services team, who took him to a local hospital. A fire crew then set a ladder against the hotel wall and helped Kelly to escape.

I'd overheard parts of Will's horrific story while swimming in and out of consciousness, but in my fevered, trippy, morphine-dosed state, it was difficult to distinguish fact from fantasy and my mind had created a whole other narrative for him: an action movie storyline, something in the Tom Cruise mould, in which Will had taken on terrorists, single-handedly, before being seriously hurt in a heroic act. I had so many questions for him. But this wasn't the time for clarifying what was real and what had been warped by the fug of opioids. I didn't have the strength to talk anymore. The most important thing was that Will, despite his suffering, had looked out for me in my darkest moment.

'Night, mate,' I said, closing my eyes, swallowing the sobs.

I was pinned to a bed and surrounded by strangers, with only a ceiling and a wraparound curtain to look at. But I suddenly felt a little less alone.

★

Sometimes I'd wake up believing, for a few beautiful seconds, that I'd experienced an all too realistic nightmare. That actually, *I was OK*. Then the truth would smash into me like a ten-tonne truck. This sensation became even more tangible during any moments where I could sense the heft of the injury as it weighted my body to the bed. During my first physical therapy session, two assistants had propped me up on what was called a sitting bag. At one point, a physio placed their hands on my back and supported the areas where my muscles had once been a functioning system. Everything was lifeless. For the first time, I felt the immense weight of my head and neck on my shoulders, and without any muscular resistance to support my skull, it was possible to comprehend the scale of the injury and the trauma trapped inside my body. It seemed so huge. As I lay there, flat on my back, waiting to be hoisted from the physio bench, I was instantly overwhelmed. I stared at the ceiling and started crying again.

A wheelchair-bound outreach counsellor called Vish came over. He was an ex-patient working for one of the many organisations that had people on the ground in the hospitals and on the spinal wards. His job, I'd learned, was to speak to any spinal injury patients coming to terms with their new circumstances. Until that moment, we hadn't connected.

'Hey,' he said gently. '*Hey* . . .'

I looked over at him.

'It's shit, I know,' he continued.

I nodded, barely able to speak. 'It *is* shit,' I agreed, stating the bloody obvious.

'But lean into it,' said Vish. 'Don't be ashamed. Don't be afraid. This is part of your journey. And you'll find that, in a year or two, even though your body's going to be in a similar place, your mind won't be where you are now . . .'

So, what do I do?

Vish smiled. 'Have faith and trust that it *will* get better.'

I was drowning in a moment of unfathomable loss; grieving for a body that was never going to work again, and an old life that I wasn't ready to say farewell to. But through the pain, I understood what Vish was saying. *Sort of.* Going forward, the only thing to do was accept the horror of what had happened and, in doing so, build a new existence for myself. Yeah, it was easier said than done. But if Vish was right, and acceptance was the only way to heal and progress, there was no getting around it. The truth of life was that, at some point, everybody arrives at their deathbed. The only choice, then, was the in-between: *Does a person give in to the fear of not living, or the fear of dying?* As far as I was concerned, the idea of *not living* felt fucking terrifying. I really didn't want to approach my final moments with a whole load of regrets and missed opportunities.

But there could be no forgetting what I'd experienced either. That night, the horrific sound of my spinal cord snapping came back to me as I drifted off to sleep.

*

I was eventually moved into another bay on the ward, alongside Will. I befriended the other people around me, even though I couldn't see them, and as they spoke, I imagined what they might look like. At one point I was rolled over to go to the toilet, and yet another nurse shoved her hand where the sun doesn't shine. From that excruciating, undignified position, I noticed that Will Pike was long-haired, with a big beard. *Probably from the time he spent in Mumbai*, I reasoned. Unsurprisingly, personal grooming was less of a priority for a person stuck in a hospital bed, unable to feel the lower half of their body. But in those brief seconds, with his scraggly barnet and shaggy beard, Will became a little more real. He was an actual person rather than a disembodied voice floating around in a room full of disembodied sounds.

And all of those sounds I'd grown to know too well. In the same way that a blind person becomes more attuned to noise and a deaf person attuned to sight, I was suddenly hyperaware of everything around me. I understood the rhythms of the beeping machine next to my bed. I recognised the approaching doctor or nurse simply by listening to their footsteps. Whenever I'd spoken to Will across the ward, I'd trained my senses in a similar way, and tried to picture more of what he might look like. My guess was that Will was a bit older than me, a friendly bloke, with a big smile. I couldn't wait to find out.

Alongside him, in the next bed, was another man, called Oliver, who had been a promising young student at Saint Martin's College of Art. I won't go into details about how Oliver sustained his spinal cord injury. I'm sure he wouldn't want me to share his full story, other than the fact that he had been the victim of a hate crime. On hearing him recount the details, I sobbed for him multiple times. As with Will, I had no clear idea of what Oliver looked like, although in one or two brief moments where I was being moved by the nurses I noticed that he had a very striking appearance: Oliver was pretty, and he looked very tall. And at one point, he seemed to be wearing a scarf made from a ferret.

As we spoke on the ward, a camaraderie grew between us, the type that forms in the military where people bond through shared moments of trauma, loss and life-and-death events. When the hospital was closed to visitors at night, the three of us told jokes and shared our thoughts on the new life ahead. It was all we could do. When the conversation turned dark, I tried to lift morale by telling stories and making self-deprecating gags, because I'd always been happy to share that side of myself. It didn't matter whether things were going well or horrifically badly, I wanted to see the funny side. I'd also decided to act selflessly for those people in need of help. That's what Will had done for me. It's how Vish had responded to my moment of suffering. Both had shared something of themselves, by providing friendship, support and humanity, and my aim was to do the same for others. Anything to make a human connection.

After what seemed like a lifetime of staring at the ceiling, a nurse handed me the remote controls to my bed. For the first time, I would be able to raise my mattress and see a little more of what was going on around me. Finally, I had some semblance of control. It felt like a milestone.

'Right, here we go,' I said, ready to assess my surroundings.

I pushed the buttons. Slowly, more and more of the ward came into view as my upper body lifted. I saw the beds, the drab colours and the strip lighting. There, across the ward, was Will. He was smiling. I noticed his arm and shattered elbow were being held in place with a grim-looking metal cage. His hip had been pinned too. Sitting next to the bed was his dad, brother and girlfriend, Kelly. I was right: he had a big grin.

I smiled back. *There you are.*

'Hello, mate,' he said. 'Everything OK?'

Wanting to put on a brave face, I nodded. But what I really needed was another human connection. It felt important to have as many allies around me as possible because there was the inescapable feeling that I was unable to do anything for myself. Typically, I didn't tell Will any of that at the time. Instead, the performer in me emerged and I cracked a joke and made light of the situation, though I can't now remember what was said. A few days earlier, I'd pulled the same trick when Marc and Greg had come to my bedside to say hello. Smiling, putting on a front, I wanted to show the stuntmen, the people I respected most in the job, that I was still a double-hard bastard and that nothing was going to dent me. Not even a broken neck that had left me paralysed from the chest down.

Externally, I was sending out a message: *I've got this.* Up until that moment in Godric's Hollow with Voldemort's serpent, Nagini, I had been a boy. A kid operating in a fantasy land where work was a playground, money came easily, and I was impervious to pain and consequence. The injury had suddenly changed all of that. I thought back to what I'd told my dad a few days previously. *I don't feel like a man.* Then I realised the opposite had happened. *I was actually growing up.* And so was everyone else around me.

I also couldn't get my head around what Will had gone through, or Oliver for that matter. 'Jesus Christ, they've been hospitalised because of hate and someone's religious extremism,' I thought one day, looking at Will's caged arm. 'I'm here from stunts. Mine was my life choice; their pain happened to them.'

The David Show began soon afterwards. Now able to sit up, I received a queue of visitors to my bedside. Mum and Dad; Greg and Marc; and eventually my brothers, Paul and Adam. Paul was able to come from the beginning, but it took Adam a little while to bring himself to see me. I understood why. I was his older brother. He looked up to me, and I'd cared for him during large chunks of our childhood. Suddenly, I wasn't a protective figure anymore and it was hard for him to accept my new, terrifying circumstances. Then other people arrived. A who's who of stunt performers I'd worked with over the years. Various crew members from the Harry Potter family. Even some of the head honchos from Warner Bros. As we spoke, I'd make sure to point Will out.

'Fucking hell, what I've been through is nothing compared to him over there,' I said. 'Will's life should be a film.'

The actor Jack Black later heard about my accident, and though we'd never worked together, he stopped by to say hello once I was well into my rehab. He listened to my story before going around the ward, messing about with other lads in the bay, making them laugh, helping them to forget what they were going through, albeit only for a moment.

On some days, there were upwards of thirty people around my bed, and the biggest buzzes were reserved for those moments when it was revealed that Dan was coming by, or Tom Felton. Dan had first visited during my earliest days in hospital, when I was still unable to raise my mattress. All sorts of tubes had been sticking out of my nose and throat at the time. I hadn't showered in over a week, so it probably wasn't the most pleasant experience for anyone wanting to sit beside me. Seeing me in such a state would have been a traumatic experience too. Even though both Dan and Tom were young back then, they handled the situation like adults. Once I'd regained consciousness and was able to chat, they never let their shock or sadness show. Nor did I want to freak them out in any way. I stayed strong for them, and they stayed strong for me.

Later, once I'd started to look a bit more human and some movement had returned to my neck and arms, both became regular visitors. Despite the challenges of a hectic filming schedule and incredibly long hours (Dan was sixteen by that point and didn't need to fulfil his legal schooling requirements), he still made sure to visit me whenever possible. No doubt it was particularly hard for him. At the time, he wasn't really looking after himself. The pressure of being Harry Potter and living his life in the public glare was becoming a bit much.

'Keep your shit together,' I said to him during one visit – or something along those lines. 'Finish this off properly.'

I didn't want him to fall apart, though I suspect his situation wasn't being helped by the fact that one of his film family had broken their neck. A couple of years later, Dan began his journey to sobriety and became as dedicated to the recovery process as he had been as a kid stepping onto a movie set for the first time. He learned from his mistakes and grew as a result. I have no doubt it's because of the professionalism instilled in him by his parents that this dedication and drive carried over into his personal life. Whenever he walked onto the ward, he made Will, Oliver and their families feel seen. And he never forgot a name.

An atmospheric shift always took place in the ward when it was announced that someone from the cast was stopping by. The nurses became excited. I heard people whispering around the beds. *Is Daniel coming? When's Tom getting here?* Before long, the press had gathered outside the hospital, hoping to grab a photo of any cast members as they came in and out of the building. Though the staff were told not to say anything to anyone about the comings and goings of various actors (and they acted appropriately throughout), I sensed an uncomfortable intensity in the ward. While it was great that Harry Potter and Draco Malfoy were coming in and playing games (like the day we tried to cram as many marshmallows as possible into our mouths at one time), it was probably a bit much for the other lads in their beds, and their friends and families.

To help matters, I passed around the staff menu that went out to the cast and crew of *Harry Potter and the Deathly Hallows Part 1* every day. One of the great things about working on a Hollywood set was the catering. The food was amazing, and Greg had promised me that I wouldn't have to suffer the hospital meals at Stanmore.

'Pick anything you want,' he said. 'A member of the team will bring it over, still warm.'

Wanting to share the wealth, I managed to get the offer extended to the rest of the ward. Every day, multiple bays on the spinal unit were fed with steaks, pies, and plates of fish and chips. I even placed extra orders for some of the hard-working nurses who were putting in gruelling twelve-hour shifts. Every lunchtime, Jimmy – who was Tom Felton's driver – arrived with baskets of food. But a few months into rehab, the steady stream of visitors and celebrity guests dwindled. At the beginning of my hospitalisation, I was receiving too many guests. As winter turned to spring, one or two well-wishers arrived on the daily. Mum and Dad always helped me with dinner, and I was so grateful to have them there. They weirdly made my hospital bed feel like home.

11

A DESIGN FOR LIFE

After my first few physio sessions, a meeting was arranged with both a spinal consultant and the surgeon responsible for completing my fixation. In a shit-or-bust event, I was to be told the medical prognosis for my short-, medium- and long-term health, as determined in a series of examinations and assessments. But I already knew the prognosis, because *I* was all the evidence I needed. My body was dead below the chest and only my arms were functioning, with limited movement. Meanwhile, every ASIA test, and the irrelevant question of whether I could feel 'sharp or blunt' across my body, had revealed a depressing truth. *I was double-fucked.* I told the specialists as much when I was taken in to see them.

'Can I just say where I think I'm at?' I said, now sitting in a wheelchair. Mum and Dad were perched on chairs alongside me. They both looked anxious.

The surgeon nodded. *Go for it.*

'I know that I'm paralysed from here,' I said, pointing to my ribcage. 'I know that the feeling is probably never going to come back because it's a complete spinal cord injury. I know that it's now my job to learn to live with the injury and to understand the adaptions . . . Am I correct so far?'

My consultant, Dr Angela Gall, nodded sombrely. *You're dead right, David.*

I was then shown a series of scans and X-rays. I saw the point of injury on my spinal cord and the metal plates that were now a permanent fixture inside my body. They were small dark grey squares with defined edges and corners. Each one was a little slab of darkness affixed to the curvature and organised chaos of my skeletal system. Finally, it was confirmed that my chances of regaining some sort of function were very, *very* slim, given my spinal injury was known as being 'complete' – in which all movements and control are lost below the point of injury. The only positive update was that, with time, the remaining muscle groups should get stronger and adapt to my new physical circumstances. All I had left was 50 per cent of a bicep on each arm, while some parts of the triceps in my right arm were stronger than the barely-there triceps in my left. Outside of my shoulders, my trapezius muscles were pretty much intact, so thankfully the gymnastic strength I had built up in Greg's Stunt Stores was being retained. This, explained the surgeon, would prove very useful when learning to transfer in and out of a wheelchair.

There were no two ways about it, my life was now in a state of flux. I had entered a chapter of uncertainty, one I couldn't have imagined on that January morning when I'd made coffee for the last time, chain-smoked three ciggies, and relieved myself on the set of *Harry Potter and the Deathly Hallows Part 1*. I was now living in a different world; my past life had happened to a different person. Meanwhile, the brakes had been pumped on any future thinking and all sort of equations ran through my mind. Yeah, I'd accepted that my career was over, and I was grieving for it, which was healthy; but there were so many questions. Among them: If I couldn't work as a stuntman, what was my purpose? If I couldn't make a new life for myself, how was I going to get paid? If I couldn't get paid, how would I survive? I was also yet to have an informative discussion with Warner Bros. regarding my financial future: *How the fuck was I going to pay my mortgage?* I'd only just bought a new house in Essex, which, despite being a bungalow, wasn't exactly wheelchair accessible. There would need to be modifications, expensive ones, but my means of financing them had been cut off.

I felt my stomach lurch. Everything seemed to be spiralling down, down, down in a vortex of shit. But there was very little time to think, because the specialists then explained that I also had work to do. *Rehab.* The kind that crushes a person's soul. I was given a list of exercises for basic functions, like sitting up independently, or rolling over in bed so that I could climb into a wheelchair. The message from my spinal consultant was to 'use it or lose it', and I was very much into the idea of using it.

With the help of a physio, I worked every day to move myself independently into an upright position. I then had to locate a sense of balance while sitting, which was something that had come naturally to me as an able-bodied person. To a new quadriplegic, however, the experience was otherworldly. I suddenly had a wobbly body. The parts of me that were still working seemed alien and bolted on, and the rest of me was a total stranger. I could only feel the top half of my arms, the movement in my triceps was minimal, my biceps had been reduced in strength by 50 per cent and there was some remaining movement in my fingers. Even the way in which I held my head had to be retrained.

All of it was overwhelming. That is, until I remembered back to Nick Inns' advice at the Havering Gymnastics Club all those years ago. Rather than becoming overwhelmed by the complexity of what I was attempting, I had to break the technique down into a series of smaller, more manageable parts. In this case, I was relearning the art of sitting up rather than a double somersault.

I gritted my teeth through the pain and pushed and pulled to achieve my goals, until I was able to transfer myself from a bed into my manual wheelchair. Not surprisingly, there was a series of setbacks. When the rehabilitation process began, weighted bands were strapped to my wrists and I was asked to work the muscles in my arm. With every push or curl, I heard a crackling sound in my neck, as if someone nearby was aggressively popping a sheet of bubble wrap.

That's not good, I thought.

My physio and weight training ran alongside a water therapy programme, and during sessions I was supported in the hospital's swimming pool and instructed to move this way and that. Supported by a series of floats, and held in place by a physio, I was yet again able to comprehend the physical presence of my injuries, and it was possible to feel the disparity between the muscles that were still plugged into my spinal cord and those that had been disconnected.

None of it made me feel good. I had been an elite gymnast and a member of the British Stunt Register. I knew exactly what my body was capable of. While moving my arms in the pool or learning to sit up independently for the first time were to be considered milestones, and significant progress on a path towards some sort of recovery, they were also reminders of what had gone before. The first time I got into bed after a trip to the pool, I stared up at the ceiling and emotionally wilted.

Yeah, I made some progress today, I thought. *But it's not the same as before. I grew up as a gymnast, I know my body, and I know what I could and should be doing.*

For a while, I felt resentful of the work. The water therapy I could get behind, but the physiotherapy was a slog and incredibly painful. Then, when I next went to the pool, I was given a harsh reminder of my immediate future.

The swimming pool at Stanmore was big, around 25 metres in length. A seating area ran along the side and a cafeteria on a higher level had a viewing window that looked down on the water. The pool was a public space that also catered for specialist therapy work and was wheelchair accessible. Anyone in the area could use it. As I rested and refuelled after a gruelling therapy session, I noticed a woman doing lengths below me. She was fully fit and confident in the water, and her body sliced through the surface in a front crawl. I noticed her powerful strokes, arms pumping like pistons.

I used to be able to do that, I thought sadly. *But better.*

As she swam, a class of disabled kids had gathered by the side, none of them able to enter the shallow end without assistance. The group were wearing neck floats to save them from drowning.

And that's where you are now.

I felt heartbroken. When I returned to the spinal ward, I didn't look at the other lads in the bay. I didn't connect with another human all day. I grabbed my iPod and headphones and played *Lungs*, the first album by the band Florence and the Machine. Then I stared out of the window and watched the birds.

★

Acceptance. I had to think positively: it was the only way I was ever going to get a handle on my situation. But I also had to recognise that life was a sometimes painful journey, and we were most tested when the things we loved were stripped away from us, piece by piece. We lost our parents. Our friends and loved ones moved on. Bodily functions deteriorated, cognitive decline kicked in, even our hair fell out. The quality of our existence depended on how we adapted and functioned in the aftermath of these bereavements. My life was no different. I needed to find a way of rebuilding my world, piece by piece, emotional brick by emotional brick. This process then manifested itself in a very literal sense when I turned on the telly one day to watch the TV show *Grand Designs* – a programme in which a person, or persons, embarked on a soul-breaking home renovation project that, at times, left them questioning their sanity. (But ultimately proved creatively rewarding.) As I watched the bones of some dilapidated church being rebuilt, or a crumbling, abandoned lighthouse transformed into an architectural master-piece, I was struck with an idea.

Building a bespoke house . . . That's what I needed to do.

I'd heard that I would be receiving insurance money for my injuries at some point, and in the not so distant future I was going to be living away from Stanmore and the spinal ward staff. I'd have to operate in The Real World as a wheelchair user, where I'd rely upon personal assistants (I'd learned they weren't called carers anymore), technological support and wheelchair access. I wouldn't be able to use the toilet freely, as I had previously. The way in which I washed, showered and shaved was going to be radically different too. Simply moving about the house was likely to be a challenge. What I needed was a home suited to my altered physical state – a modern building with all the fixtures and appli-ances tailored to my situation: a *Grand Designs* project all of my own. Every Thursday night at nine o'clock, I turned on Channel 4 to watch the presenter Kevin McCloud oversee the transforma-tion of yet another house. I became inspired.

If the insurance money comes in, there might be an opportunity to do this, I told myself.

Every night, before falling asleep, I pictured my new home. The brief was to build a house from scratch where I could live as inde-pendently as possible, and I visualised it in much the same way I used to picture a stunt when attempting it for the very first time. There were no rules or boundaries, I only had to imagine it. And when I did, I encouraged myself to think bigger and bolder with every design choice – the blueprints had to be cinematic. For starters, I knew that, even though I'd recently bought one, I didn't want to live in a bun-galow, but that life in a two-storey house was going to be tricky for a wheelchair user. *But did I want to have a specialist lift tucked in the corner of the building like a monument of shame?* No! I wanted a glass elevator that ran the height of the house, as if it were a set from Willy Wonka's Chocolate Factory.

My thinking got bigger and bolder. I wanted to be able to get in and out of my car with dignity, which I suspected was going to be hard given that someone had to transfer me in and out of my wheelchair. I dreamed up an underground car park. Having spoken to a few architects, I later realised that it was hard to find a property with the space to build a slope beneath the main structure. (It was also risky, especially if I found myself freewheeling down the ramp and towards a hard surface.) So, I made it my job to find a car lift suited for an underground space. I went down a tech rabbit hole and learned about voice-activated lights, TV controls and speakers. (This was a time before Siri, remember, and toys of this kind were reserved for the super-rich.) I didn't have a clue as to whether any of this would be financially possible as the details of insurance, settlements and payments had yet to be established, but between rehab sessions I had plenty of time left for dreaming.

There was no room in the building that I wouldn't have access to, or control over, but I knew that I didn't want my new home to *feel* like a hospital ward or rehabilitation centre. I wanted my friends and family to be blown away by it when they walked inside, and to do so I focused on the small details. The bed was going to be electric, the mattress would need to move up and down, but a lot of the products online looked as if they had been designed for an old people's home. I set my sights on designing a five-star bed, fit for a five-star hotel, with all the mechanics and wires hidden underneath. Because of my time spent in the swimming pool at Stanmore, I knew my physio and rehab work had to be water based, so I dreamed up an indoor pool. Inspired by *Grand Designs*, I pictured an art deco style that was functional enough for a disabled person and cool enough that people would want to party in it, too.

Every room was fitted with speakers. Every corner was set to be illuminated perfectly. After several months in a hospital ward, with bright lights trained directly at my eyes, I'd come to appreciate the importance of subtle lighting. I'd always had a good touch with design, and I liked nice clothes and shoes, anything with a cool line or an interesting detail. Given my time spent on movie sets, I also understood a lot about staging. I wanted my house to be full of plants, all of them backlit so that the ceilings and walls flickered with beautiful shadows and shapes. Other than the aesthetics, there were two other features I knew were vital: one for my mental health, the other for my physical well-being.

First up, I wanted a cinema room so that I could hunker down and reconnect with the movie business. The sense that, for a disabled person, nothing was going to be easy had recently been compounded when I was allowed to leave the hospital on a day trip. A specialist had asked me what I fancied doing on an excursion and there was only one thing on my mind. I wanted to go to the cinema, to escape from my world and be transported into another – an experience that linked my new self to the old me. But when I settled into the theatre, my neck in a restrictive brace, my heart sank. The room was freezing cold. The wheelchair access area was a small platform on the side of the theatre where the view was terrible. Worst of all was the sound. Because I'd been positioned on the flanks, I was too close to one speaker and too far away from the other. I couldn't make out what was being said a lot of the time, which might have helped given the film was bloody terrible.

Another addition to my house would be a specialised bathroom. After months not being able to have a proper wash, I'd learned that a standard shower for a paraplegic was a brutal experience – cold, painful, *horrendous*. I could only feel the skin above my arms and head. That meant most showers felt like water torture. I aimed to create a 'car wash' for wheelchair users where every bit of the skin could be covered in warm water. The final addition to my as yet unrealised mind palace was a steam room. In addition to the bad news that my lost muscular function was highly unlikely to return was the confirmation that my winters were likely to be spent in a near-hypothermic state. This was a physical consequence of not being able to move around unassisted. My body wasn't getting enough warmth, and in the colder months this was likely to be painful and unpleasant, as my core temperature struggled to stay above 35 degrees. However, if I could keep warm from November through to April, I'd be OK. This was where my idea for a steam room first arrived. My hope was to attach one to my bedroom so that I could get two hours of heat into my body before getting into the pool for a water therapy session. I'd then spike my temperature at night before going to bed, to help me to sleep.

Back then, as I watched yet another episode of *Grand Designs*, I didn't know whether any of my ideas were actionable. But suddenly, with a plan in place, I felt a glimmer of optimism. I had something to focus on other than my immediate surroundings. As I created from my hospital bed, music became an emotional therapist. I used artists like Florence and the Machine to help me digest the pain and articulate my feelings.* I had an outlet to soundtrack the emotional turmoil I was enduring, or a palette with which to create a more positive vibe for an event or experience. Over time, I built several playlists on my laptop, each one designed for a different

---

* A few years later, I got to meet Florence at an Agent Provocateur afterparty in London's Corinthia Hotel. It was an A-list affair. The celebrations had been organised by the fashion designer Jimmy Choo. Actor John Hamm was there, and the synthpop band Hot Chip were playing live. At the time, I was numbing my emotional pain with cocaine and alcohol, and was in a bit of a state, but I was able to pull it together to approach her. Florence was the artist of the moment, everyone wanted a piece of her, but she was kind enough to say hello when I went over. I told her about my life as a stuntman and the accident that had cut short my career. Then I told her about my time in hospital. 'Your album got me through some really tough times,' I said. 'I want to thank you for your art.' Florence became quite emotional as I spoke.

psychological state: there were songs for the hard days, songs for healing, and songs for when I was feeling nostalgic.

I still use this technique today. Quite recently, I was having a tough time, so I put on a playlist that I'd made to lift the mood. Among the featured artists were Mac Miller, Ben Howard and Damien Rice. Then George Michael played at random. I was having a massage at the time and in a lot of pain, but when I heard his voice, I was transported to a different emotional state. The track was from his album *Symphonica*, a collection of live songs performed at the Royal Albert Hall between 2011 and 2012, and George's voice lifted me. His cover of Nina Simone's 'Feeling Good' flooded my brain. I heard him messing around with his orchestra and having a lot of fun. In that moment, I was reminded that art is the best of who we are, whether we are creating with music, paint, film, a camera, or even stunt work. All of it replicated the Human Experience in some way, and it allowed us to understand ourselves better. George's vocals lifted me in a moment of physical pain, in the same way that Florence had helped me to emotionally articulate a moment of turmoil after my humbling day at the pool. Each was different in their own way. But both were offering me a path to a better place.

★

I worked through my rehabilitation until May 2009, making good progress, and my official discharge date, and the first day in a new life at my (now wheelchair accessible) Essex bungalow, had been set. Then life took a disagreeable turn, and I experienced a series of crushing headaches that kicked in whenever I sat up or was transferred from my bed to a wheelchair. Lights flickered in front of my eyes; a wave of nausea surged through me. Eventually, an MRI scan revealed that I'd developed a syrinx in my spine – a cavity in the brain stem spinal cord that filled with fluid, causing a series of unpleasant symptoms. I was told that unless an operation took place very quickly, the syrinx would kill me, and to drain the fluid I would need another operation where the back of my neck was sliced open, with more metalwork and a shunt fixed to the middle of my vertebrae. I cursed my horrendous luck. I was back at square one, and after healing from the surgery, I'd have to relearn the basic processes that had already taken several weeks to master.

Then, following my second round of surgery, I was given yet another shit sandwich of a diagnosis. The good news arrived in two parts: the operation had been successful; I wasn't going to die. The bad was that my condition was now going to get worse with time.

My heart sank as the consultant relayed the details. *Wait* . . .

. . . *Deteriorate?* The word felt like a kick to the balls.

'Yes, David,' she said. 'Your remaining muscle strength will fade. Breathing, speech and swallowing independently . . . Eventually, you'll be lucky to keep all three.'

In the aftermath, I clung to my sense of humour like a life raft, because, really, it's all I had left. Will and Oliver were discharged, and in my new ward I was surrounded with unfamiliar faces. There were new names to learn. As I had done during my first weeks in Stanmore, I leaned into self-deprecating humour to deflect the pain, and rather than wallowing in my situation for too long, I attempted to alleviate the emotional heft with a gag, or wry comment. I became the first one to laugh at myself when something went wrong.

This is bad, I thought, whenever I was clotheslined by a fresh set-back. *But there's a place where you can put it. You can use it.*

If ever I lost control of my bowels, I made a joke. If ever I forgot my body and attempted something that would have been second nature to an able-bodied person, and fell flat, I did my best to laugh about it. As mates from the film industry, like Daniel, Tom and Marc, came to visit me, these moments of levity helped to kill the awkwardness stone dead. They also helped my family. Seeing the pain in a loved one's eyes was too much for me to bear, especially when it was Mum, who couldn't even wrap her arms around me because of the precarious nature of my recovery. I hated to see her cry, so I lifted the mood with optimism, or a laugh. If my experience with bullying at school, and in the film industry, had taught me anything, it was that positivity was a tool I could use to shield me from hurt. It became an effective defence mechanism.

Luckily, there was plenty of material to work with. It was horrendous to have someone manually assist me with a suppository when going to the toilet. These days, I have little sympathy for anyone who complains about their bowel movements, or piles, and I learned that having a socially aware rectum was a gift, as was the early warning system that alerted an able-bodied person to an incoming dump. The uncontrollable boner I had experienced in the immediate aftermath of the accident was also a frequent guest, and it usually arrived without warning, often in situations that created acute embarrassment for anyone within viewing distance. One afternoon, with Mum and Dad at my bedside, I worked on my rehabilitation, practising the gruelling techniques required to move my body from wheelchair to bed. This process required assistance from one other person, as I needed to lift my legs before sliding my lower half onto a wooden 'transfer board' affixed to the mattress like a ramp. To reduce friction, its surface had been covered with a plastic sheet. I then had to slide forward, by pushing myself from the back of my chair. It was important that my parents became familiar with the procedure because there was every chance that one of them might have to help me with it at some point.

As I slid over to the bed, I noticed the dressing on my pubic area needed changing. About a month previously I'd had a suprapubic catheter fitted, a process where an incision was made in my belly and a hole cut into my bladder. A catheter tube was then fitted. The hope was that this device would help me to regain some sort of connection with a penis I couldn't feel. As my mum and dad fussed around me, I realised they were taking a lot longer than normal. When I used the electric bed to raise me up for a better view, I noticed the boner rearing up in front of me. Mum was having to backhand it out of the way while Dad set the dressing in the right place, and the embarrassment was excruciating. So, I made a joke about it.

'Lads,' I called out to the ward. 'I've got a boner in front of my mum. Do you reckon I've reached rock bottom yet?'

As these events happened more frequently, I learned more about the symptoms of my uncontrollable stiffies. Apparently, they could sometimes last for hours. (My record was an impressive eight.) Though if an episode went on for too long, it was important to seek medical assistance, because deep vein thrombosis was a dangerous side-effect, and nobody wanted to die because of an erection. During one marathon stiffy, I was told that an injection at the base of my penis was needed if it was to droop. *Fuck that*, I thought. And I set about finding a self-administered antidote to a very embarrassing problem. I tried to whack it down; I pulled my leg hair out in chunks; and I struck my thighs with the palms of my hands as hard as I was physically able. In a last-ditch attempt, I leaned forward and bit into my kneecaps, chewing angrily at the flesh. Miraculously, the stimulus put my pecker to sleep, but my skin was black and blue with teeth marks.

Rather than drowning in depression, I focused on the future, and there were other, more challenging tests ahead. As I slowly caught up with my rehabilitation, the time came for me to move back into my Essex home. Firstly, though, I had to come off the prescription drugs that had been keeping my pain under control for several months. This was particularly tough given I was on the lot, including morphine, a powerful opioid that kept much of my post-surgery pain at bay. Once a person was taken off it, the excruciating hurt seemed to come back doubly hard. *Something given, something taken.* Also on the list was dihydrocodeine, a weak opioid painkiller that was OK if you didn't want to shit for a month. But ketamine was the best and harder to quit. I loved the buzz, and I was able to knock myself out and have some fun along the way. I used to have a friend who was addicted to the stuff, and they regularly dropped a dose at the start of every morning, in a process they referred to as the *wake and wonk*. Beginning the day like that wasn't for me, but I could understand the appeal for someone wanting to remove themselves from reality, especially if the horrors of everyday life were too much to bear.

I approached my opioid withdrawal cold turkey-style, and the process was typically tough. Pain came at me in phases, building slowly at first, before striking me in a succession of body-quakes, each one more violent than the last, until it was almost unbearable. One morning I woke up in agony and prayed for the hurt to stop.

I'm just in too much pain, I thought. *I can't get through today without some help . . .*

Then my brain found another gear. I didn't want to be reliant on prescription drugs.

No, this is it, I told myself. *You either get off of everything now or you're going to be chained to it for ever.*

The sleepless nights and racking pain soon faded away. But the hardest thing to quit was the ciggies. I hadn't had one in months, and I missed the ritual of going outside, sparking up and chatting to anyone with the same addiction. In a hospital, unsurprisingly, there was nowhere to go for a smoke. This was particularly noticeable if you were unable to move. My habit was eventually crushed by circumstance rather than willpower.

What had also become obvious was that I'd have to become less reliant on my parents, especially when seeking out home care once I'd left Stanmore and their amazing team of specialists. Mum and Dad would have done anything for me, I knew that, and I loved them dearly for it. But other than cooking my meals, there wasn't a lot that either of them could do to help. My injuries, and their implications, were so complicated that a team of experts was required for the most basic of functions. I was advised by the hospital that it was best if any personal relationships were kept separate from the care aspects in my life because, when entangled, it had the potential to get very messy indeed. This information helped to establish an important boundary. My disability wasn't on anyone to fix, least of all my parents. So they should stop worrying about whether they were acting in the right way, or not.

One family member who didn't give a shit about boundaries was Rosie, my six-month-old Yorkshire terrier, who I hadn't seen since before the accident. Whenever I lay in bed wondering about an inevitable moment, several years in the future, when I wouldn't be able to breathe, speak or swallow without assistance, I snapped out of it by thinking to a happier time just before the accident when I'd walked Rosie through the park behind my bungalow. As we'd strolled, I spotted a neat row of houses in the distance. *The sort of place that would be perfect for my* Grand Designs-*style home.* The sunset was just perfect there, it pinged off the rooftops, and Rosie had loved racing across the grass. I missed that dog so much. She hadn't seen me for ages and was being looked after by friends. *Would she even recognise me now?*

But dogs, as Ricky Gervais once famously said, are amazing and beautiful. *They have soul.* When Rosie was finally allowed to visit, shortly before my discharge from Stanmore, I was taken into the corridor. I saw her at the end, sitting by my parents. She was looking around in a confused state. Then she spotted me. I saw her tail wagging, slowly at first, and then frantically. She strained at the lead to get closer and charged down the corridor, licking at my feet and ankles once she'd arrived by my side. Then, when the lead was taken off, she jumped into my lap and licked my face, over and over and over. It was good to feel the sensations of her rough tongue on my cheek, and her warm breath on my neck.

It was the happiest I'd felt in months.

12

THE POTIONS MASTER

I moved into my bungalow, complete with its newly fitted specialist bathroom and just enough wheelchair access to move about. My first day back was memorable because it was so weird. Barely able to squeeze through the front door in my chair, I moved from room to room as best I could, with the help of two personal assistants. Because of my chair, the bungalow seemed to have shrunk in size. I barely had the room to turn in a full circle, and on the first night it was decided I should sleep on a makeshift bed in the living room, until the obstacle course around me was made safe for someone on two wheels. Later, mates carried me into the bathroom so I could wash myself. Like I said: *weird.*

No surprise, my brain was in a discombobulated state. I was in my house, but it wasn't home, and everything seemed alien. In a homecoming celebration, someone had rolled up a massive spliff, and as it was passed around, the weed hit my bloodstream and a blissful high settled my jittery brain. Finally, there was calm. The muscle tremors that had jerked my body all day stopped, and my nerve pain melted away. Over those first few weeks away from Stanmore, I realised that cannabis was a temporary salve for my problems, and with a joint I was able to connect to some of the human experiences still left available to me, like a beautiful sunset, a cuddle with Rosie or a great piece of music. At times I probably smoked too much. I'm sure there might have been one or two occasions where it made me doubly vulnerable as I settled into a new way of life. But it also helped me to be open and honest with people. More than anything, I wanted to share a smoke with my folks, to break down the parent–son barrier and deep-dive into what had happened – and what was happening. There was fat chance of that, though. Mum and Dad were too grounded.

Emotionally, I was a mess too. The sound of my spine cracking still came back to me in nightmares, and I mourned the life that I'd lost while simultaneously fearing for my future. A huge cloud of guilt trailed me wherever I went – I felt terrible for the hell I'd put my parents through, not to mention my friends, loved ones and work family. One or two people encouraged me to have therapy, and I took a handful of sessions, but the vibe wasn't really my thing, and as I tried to piece together my life, the film industry moved on. Marc grew out his hair and stepped in as Daniel's stunt double, which wasn't an easy decision for him to make. In the wake of my accident, he had originally wanted to quit working on *Harry Potter and the Deathly Hallows Part 1*. There was another, less traumatic gig waiting for him on Russell Crowe's *Robin Hood*, and my misfortune had upset him so badly that he wanted to go there instead. In the end, he only agreed to take on my role after I'd asked him to do so. I really wanted Daniel's safety to be in the hands of someone I trusted.

At the heart of this psychological turbulence was my legal set-tlement with Warner Bros. As part of my compensation package for the injuries incurred while working on set, a three-year process was put in place, during which the financial value of my wrecked life was established. While I'm not allowed to discuss the numbers, or some of the details of the eventual settlement, I can say that it was an unsettling, bewildering and, at times, downright terrifying experience. At various moments I felt disgusted, hurt, abused and utterly worthless. My overall opinion by the time everything had concluded was that the law worked in a very cynical way.

The process had begun in my hospital bed when, shortly after my accident, one of the studio's head honchos informed me that a compensation process would be set in motion. It would involve insurance companies and lawyers, but I wasn't to worry because I would be looked after. Furthermore, my care requirements were going to be taken care of, which, as I was slowly coming to realise, would need to be around-the-clock and 365 days a year. In other words: *mega money*. Then came my first meeting with an injury lawyer from the firm Irwin Mitchell. Having been taken in to see him, I slumped in my wheelchair, with barely enough strength to sit upright. I then had to relive the worst moment of my life as notes were taken and details established. Though I'm sure the lawyer was very nice, the experience felt more like a police interrogation. I took my mind off the horror of picking over the sights and sounds of my accident by focusing on a nearby window. Outside, a robin flittered between the bird feeders.

Fuck me, I thought. *What I'd give to have that bird's freedom . . .*

The global stunt community rallied around, as did the British Stunt Register, the association I had worked so hard to become a member of, and they financially invested in my rehabilitation. I even received a cheque from the Red Bull Stunt Foundation, the people behind the awards that celebrate the fall guy industry. The money they kindly donated paid for an electric wheelchair. Pretty much everyone who risked their life alongside me in the business had visited my bed at Stanmore. Meanwhile, several stunt directors and coordinators delivered references and projected earnings packages – financial estimates that, with the lawyer's help, would establish the compensation levels I might expect to receive from the studio. Once I was out of hospital, the team at Irwin Mitchell gathered statements from medical experts, doctors, physiotherapists, care coordinators – specialists with a unique understanding of exactly how hard and how expensive it was to live any sort of life as a quadriplegic.

Meanwhile, *The Deathly Hallows Part 1* was released with typical fanfare and became another box office sensation. I even went to the premiere, under hospital care with Mum and Dad, and before the film started, one of the producers, Dave Barron, announced me to the audience.

'There's a young man here that gave everything for this film, and I want everyone to recognise that . . .'

The cast and crew applauded, and I felt a little overwhelmed, but I'd gone through so much to get to a point where I could even sit in a cinema and watch a film that the emotions eventually bounced off me. It was a different experience for Mum, though. She hadn't wanted to go, and when the scene in Godric's Hollow played out, Harry flying backwards during his encounter with Nagini, I consoled myself with the fact that the style of stunt work that had left me paralysed was no longer being practised in any major studio in the US or UK.

There was also a new sense of conviction about me. The accident could have left me feeling powerless, but if anything, the opposite had happened: *I was taking the power back*. This was especially so with Greg, my film father, the man I'd once been so afraid of failing. At work, our relationship definitely wavered between professional and paternal; I'd push for bigger stunts and higher risks I shouldn't have considered. During the early phases of my recovery, in April 2009, I went to visit Leavesden and the Stunt Stores during another day trip from the hospital. I was still wearing a neck brace; a feeding tube dangled from my nose because the medical team at Stanmore were loading me up on calories to help power up the healing process; and as we sat in the staff canteen, everyone staring, he fed me lunch. Just by looking at him, I knew Greg was nervous, so when he jabbed a fork into a mountain of chips, I shook my head.

'I'm going to need a bit more ketchup on that,' I said, breaking the tension.

Later, we chatted in the Stunt Stores, and Greg broke down in tears. He had been trying hard to keep his emotions together, but I knew that he was having a tough time. He couldn't look me in the eye. In that moment, I realised that I was the bigger man. *The stronger man.* And I would never ever need his approval ever again.

Before long, a periodical payment was secured – a regular sum of money that would be dispatched to my bank account by an insurance company employed by Warner Bros. This money allowed me to refit my bungalow. It would later pay for another electric wheelchair, accessible vehicles, home care, and a deposit for my *Grand Designs* home. All of this was adding up to a lot of money. There were moments when I questioned the point of it all.

What's the use in fighting? I thought. *It's not as if my physicality is coming back.*

This was particularly so when every building requirement in my new home was questioned by a lawyer. *Why did I need a sauna?* Because I would be dangerously hypothermic in the winter. *Why did I need a swimming pool?* Because aqua therapy was a vital part of my rehab. And so on, and so on. The low came during a meeting in London when I was told that if a settlement wasn't reached and my case went to court and I lost, the consequences could be a life without financial support for my injuries. I would also have to battle one of the largest entertainment entities in the world and their team of legal minds.

The thought made me want to puke.

Even without a court case, there were arguments and counter-arguments. I saw statements and expert opinions. For three years, my future seemed to be in the balance, numbers were passed back and forth, until, eventually, *mercifully*, the quality of my existence was finally decided by two men over coffee, in what sounded like a very informal meeting. I was to be properly compensated, but no cheque was going to make up for the pain and suffering I'd endured. The results of my payout were relayed to me while I was in Valencia on a holiday with mates. Given I still retained the use of both hands, I'd decided to travel the world, where I could drive cars way too fast, before getting fucked up on booze and drugs to forget my disability. To celebrate, I spent the day snorting white powder up my nose while cruising through Spain's largest aquarium.

But later that night, through the fog of class As and champagne, I imagined the coffee at the meeting as two faceless men decided the value of my life. *Had it even been drunk?*

I pictured two cappuccinos going cold. *What a fucking waste.*

I saw them laughing and smiling afterwards. *What had they spoken about? The fucking football?*

I put on a pair of sunglasses, snorted some more powder, and cried in the corner where nobody could see me.

My old life was over. But I wasn't yet ready to start the new.

*

Maybe as a consequence, maybe not, The Little Man Syndrome returned, only this time it took on a different method of expression. Rather than driving me forward, towards feats of bravery or athleticism – gags that other stunt actors were reluctant to try – it convinced me that I was still the same person. That, yeah, I was disabled. *But I was also financially secure.* I brought in my friend, Thomas 'Tommy' Wells, as a full-time personal assistant, plus Maggie.* When my new home was finally in full working order in November 2013, complete with its Willy Wonka glass elevator,

---

* When I first returned home in 2009, I was under the care of a specialist spinal cord injury care agency. My life was full of checks and balances. After my legal case had concluded, I approached Tommy, who had been one of my best friends for many years, and offered him a job working with me. Not long afterwards, I found Maggie (or Malgozata, to give her full name) on Gumtree.

I went from room to room, alone, as Pavarotti's 'Nessun dorma' played at full blast through the speakers dotted about the three-storey building. Then I sat by the front door and sobbed.

I fucking did it, I thought. *This is mine. I made it happen.*

Emotionally, there was plenty to block out for me too, particularly the realisation that my sex life was over. This felt like an extra special kind of fuckery, but apparently a nasty side-effect of a high-level spinal cord injury is a terrible thing called autonomic dysreflexia. Any time I get a very extreme nerve stimulus below my level of injury, my blood pressure and heart rate spike to dangerous levels. I had already experienced this excruciating and very scary side-effect when trying to pass one of the largest shits of my life in hospital. Because of the morphine, I had been severely constipated, and at one point a crash team was called to my bedside. My head pounded and my vision blurred – I thought I was having a stroke. Eventually, the anaconda wedged up my backside passed and the symptoms subsided but, judging by the faces of the medical team standing around me, it had been touch and go for a while.

Then I learned the same thing could happen during orgasm. *Death by ejaculation.* At first, the risk-reward setting in my brain viewed the condition as a spicy challenge. Maybe I could get away with it, like a risky wire gag, or a jump from a fast-moving car? For a while, I worked bloody hard to push through the pain barrier, until the intense headaches that engulfed me became so painful and overwhelming that I screamed and cried afterwards, my heartbeat ricocheting around my skull.

Getting fucked up on booze and drugs was an understandable, if somewhat unwise, trauma response and a logical next step. Everything I knew was upside down, and while I tried my best to adjust to a new life, I was mournfully saying goodbye to the old. The plot twist to this story was that, when starting work on *The Deathly*

Hallows Part 1, I'd become bored with the hedonistic scene fostered during my early twenties – the drinking and the drugging, the parties, and the endless search for a new buzz. As I approached my thirties, I was all raved out, bored with the hangovers and ready to move on. Then the accident changed everything. I suddenly wanted what I couldn't have, and in a moment when convalescence and self-discovery made perfect sense, I went the other way because the idea of slowing down felt bloody depressing.

This process started with a series of trips to Ibiza and a number of house parties. I had a lot of loose money to throw around and plenty of mates who wanted to hang out, and during benders we'd play music, share mind-altering substances, and dig into our own souls in a series of profound conversations. I found that MDMA helped me to open up about my trauma, but the partying soon spiralled out of control. I visited exclusive parties and treated mates to the VIP service at clubs. At one point, I found myself at an Agent Provocateur fashion event, having been invited by my tailor, who operated out of Savile Row and seemed to be a well-connected bloke. The exercise of buying a suit had been an experiment in itself; I found out that I was the first wheelchair-bound client to have visited the Spencer Hart outlet, and I'm probably one of very few, if not the only quadriplegic to have had such a suit fitted. But the outfitter charged with the job, a tailor called Joe, was more than up to it. (And I knew, because I had spent plenty of time hanging out in the wardrobe department on film sets.) This was a relief, given there was so much more detailing involved when making a suit for a quadriplegic. For starters, the cut of the suit was much shorter in the body than it would be for an able-bodied client. I also needed an accessible opening on the leg so that my catheter could be accessed and emptied discreetly, plus a neatly tapered ankle cut into the trousers. I'd always had an eye for fashion and whenever I saw people in wheelchairs wearing suits, the fabric seemed to swamp them. That was not going to happen with me.

For the fittings, I was taken to a private room and lifted in and out of my chair, while Joe took measurements and made adjustments. There were canapés, flutes of champagne and the occasional shot of tequila. In the end, I splashed out a silly amount of money on five suits, one of which was a blue velvet smoking jacket. Getting a sense that I liked the finer things in life, Joe then sweetened the eye-watering bill with a kickback.

'Would you like to go to an Agent Provocateur catwalk show later?' he asked casually, like it was an everyday occurrence.

I jumped at the chance, admired the models in their barely-there lingerie and then made a bid of three grand in a silent auction for a bespoke stay at the Osea Island Hotel – a secluded outpost on a beautiful tidal island in the Blackwater Estuary. The accommodation looked like something out of Downton Abbey. The island, and its famous connecting causeway (which disappeared whenever the tide came in), felt like a horror movie trope. When I unexpectedly won the auction and announced that a mob of mates would be accompanying me for the adventure, plus a shitload of drugs, the vibe promised to be something akin to the controversial movie *Saltburn* – a hedonistic, sex-fuelled, psychological thriller. Ironically, the island also housed a successful rehab centre, as used by Amy Winehouse, and was the location for *The Woman in Black* – the 2012 film starring Dan Radcliffe. It was the perfect spot in which to lose myself and forget my situation in the mother of all blowouts.

Our home for the weekend was a twelve-bedroom mansion, though given I wanted to bring a large crew with me, I booked several additional cottages that were positioned near to the main residence. Forty people showed up and together we recorded our version of Lou Reed's hit single 'Perfect Day' in the nearby studio, the 'singers' snorting lines of cocaine from the mixing desk during breaks. For a while, I wondered if my life could get any more debauched. The answer, unsurprisingly, was: *Yes, it bloody well could.* A DJ arrived to play tunes for forty-eight hours and I moved from room to room in my wheelchair, spotting one drug-fuelled act of mania after the next. Bodies were sprawled in every chair. In the snooker room, a woman was lying face down on the baize, while a friend snorted a line of gear out of her arse crack. In the kitchen, two friends threw knives at one another after chomping their way through a bowl of magic mushrooms.

To top off the night, someone offered me a mug of hallucinogenic hot chocolate, accompanied by a sugaring of ketamine. Ordinarily, this would have made for the perfect nightcap, except at four in the morning I was woken suddenly by my mate Kenny, who was screaming that his room had been invaded by a rat. Apparently, it was the size of a tabby cat. The house passed it off as a spangled chemical vision, but when Kenny showed us a photo of the intruder the next day, he hadn't been exaggerating. *The rat was huge.* Though Kenny only had himself to blame. To stave off any early-morning hunger pangs, he had taken an open tube of Pringles to bed. The smell must have drawn in the vermin and when he was awoken by the sound of rustling and chomping, the rat had polished off the crisps and was working on the carboard tube for dessert. I couldn't stop laughing when I heard the full story. Though really, I should have been counting my blessings that nothing had gone wrong. I had been off my face for the whole trip. Worse, I'd been cut off from the mainland by the tide for large chunks of time. If anything had happened, it's unlikely an ambulance would have been able to reach me. With hindsight, I'd put myself into a very risky position.

Which was just how I liked it.

★

No doubt about it, getting off my head helped me to escape the idea that I was trapped in a wheelchair, and in the summer of 2013 I booked a ridiculously expensive villa in Ibiza, with the intention of partying hard with friends for three weeks. Upon arriving, my first phone call was to a local dealer, who arrived with a briefcase full of drugs. I blew £2,000 on every mind-altering substance this side of heroin and crack cocaine. Collectively, we snorted and smoked our way through the lot in two days, before the man with the briefcase returned. I was determined to keep the buzz going.

Ibiza was a lavish experience from the moment we arrived. One night, I booked a VIP table at the island's infamous Ushuaïa night-club, in Playa d'en Bossa – an opulent outdoor venue, built around a swimming pool, that described itself as being *naughtier, more discriminating*, where the likes of Sasha, Richie Hawtin and Calvin Harris spun tunes. The booking cost me a stupid amount of euros, and when a group of models sashayed over to party with us, I bought another table, extended my minimum spend and went at it hard.

With a cocktail of booze and class As (and Bs, Cs, Ds and, of course, Es) whizzing through my system, I felt cocooned from everything that was going on around me. The VIP area overlooked the dance floor, and the thousands of people moving below, all of them losing it to the music, resembled a field of ants. The music peaked and throbbed. The visuals pinged off the stage and set my brain on fire. The surging charge of drugs in my system pulsed and intensified, and when I accidentally brushed the tip of my penis with my elbow, a muscular jolt caused me to kick down on the plate of my wheelchair, setting off a physical chain reaction through my body. My spine arched over the back rest of the chair. Every nerve and muscle in my body twisted and clenched in an agonising spasm. When the tremors eventually passed, I felt even more broken than before, and tears of pain streamed down my face. I put on my sunglasses to mask the emotional turmoil, but it was the first warning sign that I'd pushed things too far.

Did it encourage me to slow down? Did it fuck. A newspaper photographer snapped photos of us as we partied, one of the lads raising a bottle of Grey Goose vodka in celebration, and our faces were plastered over a Sunday broadsheet the following weekend. Topped with the headline 'How the Super-Rich Took Over Ibiza', the accompanying photo was a snapshot of Balearic debauchery: my mates and several unknown beautiful people falling over one another, soaked in sweat, grinning and smashed up on drugs. Everyone was there, having the time of their life. Except me, the guy who paid the bill. Rather than moving to the front of the photo, I'd tucked myself behind the group in my wheelchair, trying to look cool and not disabled.

The following day was my birthday, and we celebrated by hiring a local chef to make sushi, which was served on the flesh of a naked woman who had positioned herself on the dining-room table. As everyone dined on delicious food and supped saké, all I could think was: *If anyone deserves to get laid in this villa, it's me.* And so I contacted the guy I'd hired as a personal concierge for the holiday. It was his job to act as a fixer, and he'd arranged the VIP service in every bar we visited. He ordered cars and arranged drug deals. He employed women who doubled up as sushi tables. He also knew how to engage with just about every sordid pastime on the island. *Could he arrange for a girl to visit my room the next night?*

When I made the request, he smiled. 'Of course I can, David,' he said. 'I will come around tomorrow with something that will help you to make a decision.'

The following morning, he arrived at our villa with a ring binder as thick as a brick. Inside were A4 profiles of women from around the world, all of them beautiful, and all of them with a price tag attached. It was the Argos Catalogue of Sex. The numbers were eye-watering. Some of the girls were already on the island, others were as far away as Australia and America, and as I flicked through the pages, I wondered whether to go for a blonde, a brunette or a redhead. Full disclosure: at the time, I wasn't really considering the implications of what I was considering. I was about to involve myself in a crime of moral turpitude, and while I don't have a problem with sex workers and the service they provide (providing it's between mutually consenting adults), I do have a problem with the mechanics behind the industry – the pimps, the abusers, the human traffickers. I reassured myself that I was a traumatised man trying to reconnect with my old life, and that if I lived in Germany, I could have offset the cost of an escort against my taxes as a disabled adult.

Then I pointed to the photo of a gorgeous Russian woman called Georgia. 'I'd like to meet that one,' I said.

The fixer nodded, approvingly. *Good choice.* It was as if I'd ordered a wine of exquisite taste and vintage.

I had a condition to set. 'I want a dinner date,' I said. 'I don't want a woman to turn up and not have any connection.'

When Georgia arrived, she was every bit as gorgeous as her photos had suggested. Tall and slender, with a severe shoulder-length bob, her dark brown eyes were like deep pools, and I wanted to lose myself in them as we ate pasta and sipped wine. The buttons running down the front of her tight-fighting summer dress looked set to pop; the heels on her Roberto Cavalli shoes accentuated the muscles in her sleek calves. Every now and then I took a bump of cocaine to keep my courage burning, until, eventually, the time arrived for us to go to bed. As my friends carried me to the bedroom, Georgia excused herself to use the shower, and when she emerged, naked apart from those shoes, it was impossible to hide my nerves.

'David, what would you like me to do for you?' she said in a tone that suggested anything was possible.

I crumbled. Nothing was stirring from the neck down and any faint hopes I'd had of experiencing an intimate connection faded away. Because of the transactional situation I'd put myself in, I also felt insignificant and weak. Then the little boy inside me returned.

'Can I have a cuddle, please?' I said, feeling lonely and scared. A tear trickled down my cheek.

The hug cost me two and a half grand. When I retold the story later, I didn't have the heart to go into details. As far as everyone else was concerned, I'd had a great time.

A footnote to this story: When I recall these stories now, I see myself for what I was back then. *A scared little boy.* I was fearful of being alone, and I was trying to hold on to every aspect of my masculinity. These fears were understandable, however. I just hadn't yet learned to manage them. For many years I made the mistake of thinking that the opposite sex only found me attractive for *what I had*, instead of *who I was* as a person, and the way in which I carried myself in life. But in making that mistake, I've since learned a lesson: what makes you a man above all other things is accountability. I'll openly admit that for far too long I was not accountable. I did things that I am now ashamed of, and having a broken neck is no excuse. The bottom line is, I could have done better. These days, I work bloody hard to make sure that I do.

*

The warnings were coming at me like spasms. I was going too far. And then in 2014, I had a terrifying run-in with the law during a stag do in Amsterdam. At that point, I'd already endured a couple of upsetting incidents while travelling by air, because anxieties and stresses I'd never previously considered as an able-bodied person were unlocked, such as the paranoia of a turbulent flight when a bowel accident was a very real possibility. Having learned that air travel as a paralysed man required an extreme act of bravery equal to the days in which I'd set myself on fire for a living, I decided to drive to Holland in my Mercedes-AMG C63, a beast that ripped at 150 miles per hour with one of the greatest noises I'd ever heard. To add an extra buzz to the occasion, I attempted to hit the 155mph mark in northern France, while smoking a joint with the windows rolled down. I'm not sure whether I cared if I lived or died at that point, which can't have been a fun experience for anyone sitting alongside me in the car.

Another European city, another drug deal. Having arrived in Amsterdam, I connected with a courier who arrived with a briefcase full of party favours. I swear the contents glowed as he flipped open the lid and I took my pick, buying a large stash for the stag and his mates: eight bags of cocaine, four baggies of ketamine, twenty ecstasy pills, four MDMA pills and a shitload of laughing gas – in case things got dark. I didn't need to buy any weed. It was legal in Amsterdam and picking up a joint was like buying a packet of mints. The party started soon after and before long I'd secured a VIP table in a nearby club. God knows what I must have looked like. Navigating Amsterdam's cobbled streets in a wheelchair was a painful experience. At times it felt like I was riding a bronco, and every jolt sent a spasm blasting through my body. I kicked, screamed and swore. My eyes went wonky behind a pair of sunglasses that were falling off my nose with the vibrations. I was hammered, swearing as if I had Tourette's while fighting to stay in my chair.

When a bouncer ushered us into the club and kindly offered to carry me up a flight of stairs, I took it as a sign that we were in for some next-level service. Then he dropped me. Thankfully, I was able to react in time and put out an arm to limit the blow, but the impact to my torso was so severe that the skin around my ribcage was black and blue the next day. Not that it deterred me from pushing through.

The morning after the night before, I piled into the drugs again and went to a dance festival at the city's Millennium Park, not caring that it was a 40°C day and I was unable to control my body temperature. According to the doctors, dehydration and sun exposure might cause me to fit, spasm and maybe go into a stroke. But I had bigger things to worry about. Like how we were going to smuggle our drugs past the bag searches taking place at the festival gates.

Then I had a dumb idea. 'Shove it into my wheelchair,' I said to the group boldly. 'No one ever searches a disabled person.'

Various baggies were positioned around the chair as my mates separated, so as not to look like a big gang of troublemaking lads, and I was wheeled towards the checkpoint. Then a bouncer called me out of the line. The bloke looked like he wasn't one for messing around. He sized me up and down and asked if he could check the chair. Clearly, this wasn't his first rodeo.

Shit. Shit. *Shit.* 'Sure,' I said, presuming he would only check the front, which we'd deliberately left empty. '*Go for it.*'

He went for it. The wallet was the first thing he looked through, and the first sign I'd been operating as a rolling drug mule. It bulged with plastic baggies. The container at the rear of my seat was searched next. More baggies, more drugs. When I was then taken into a security tent for a more thorough search, the combined haul was laid out in front of me. Not even Hunter S. Thompson at the peak of his powers could have handled the stash.

The bouncer looked at me sadly. *I was not going to be admitted into the festival.*

Then he apologised. *He was going to have to call the police, given the amount of narcotics I'd attempted to bring into the event.*

I was screwed. They had me down as a drug dealer. Suddenly, the bump of cocaine I'd taken for courage in the queue seemed to shift into a higher gear. My decision not to wear a sunhat also seemed incredibly dumb, and all at once dehydration, the heat and a grinding hangover from the day before caused me to meltdown. I couldn't breathe. The edges of my vision were caving in. I was over-heating, and if I passed out there was a good chance I'd go into a fit.

'Water,' I croaked. 'I need water. And ice.'

The security guard looked at me in a panic. He could tell I was having a medical issue.

'Fuck the drugs,' I said, now panicking. 'If I don't bring my tem-perature down quickly, I'm going to die.'

One of the other lads from the stag do noticed my predicament and rushed to my aid. When I looked up, I noticed that he had popped at least one of our ecstasy pills, and it was kicking in. His eyes were on stalks; his jaw was gurning so vigorously that he looked to be chewing on a tough piece of leather. I couldn't have imagined a worse person to help me in such a precarious situation.

Fuck, I thought, *I've got to get rid of him or I'll be charged for drug-ging my friends, too . . .*

Using every ounce of remaining energy, I called over a security guard. 'This is not my official carer,' I said, now panting. 'He went through with another group of boys. I need to send this person to find my official caregiver, who is medically trained to look after me . . .'

Before long, Tommy Wells, the person I most trust with my life, was by my side and I was escorted to an air-conditioned police van. (At this point I'd like to point out that Tommy was, and still is, the most angelic member of my circle of friends, and his vices extend to a glass of red with his dinner. He was definitely *not* having as wild a time of it as the rest of us.) Having cooled down a little, I was transported to a nearby police station where I could be pro-cessed. My head was still rushing from the cocaine, and the journey was excruciating. I was separated from my chair and placed in a seat next to Tommy, where I slid and spun, unable to hold myself down, all while taking in the sights of Amsterdam that I hadn't yet been able to see. Eventually, Tommy hooked his arms around mine for stability. As far as tourist experiences were concerned, this one hadn't yet been listed on TripAdvisor. Both my arms had gone numb. My vision was darkening again. Once at the station, I was separated from Tommy.

'If I'm not out in an hour, get me a lawyer,' I slurred, as a copper wheeled me away.

Tommy looked terrified. 'Who?'

'Any fucking lawyer.'

Close to blacking out, I was placed into yet another air-conditioned room.

'Please don't leave me in a cell on my own,' I said, the gravity of the situation bearhugging me. 'I don't know what's going to happen to my body if I don't cool down, and I'm scared.'

The police officers nodded and took me into the corridor. They knew I was experiencing a medical issue and promised to get me help as they inventoried my drug stash. But if I was going to be charged, I'd rather it happened in a hospital bed where I could be cared for than in a police station where I might die.

'This yours?' said one, holding up a bag of cocaine.

I shrugged. *Don't know.*

'And this?' It was another baggie of white powder.

Again, I shrugged. *Don't know.*

By the time they'd finished, and a small mountain of drugs had been piled up on the table, it was clear that I could have supplied half the festival with chemicals. As far as the cops were concerned, I was Pablo Escobar in a wheelchair. Thankfully, my body temperature was starting to regulate itself again. I guzzled water, the cocaine left my system, and I was beginning to think more rationally. From what I could tell, I was in some serious shit, and about to face a dealing charge, which carried God knows how many years inside. Given my time was limited, and my health was likely to deteriorate in the coming decade, I didn't really want to see out the last of my days behind bars. I had one option, a Hail Mary pass, and it involved me playing to my strengths. *Storytelling.* Something I understood very well given my years spent on Hollywood sets.

Over several minutes, I spun a cock-and-bull story: *The guys I was with are new acquaintances. I met them in Ibiza a week ago. They wanted to see Amsterdam, I encouraged them to go, and even bought their festival tickets through my concierge service card. We met again, we partied. But I barely know their names, honest. One of them might be called Fitz. Or Rick. Because everyone calls him Fitzpatrick Rick. But other than that, I'd only heard nicknames. When we arrived at the festival, I asked one of the guys to put the money for the tickets into my bag at the back of the chair. My guess is that they stashed their drugs in there too, thinking I wasn't going to get searched. And here we are.* To prove I was unable to control what went on at the rear of my chair, I performed a show and tell of my limited motor functions in the look-how-disabled-I-am dance.

The police officers nodded. One of them took notes. I hadn't been laughed at yet, so I pressed ahead.

'If you check the wallet, there should be exactly €200 in there,' I said. 'It's the money for the tickets. I didn't have cash on me beforehand . . .'

A cop reached for my wallet and counted out €200. 'OK, so . . .'

'So, I'm saying I've been used,' I said. 'I am the world's most vulnerable, unknowing drug mule. These people took advantage of me, and my disability.'

The police officers listened to my story patiently. Then one of them called a prosecutor to relay the situation. As a series of instructions were relayed, he nodded and looked across at me. The conversation must have only lasted a minute or so, but it felt like an hour. I was shaking.

'OK,' said the policeman, putting down the phone. 'Our prose-cutor has stated that you will have to sign a form saying that we are allowed to incinerate the drugs. Then we are to let you go.'

If I could, I'd have leaped out of the chair and hugged him. I had catastrophised to such an extent that I'd imagined my life in prison as a disabled person, vulnerable, and unable to fend for myself as I was passed around like a sex doll. (Though the good news was that I couldn't feel anything below the neck.) Tommy must have had the same vision, because when he saw me leaving the cell as a free man, he looked close to tears. A surge of guilt hit me in the chest. I felt awful for putting him through so much stress, but I still couldn't stop myself from messing around. Having signed my statement with an 'X' – because I wasn't physically able to write out my name in full – I asked if there was any chance my weed could be saved from the fire. *It was legal in Amsterdam, after all.* Tommy stared at me like I'd lost the plot. *I probably had.* Then he pulled away from the station, before my mouth landed me in even more trouble.

We went back into Amsterdam city centre, where I smoked a joint to calm my nerves before taking Tommy on a shopping spree to make up for my misbehaviour. In the splurge I picked up a crack-ing pair of Björn Borg high-top trainers in blue. I barely wore them. Several years later, when Dan Radcliffe stayed at my house before the filming of *The Boy Who Lived*, he showed up wearing a tatty pair of gym-worn shoes.

'Mate, you can't wear those,' I said, handing over the (nearly) box-fresh pair of Björn Borgs, before retelling the story of my Amsterdam adventure.

He wore them for ages. If you want to know what they look like, they're on the cover of this book.

13

LOSING MY HORCRUXES

I travelled, even though bustling airports weren't the best place for wheelchair users and plane toilets were a living hell for a quadriplegic with a disconnected bowel. No way was I going to allow the fuckery to slow my wanderlust, though. I took holidays to Australia, Toronto and Mauritius, but I was pushing too hard and something had to give. It finally did in 2015, on a lads' trip to southern Spain, when a pharmaceutical rush sent an agonising spasm through my arm. Electrifying pain then ricocheted across my chest, as every major organ seemed to jangle, and I was forced to spend the rest of the day in bed. Yet again, I'd been pretending that I wasn't disabled, while pushing the boundaries of what I could and couldn't do. No doubt about it, a crash was coming.

By that point in my life, the warning signs were everywhere. Having settled into the *Grand Designs* house, my parties had become a regular event, and every Friday began with a visit from the local dealer, though following my spasm in Spain I'd dialled back my intake and I only ever did one or two rails myself. The rest I dished out to the guests and I certainly wasn't getting my money's worth, but that didn't matter because the thought of being lonely was terrifying – I'd become convinced that if the party stopped, the important people in my life would drift away, but my thinking was upside down. I had friends who loved me, regardless of my disability. I also had physical priorities to consider. Weekend by weekend, comedown by comedown, the truth became impossible to ignore. My lifestyle was dangerously dysfunctional, and the drinking and drugging was ruining me. I soon realised that I'd had enough, so I quit the booze, and I quit the class A drugs. The party was over.

Throughout this new phase, and for much of my life, Dan Radcliffe was a constant source of support. Following the conclusion of the original Harry Potter film franchise, he'd broadened his range as an actor, on both the stage and screen, appearing in the 2013 goth horror *Horns* and *A Young Doctor's Notebook & Other Stories* alongside John Hamm. He'd also appeared in the 2011 Broadway reworking of *How to Succeed in Business Without Really Trying* and was preparing for the off-Broadway show *Privacy*, in which he played a writer. Unlike a lot of actors who became famous at an early age, and in an iconic role, Dan had shaken off his breakout character and was establishing himself as an artist with some serious chops. I felt incredibly proud of him. If ever he was in London, I visited him at his flat. Then, as he spent more and more time in New York, we connected every week. When one of your best mates is an A-list movie star it can be hard to navigate the friendship, especially as Dan was constantly jetting around the world on some new film or project. But he was incredibly committed to the job of acting, I respected him for it, and FaceTime helped smooth the experience.

Free of the fog of booze and class A drugs, I became acutely aware of everything around me – the good and the not so good. My parents were still consciously separated from the specialist aspects of my care, and though Mum would have done anything for me, had I asked, some of the basic, beautiful aspects of a mother–son relationship had been painfully altered. Because of my wheelchair, she was unable to get her arms around me for a cuddle. At first, this barrier was heartbreaking for the both of us, but we soon found new ways to show our love for one another. Every few days, Mum insisted on washing my bed sheets, and when I went to sleep at night the sensation of clean linens on my skin felt like a hug. I couldn't squeeze her back to say thanks, so I wrote my feelings in a note:

I know that it's hard for you to see me live my life and go through my struggles. But every night I get into bed, I pull those bed sheets up. I smell you and it gives me a sense of comfort.

I only ever broke down in front of her a few times. As my body deteriorated during 2016, moving around in a manual wheelchair – an activity that had been manageable during my first few years out of hospital – was starting to become incredibly difficult. This was the first of my Horcruxes to go. I then stayed in a manual wheelchair for far too long, and this no doubt added to the pain I was living with. But I was in a state of grief and denial. A few years later, on 14 April 2019, I sat in a manual wheelchair for the very last time. Saying goodbye to that chair was like saying goodbye to a piece of my soul. I knew that everything would become that much more difficult when using an electric chair – travel, independence, and almost every aspect of daily living would be affected by this change. Electric chairs are heavy and cumbersome, they are harder to navigate on different surfaces and terrain because of their weight, and interacting with society fundamentally changes because people have a different opinion of your disability.

My next Horcrux was destroyed when I then couldn't manually transfer myself in and out of my wheelchair. Instead of the process taking a couple of minutes, as it had done previously, I was now taking at least three times that long, and the daily amount of time used up by the ritual was frightening. I worked out I was set to lose thousands of hours of my life just through getting in and out of bed. With every step of neurological loss, a new adjustment and change to my lifestyle needed to be made. From eating with my right hand to eating with my left. Likewise, brushing my teeth and using the remote on my wheelchair. With every change, or muscle group loss, the adjustment period felt excruciating, and I experienced the five stages of grief with each one – denial, anger, bargaining, depression, and then, finally, acceptance. The nightmarish, once faraway event where I might require mechanical assistance to breathe, speak and swallow seemed worryingly nearby. When Mum came by on one of her visits, the emotions welled up.

'It's going to go, Mum, I'm going to lose this as well,' I said, raising my arm mournfully.

She kneeled beside me, and I lifted the armrest on my wheelchair, holding on to her as best I could.

'I can still feel it,' she said, as I squeezed her with my stronger left arm. 'It's OK, don't worry.'

'I just don't know if I can do it. I don't know if I can have a life where I don't have two arms . . . Where I maybe can't swallow or breathe.'

She tried to soothe me, but it wasn't working. 'Mum, I think if it gets to that stage, I don't want to be here,' I said finally.

She looked at me sadly. 'We really don't want you to do that,' she said. 'But at the same time, it's your life, and you know we're going to be your parents and love you, no matter what.'

When I had first mentioned my decline to the doctor in 2016, it was suggested I take an MRI scan. The fear was that the shunt that had been installed around my spinal cord in 2009 wasn't draining properly and the syrinx had returned, only bigger this time, which would have been incredibly dangerous given the last one had required the surgeons to bore a hole in my spine that went all the way up to my C1 vertebra. When the scans came in and it was confirmed that, thankfully, there was no syrinx, my symptoms were discussed by the British Neuroscience Association in London. Various treatments were suggested for my condition, among them an extra round of surgery, but in the end it was decided that I should be left alone. An operation was deemed too risky, especially given that my arms had some remaining function, and it was unclear as to whether the procedure could even save my deteriorating limbs.

Between 2016 and 2019 I had endured the pain and loss of every muscle group on the right side of my body as it atrophied. The process was incredibly painful. It began with a wet sensation. Then the muscles went into a state of cramping, before finally all the function and strength was lost as they deteriorated into tendon-like strings. It was at that stage that they were gone for good. The agony was physical and emotional. Then, while moving through the house, I realised that everything was too painful. Each push and pull caused me to cramp. Enough was enough.

Fuck the risk, I thought. *I'm rolling the dice and pressing ahead with an operation.*

There were warnings; the procedure was fraught with danger. Firstly, the heavy scar marking the back of my neck, a visible reminder of my past surgeries, had to be reopened, and the metal fixating point holding my spine in place removed. A surgeon then had to cut through the outer layers of my spine, an area that contained cerebrospinal fluid – a liquid in the tissue surrounding the brain and spine from top to bottom. With the inner neurological core exposed, any scar tissue around the edges of my spinal cord had to be scraped away. Finally, I was to be sewn up again. If all went well, the work would allow my nerves and arms to remain connected, while slowing the deterioration in my body. But there were downsides: an operation of this nature was known to take around eight hours, and there was every chance I might die on the table. There was also the possibility that the work could worsen my condition. (Or, that it wouldn't move the dial one way or another, and it would have all been for nothing.) As far as I was concerned, the pros far outweighed the cons. Anything to prolong the mobility in my working limbs.

Through all this time, Rosie became the ultimate companion. (Likewise, her little sister, Beverley, who came into my life just after I moved into my new house.) As a therapy dog, she was perfect, though she was useless at everything else – after years of trying, she'd yet to master the basic human-to-dog exchange of catching or fetching a ball. A mate of mine once joked that were a vet to cut Rosie open, they'd probably discover a body full of cotton wool and fluff, like a teddy bear's, and a brain that was nothing more than a jumble of candy floss. But even though she wasn't all there, Rosie was forever finding new ways to get into my chair for a cuddle. If ever I was feeling down, she would pick up the signals and wait patiently in her spot. Once I'd got close enough, she would hop up and lick away the tears.

These beautiful interactions made my need for an operation seem even more pressing. I wanted to be able to hold and comfort Rosie for her whole life, in the same way that she had always comforted me. The physical connection between us both was a godsend. Knowing that a time was approaching when I might not be able to experience those moments anymore was one of many reasons I pushed for the operation.

A date for surgery was set in November 2019 and given it might represent a death-or-glory event, I decided to go on a proper safari holiday, an expedition that had been on my radar for a while. If I was going to die, I wanted to know, undeniably, that I'd lived. But even with this defiant mindset, there were emotional wobbles. The night before departing for South Africa, my body spasmed in agony, and I wondered if I'd made the right decision. *Had I bitten off more than I could chew?* It was October, the cold and the damp of a chilly English autumn had crept into my bones and muscles, and when I mentioned my concerns, Tommy, plus my brother Paul and my mate Danny Lawrence – my travelling companions for the trip – convinced me to stay the course. It was the right call. The following day, after a horrendous long-haul flight to Cape Town, I felt the warm sun on my body. My mood lifted. *This was a new space.*

From then on, the trip was everything I'd hoped for. We flew on a private plane into the Kruger National Park where we stayed in the Sabi Sabi Earth Lodge – a luxurious subterranean building constructed from concrete and straw, where elephants roamed across the ground-level rooftops. Given the proximity to some of the world's most dangerous animals, there were all sorts of guidelines in place to keep us alive. For example, I wasn't allowed to move from my room to the main lodge without an armed guard, because I would likely become something's lunch, or trampled to death. I soaked up the potential danger and spent every waking minute with my eyes on stalks, surveying the land as yet another creature strolled into view – some animal I'd only previously seen on David Attenborough's *Planet Earth*. As my mates relaxed at night and, inexplicably, watched an international rugby match or football on the big TV, I got high on weed and waited. I saw hyenas. I watched a pride of lions saunter past. And I saw elephants, loads of them. *My favourite animal.* When we went out on an early-morning drive, one lumbered up to the car and looked me dead in the eye, and I sobbed with the emotion of it all.

I was in a strange headspace. In mourning for the life I'd lost, scared for the future and the implications of my forthcoming surgery, and uncaring of whether I lived or died on the Kruger savannah. As far as I was concerned, getting eaten alive or crushed by one of the big five (lion, elephant, leopard, rhino and buffalo), while unpleasant in the moment, was a cool way to go out – a far better story ending than everything going wrong on an operating table, my spine exposed. When we later visited an off-grid resort called Cheetah Plains, a guide pointed out that a green boomslang snake was sleeping in a tree not far from my shoulder.

He leaned forward. 'You know, if that bit you, you'd be dead in six minutes . . .' he said ominously.

My reaction: *Cool.* People would talk about my death for ever.

The more I saw, the more connected to nature I became, and it was an overwhelming experience. One day at the Sabi Sabi Earth Lodge, a herd of elephants stopped off at the swimming pool outside my room to drink. The Earth seemed to stand still. My body thrummed with love. It was as if Mother Nature had presented me with a gift.

'Thank you for giving me that time,' I said under my breath. 'Thank you for trusting me.'

Whenever we went out with the trackers in our silent electric vehicles, they seemed to carry an unspoken link to one of the wildest places on Earth, reading the ground and broken grass for information in much the same way the rest of us check our weather apps. At times I even experienced the smothering sound of absolute silence, a sense that was heightened because so much sensation in my body had been taken away. When I eventually returned to Johannesburg for the flight home, I felt totally depressed. There were humans everywhere, all of them unknowingly destroying the environment outside their daily bubbles. (Or knowingly, and not caring.) I cried throughout the twelve-hour flight home, partly out of sadness for what we had done to the world, partly because of what might happen to me over the next few weeks.

*

I was back in Stanmore a few days later, wondering how to divide my money and assets if the worst came to the worst. Part of me wanted to bestow untold wealth upon Rosie and Beverley, making them the richest dogs in the world. The more rational side of me decided to leave my cash to all the kids in my life, the nieces and nephews, and my friends' children, though only once they'd reached the age of twenty-five. I didn't want them hoovering it up their noses like I had, or blowing it on naked sushi lunches in Ibiza. The experience of planning for my death was rewarding and sobering in equal measure, as was my conversation with the specialists who were performing my latest spinal procedure. I'd read that when somebody undergoes a risky life-altering operation, it helps to psychologically connect to the person wielding the scalpel. The thinking was that if the surgeon is viewed as a stranger, with no vested interest in their patient, the anxiety and trauma of the experience will be more impactful. However, by seeing them as *A Real Person*, with a family, passions, and a world beyond the job, a more robust emotional connection can be formed. There was even evidence that this psychological perspective reduced the amount of pain experienced by a patient, post-procedure. How much of that was true, I didn't know. But I was willing to give it a try.

I asked the specialist to hold my hand and looked him dead in the eye. 'I trust that you've got me,' I said. 'And I trust that you are the best person for the job. I'm putting my life in your hands.'

Then I asked him about his day, his family and his life, praying that everything was going to be OK.

It wasn't. I spent two months on the brink of death, and after the first round of surgery, from which I'd emerged physically unscathed, it was revealed that cerebrospinal fluid was leaking from my spine. My old wounds would have to be reopened again. This happened three more times, and on the last occasion a gauze was placed across the front of the cerebrospinal fluid sac in the hope that it might plug the leak. When that didn't work, I was told a brain drain was needed. This was yet another dangerous operation in which a hole was drilled into the top of my head and a device inserted into the cavity. This then drained away the fluid, reducing any pressure as the internal stitch in my spinal cord slowly healed.

I was in agony. During one conversation with my surgeon, I announced that if I were to die on the operating table, I'd be OK with it because the experience had broken me. He brushed aside my doomy outlook.

'No,' he said firmly. 'I've never, ever seen any negativity in you before, David. You, more than anyone, have an unbelievable determination to survive. Remember: this is a battle.'

I sucked up the pain and the fear. The Little Man Syndrome flickered inside. Then I pressed ahead.

*

Adding insult to injury, the liquid leaking from my spine also caused meningitis-like symptoms and my brain became super sensitive to light and sound. I then developed tinnitus and, at times, became overwhelmed by an unshakeable sense of dread. To ease the agony, I wore soundproofed headphones and draped a flannel over my eyes. My senses seemed as amplified on a spinal ward in Stanmore as they had been in the silence of the Greater Kruger National Park.

Once again, I was pumped through with hardcore painkillers, the kind I'd worked so hard to quit during my first stint in hospital. Oxycodone. Ketamine. Morphine on a timed administration drip. There was also fentanyl. Most of the time, I didn't know who or where I was, though in my more lucid moments a weird state of hyperconsciousness kicked in. Or, at least, I thought it had. Though I was temporarily deaf and nearly blind, I knew exactly who was in the room with me, even when they'd arrived silently, or unannounced. If it was Tommy and Maggie, my personal assistants, *I knew*. If they were smiling or frowning, *I knew*. If somebody was laughing, crying, or telling a story, *I knew*. Suddenly, I was blessed with Spidey Senses. The keenest feeling of all, though, was the sense I'd been locked in a fight for survival. Maggie and Tommy kept me going when my parents weren't there, and they made me as comfortable as possible, and it gave the (always brilliant but sometimes overworked) nurses more time to check in on other patients. As I drifted in and out of consciousness, my job was to focus on breathing, staying calm, and making it to the end of the next minute.

In those moments where I was alert enough, or my tinnitus faded, I listened to podcasts, quietly, and reached for inspiration. I thought back to the beauty of Africa, and the elephants, clinging on to the experience like a life raft.

'I need to live like that again,' I told myself, over and over. 'When I get out, I need to have more experiences like that one . . .'

I also understood that the latest traumatic setback was hurting everyone around me. In those moments where I emerged from my druggy haze, I told the people I loved to seek help for themselves. I knew that speaking to hospital staff or the in-house psychiatrist for advice would help them to stay mentally well. I didn't want anyone falling into an emotional hole because of me. Then I decided to come off the drugs again because they were driving me bloody crazy.

'I'd rather make peace with the pain than lose my mind,' I told the specialists who were advising me not to go cold turkey.

The next day, I woke up in a world of hurt. My skin crawled, as if an army of red ants were skittering across my body, taking small bites from the flesh. My jaw ached. My eyes burned. The only thing I could stomach for food was watermelon. Everything else turned my tummy inside out. (Though it helped me to move past the constipation clenching my insides, as did the 2 litres of water I was taking in through an IV drip.) There were also other complications that came with recovering from an invasive and life-threatening operation. I was peeing through a catheter and the insertion point sometimes became infected; and my stitches and sores had to be tended to prevent them from going manky. Given the most basic swab or needle swap could lead to a mortal complication, I became understandably paranoid. But it was important to stay calm: if I experienced an episode of autonomic dysreflexia in such a weakened state, there was every chance I might suffer a stroke. With a clear mind, I was able to focus only on my breath. Every survived second was an achievement, every minute a conquered hurdle, every hour a finished marathon. If I reached the end of the day, I considered it a psychological landmark, like an astronaut setting foot on the moon.

Then on Christmas afternoon, with my recovery in motion, I lay in bed, surrounded by my family, a home-cooked dinner in my lap. It was the first time I'd been able to eat a full meal in nearly a month. Turkey, roast potatoes, sprouts and gravy: Mum had made it, and polishing off the lot was as much a gift for her as it was for me. She was so pleased to see me stuffing my face after two months living on watermelon and opioids, especially as I managed to demolish one of her mince pies too. Then I was reminded of the power of storytelling. I'd been given a private room, with a flatscreen TV on the wall. As we flicked through the films on offer, we settled on *Oliver!* – the original cinematic version of *Oliver Twist* – starring Oliver Reed as Bill Sikes and Ron Moody as Fagin. Immediately, we were all transported away from the hospital and into another world. Mum started singing along, so I joined in. When I looked over, Dad was tapping his feet and smiling. No words were spoken between us, but nothing really needed to be said. *We were happy.* One story had saved us all that Christmas.

It was down to me to make some new ones of my own.

14

IT'S ALWAYS DARKEST
BEFORE THE DAWN

I was discharged again on 10 January 2020, my brain buzzing at the thought of another adventure: *I was going to Thailand for the winter.* For someone in my position, the UK's bleakest months were psychologically demoralising and physically punishing – the cold chewed at my bones and muscles, even though I was able to use the specially modified sauna in my new home. The heat and humidity of Thailand, I knew, would be great for my recovery. When I told my spinal consultant at Stanmore of my travel schedule, he looked sceptical.

'David, I'm not sure if you're aware of this novel coronavirus that's coming out of China?' he said gravely.

I nodded. *Covid-19.* It had been all over the news. I'd seen video footage of people in hazmat suits spraying down wet markets and listened to the stories of victims dying in grisly circumstances. Hypoxia. Strokes. Cytokine storms. *But what did that have to do with me?*

'Well, given the symptoms and the way it's spreading, if you were to contract Covid in Asia, the implications would be grave—'

How so?

'It'll probably kill you.'

'Yeah, but Thailand's the best place for me to go for the winter . . .' I said.

'Well, yes, that may well be,' said the consultant. 'But if you do go, whatever happens, do your best not to get Covid. You'll be placed on a ventilator, you'll be given a tracheotomy, and I don't think you'll survive it.'

His assessment was sobering, but I wasn't risk averse; I certainly didn't make fear-based decisions, and given my determination to write new stories for myself, I decided to push his advice to the back of my mind. A couple of weeks later I flew out to Thailand with my personal assistants and a couple of mates. 'It's time to live in the moment,' I told myself. 'This is the new mindset: I've been given a second chance at life, and it's important I push past my new fears.' Then I remembered the stuntman motto. *You're only living when you're nearly dying.* But once I'd landed and settled in the villa for what was supposed to be a restorative six-week stay, a heartbreaking realisation nagged at me. *The surgery hadn't worked.* At first, it came to me in flashes – and I ignored it. Then it weighed me down – and I was overwhelmed by it. The neurological warning signs that had prompted me to go for the surgery in the first place were flickering again, like blobs on a radar. My skin felt wet, the muscles in my arms were cramping painfully, and I felt the function and strength in both limbs leaking away. The decline was traumatising.

Fucking hell, I thought. *I nearly died in hospital for nothing.*

I was necking the bitterest of pills. Within weeks, I was back in Essex, having raced home to get ahead of what would prove an emotionally brutal lockdown for everyone, as the planet stopped to contain the spread of Covid-19. We were all being confined to our homes, separated from The Outside World, which was a horrible experience for everyone, but it felt acutely threatening for anyone living in a wheelchair. Instantly, my already complicated life became an existential crisis, especially as I wasn't yet ready to share the news of my failed surgery. The people closest to me had all gone through so much heartache on my behalf; I didn't want them to hear of my deteriorating state in what was an incredibly stressful time for everyone. Luckily, one of my best mates, Tom Di Cap, a freelance artist, had offered to isolate with me. He'd been going through a painful breakup at the time and didn't want to be on his own. Tom's arrival made me feel a whole lot safer, as did the commitment of my personal assistants, Tommy Wells and Maggie, but as my body seemed to wither, a dark internal monologue began. I asked the same, morbid question of myself . . .

Was it even worth it?

At the time, nobody knew of the full complications of the pandemic, but the media was painting a terrifying picture. It was a killer. There were no tests. Vaccines were another year away, at least. Even the basic details of the virus's incubation period remained a mystery. The most important thing, according to the bellends in charge of running the country, was to avoid all unnecessary contact with others. Under those circumstances, the last thing I wanted was for people to risk their lives because of me. Generally, wheelchair users relied on human support, to varying degrees, so they could have as normal a life as possible. I needed help to bring in food and supplies; I relied on carers to provide basic medical care. Suddenly, the most basic of my everyday activities seemed loaded with risk. The thought of Mum, Dad or one of my brothers running errands for me and getting sick as a result filled me with horror. Whenever Tommy or Maggie came by, I felt smothered by guilt. At one point, I sat at the top of my stairs and looked down.

'I could take my final stair fall as a stuntman,' I thought. I'd done plenty of them as a performer, but as a disabled person, the tumble would likely kill me.

I pulled myself away. Later, having spent too much time catastrophising about what might happen to me were the world to fall into a dystopian post-pandemic hellscape (and my personal assistants understandably chose to spend their final days on Earth with loved ones rather than me), I placed a sheet of diazepam on my bedside table. If the worst came to the worst, I thought, I'd at least have some control over my final moments. I'd rather that than die of starvation, a dysreflexia-induced stroke or a fatal infection because I couldn't change my own catheter. What a fucking horrible dilemma.

The thought haunted me for ages; I became conflicted and angry. I knew that taking my life was a permanent solution to a temporary problem, but were I to lose the ability to breathe, speak and swallow, was I even living? I became weirdly envious of people living in Switzerland, where the terminally sick were allowed to go out on their terms at a location like Dignitas,* or to die peacefully in their own homes. But because of the values in Western society – a lot of them founded in religious beliefs – that type of ending was considered immoral. According to Dad's faith, if I died by suicide I would likely end up condemned to eternal damnation, which would make him miserable. He believed in Heaven. What happens to a parent if they know they're not going to be reunited with one of their kids in the afterlife?

At the height of my lockdown misery, during a FaceTime call with some of my closest friends, I shared what I had been going through and we played a morbid game. *How was a quadriplegic like me supposed to die by suicide?* The act would pass on some trauma to whoever found me, especially if it was a mate or family member. I imagined the emotional impact upon their life and it felt too upsetting. The idea of rolling in front of an oncoming train or, worse, asking someone to help me achieve my final act didn't bear thinking

---

* In 2022 I went to Switzerland with my mate Jay, another 'quaddy' – he controls his wheelchair with his chin. As we explored Zermatt, he couldn't get over how nice everybody was being to us. 'Why do you reckon that is?' he said.

   I laughed darkly. 'It's because they think it's our last ever holiday. That we're here for Dignitas.'

   He pissed himself laughing.

about. In the end, I settled on the concept of hiring a hitman with a sniper rifle. My plan, which was a joke between mates, nothing more, felt like a movie script. As I slept with my bedroom door open, the assassin would do their work before calling the police to my address. That way, my personal assistants would be spared the horror of finding me, my brains splattered across the headboard. The game was screwed up. And while it wasn't something I was seriously considering, it proved morbidly entertaining in a dark time.

Though lockdown physically detached me from so many people, I weirdly wasn't alone in my suffering. For once, everyone in the world was getting a sense of what it was like to have their most basic freedoms stripped away, as I had after my accident. Other than the occasional walk, they weren't allowed to leave the house; it was impossible to move around as freely as before; even the simplest of processes, like receiving food deliveries at the front door, came with a health risk, like infection. I received so many phone calls from people who were suddenly feeling an amplified sense of empathy for what I'd gone through. The simple experience of an enforced lockdown delivered a bruising insight into what it was like to be me. People understood why I'd built an underground car park for my house. (That way, I could be lifted in and out of my car without shame or discomfort.) They realised that my steam room wasn't a design state-ment, it was a health requirement. They grasped how every quid I'd spent on my *Grand Designs* home was an attempt to claw back some semblance of self-sufficiency, rather than an act of showmanship.

I was in a bad place, and I knew it. I had to break free of the negative chatter, and to do so I tried to think back to Africa again and my experience with the elephants. I remembered the posi-tive marks the adventure had left on me, the beauty of nature and what it meant to be alive. It had been a lesson: I had to live again. *But how?* At first, the reality of losing more and more of my physical self each day forced me to be more present. I wanted to savour what I had while I had it. *Why lose an hour going over my problems when I could do something productive instead?* I decided that caring for others would become my therapy. What I really wanted was to be creative again. As a stunt performer, I'd used my talents to tell stories. *What was stopping me from using my imagination to bring joy to others – like I had before?* After a few months indoors, I discovered a renewed sense of appreciation for nature, people and the arts. The stuff I might have taken for granted previously.

I was also beginning to understand the implications of lockdown for generations of artists around the country – the painters who couldn't go to galleries, the actors who couldn't tread a theatre stage, and the musicians with no venues to play in. That's when I came up with the idea for a series of live shows called the *Concert for One* – a programme of intimate gigs in my back garden, where performers were paid to play a short set, and people could watch the shows online, from the safety of their front rooms. Through local contacts, I connected with singer-songwriters, spoken word artists, comedians and poets from Essex and east London. Everyone was paid £100 for fifteen minutes and as I watched from behind the glass doors of my kitchen, cameras streamed the performance across the internet.

I ran shows every week. Once the restrictions were lifted, and people were able to mix with one another again in 2020 and then into 2021, I invited friends into the house to share the experience. My best mate's dad had stage four cancer at the time, and he sat in my house as a singer called Darren Jones covered some of his favourite artists, including David Bowie and James Taylor. My mate's dad had a tumour in his throat, and it was badly swollen. Even though he could barely speak, it gave me so much joy to see him laughing and smiling. When the sun set in the evening, I made sure to capture it on camera. As the cold weather came in, I lit up the garden with my fire pit to create a welcoming vibe.

Eventually, the *Concert for One* became a protest against the Tory government. As they partied – all while telling us we couldn't mix with our dying relatives – I wanted to create an environment where artists felt supported. Meanwhile, the likes of Boris Johnson and Matt Hancock had made such a shitshow of the pandemic – especially in their treatment of the NHS, and the care workers operating across our communities – that I wanted to make a statement. The selfless had kept society going during its moment of need; the government had tried to financially undercut their services. In my case, I had the NHS to thank for my life. *I owed them everything.* And yet, all they were receiving for their efforts was a round of applause once a week, as the nation stepped onto their doorsteps to clap. What the UK's doctors, nurses and carers really deserved was a massive pay rise. *Concert for One* did its best to increase awareness of what was needed. I paid the artists for their shows and donated money to the NHS out of my own pocket.

The subject of caregivers was one I felt particularly passionate about, given my circumstances. When Tommy and Maggie came in as my personal assistants in 2009, their work was so much easier. I could still move around in a manual wheelchair while performing several basic functions unassisted, such as cooking or changing my catheter. Following on from my failed surgery in 2019, that had all changed. My needs became greater. With a financial settlement in place, I was able to make Tommy and Maggie my full-time carers, while bringing in one or two others.

Nowadays, whoever I am working with has to work bloody hard. I require assistance in all aspects of my daily life. Every floor is primed with potential booby traps. I need to be set in a certain position just to sleep safely. In the morning, someone must help me get out of bed. I also require assistance to go to the toilet – one of my favourite jokes is that I've had more hands up my backside than the cast of *The Muppet Show*. If an emergency happened in the middle of the night, it was important someone was in the house to call upon. Being a personal assistant or caregiver is a job that requires patience, humility, courage, attentiveness and, above all, compassion.

Tommy, Tom Di Cap and Maggie had these qualities in abundance. They have been and still are brilliant for me. I have never been someone to give in to fear; there are aspects of my life I refused to give up, and I have asked a lot of my staff. Tommy, Tom and Maggie have been beyond exemplary over the years. Both Tommy and Tom have whale-sized hearts. But I understood their time with me is finite. (In 2024, Tom Di Cap retired with his Italian passport, got into his camper and moved to Portugal. I was happy for him. The bloke has an adventurous spirit, and it filled me with pride knowing he was going off on an adventure. I just had to find mine. I'm hoping Tommy will stay with me until retirement. He's my rock.) I now have two more lovely personal assistants and, since joining my team, Jon and Luke have brought many great qualities to my life. A good caregiver can change someone's life, and I have been fortunate over the years. I have worked with some truly beautiful human beings; I am grateful for them all and everything they have done for me. I can honestly say I would have given up a long time ago without them.

★

Like everyone during lockdown, I took some time to reflect. I assessed my life. My partying days, while not over, were very different to how they had been previously. Other than a joint or two here and there, and the occasional beer, the drugs were done with – and even those two minor vices had lost their appeal. With sobriety came a clear head, and with a clear head came more energy. My testosterone rocketed. Rather than burying my problems in a shroud of smoke, I was able to face them head on. Getting fucked up didn't carry the appeal it once had, and with a sharp mind I was able to draw several lessons from the trauma of the past ten years.

The first of these was to live in the present, because, really, what other option did I have? When I first learned of my diagnosis, I heard someone claim that adapting to such a life-changing injury generally took two years. What a load of bollocks. The process was a hell of a lot longer – a never-ending, uphill battle, with no end in sight. There was very little point in me focusing on some imagined destination in the future, one where everything might be OK. Instead, I trained my thoughts on the present, because it was the only thing I had. (The same goes for all of us.) The good news was that I'd had some training in this process. As a stunt actor, I'd learned to manage my fears by focusing on the now. It helped me to deal with pressure and challenge myself, all while becoming obsessive about my self-development. It turned out that this was the perfect preparation for being a quadriplegic.

Just as I had done when preparing to perform on a dead man's wire, or exploding from a hydraulic air ram, there was very little benefit to me ruing my previous fuck-ups or worrying about the what-ifs. I had to focus on the task ahead, and nothing else. That now meant accepting some harsh truths. I was living in a body set on a path of neurological decline. My left arm was the only remaining connection I still had to some sort of independence. At some point I would have to say goodbye to that, and if I was going to survive the emotional tumult, I would need a huge amount of mental strength. That's when I decided to make the most of what was remaining.

My first few actions were psychological. I made sure to be gentle with myself because perception was truth. I couldn't remember the number of times I'd heard someone beat themselves up with negative self-talk and it drove me mad. They'd drop something and call themselves an idiot. Or they'd make a disparaging comment about their work, life or home, and, in doing so, put themselves down. Through being flat on my back in hospital, and having survived several life-threatening surgeries, I'd learned that the language people used about themselves, and the world around them, directly affected their personal lives. It shaped their world views. It impacted upon their actions and choices. My attitude was to start the day by thinking positively because it would shape everything going forward. If I did the opposite, my life would probably go downhill, and quickly.

For that same reason I stopped reading negative news, because there was just too much of it. The world was a screwed-up place for sure, but there was also plenty to be excited about. Despite the wars, pandemics and scandals, there had been some amazing advancements in science. For starters, fewer children were being born into poverty around the world than ever before. There were new treatments for cancer and Alzheimer's. Even polio, a disease that had confined some of my mates to wheelchairs, was close to being eradicated. Whenever someone moaned about the state of the 21st century, I made sure to push back. A saying that I leaned into was: *We're just advanced monkeys, on a rock, spinning in space.* It helped me to put things into perspective. Up until the First World War, most people died after suffering a spinal cord injury. The fact that I was still able to speak, laugh and travel the world was a bloody miracle, and I treated it as such.

With that in mind, I decided to refer to myself as a survivor, not a victim. Yes, something terrible had happened to me and my life was altered for ever. But my experience also reminded me I'd been a thrill-seeker. I'd embraced the stunt performer image, and I loved taking risks. At the same time, I'd known all too well what the consequences of those risks were, and I'd been more than aware that one of the downsides of being a stunt performer was the constant threat of serious injury or death. When I thought back to some of the lads I'd met in Stanmore, their injuries had happened through no fault of their own. All of them had shown kindness and support during my darkest moments, even though they had been suffering themselves. I decided to take on the same attitude. I wanted to come from a place of positivity in everything I did, because there was no space for anger or resentment. If ever I did feel rage or frustration, I made sure to turn it into positive energy by working harder in rehabilitation, or by putting even more of myself into a project. Pain was inevitable, but suffering was a choice.

The more I looked towards the optimistic outcome, the more happiness I found, and I actively sought out the light in every gloomy situation. Often literally. I watched the sunset every night. I positioned myself in the house to catch the fading light as it shone through my patio windows. Whenever I flew abroad, I always enjoyed those dark grey travel days, the cabin flooding with brilliant sunshine as the plane broke through the clouds. Most of all, I tried to laugh off the misfortunes, just as I had as a schoolkid when the bullies came for me, or while dusting myself down after a bruising fall on set. Making a joke after a public erection or an uncontrollable bowel movement killed any discomfort for me, and anyone nearby. Laughter brightened an event that might have ordinarily been considered excruciating. Besides, I didn't have time for any embarrassment.

To solidify this new mindset, I made the rational decision to accept those problems that were within my control and to relinquish any stress about those that weren't. One step towards reaching this point was to focus on my breathwork because I'd become painfully aware that, at some point in the future, I wasn't going to be able to breathe without mechanical assistance. I didn't want to think about what that might look like. So, to give myself a fighting chance of delaying the moment, I decided to control the controllables by strengthening my lungs. This idea first came to me while doing aqua therapy at my home pool, as I sat at the bottom with a scuba tank and a rebreather. While underwater, the weight of my head seemed to dissipate, I felt supported, but I also experienced a sense of inner peace. There was no noise – my inner dialogue, which was normally dialled up to eleven in volume, was reduced to a whisper. I felt calm and, more connected to my body, I could assess my injuries. And after a while I took my regulator away, and practised my breath holds.

In a weird way, this echoed the work from my previous career, in the indoor tank at Leavesden Studios while filming *Harry Potter and the Goblet of Fire*. But rather than swimming around as Harry, I sank to the floor. Tommy stood on the edges of my swim shorts to tie me down and watched me like a hawk throughout. I couldn't blame him. A couple of years previously, in a moment when I'd enjoyed more mobility in my arms, I made the stupid assumption I would be safe to swim alone and unsupervised. I'd asked him to drop me in the pool and insisted he cut the lawn. At first, I'd kept myself buoyant by sucking in a lungful of air. But as Tommy walked up and down with the mower, I also sucked in a mouthful of water, which caused me to choke and splutter. I felt myself going under.

'Tommy!' I yelped. '*Tommy!*'

But he couldn't hear me. The lawnmower was too loud. Deliberately, I sank to the bottom, using my elbows to crawl along the floor of the pool. I then dragged myself up the steps and towards the side, where I coughed my guts up.

'Better not leave me alone again,' I said, as Tommy ran over, looking horrified.

Near drownings aside, I found a sense of peace underwater, and I was soon able to sit beneath the surface for ages and hold my breath. On the first few occasions, my mind raced; I felt a panic fluttering in my chest. My pool sessions became a mental challenge, during which I wasn't allowed to freak out, even when my brain was screaming at me to surface. In those moments, a three-word sentence rattled around my head. *You're not breathing! You're not breathing! You're not breathing!* Eventually, I was able to silence the fear by counting. My first target was to get to five, then ten, until eventually, I began thinking in terms of minutes rather than seconds. As I focused on the lactic acid burning in my remaining muscles, and the growing strength in my lungs, all the negative shit in my mind faded away. Any problems I might have been facing that day seemed inconsequential, and before long I was breaking barriers at one minute, then two, until I'd reached four. Four and a half soon became a personal Everest. Once I made it to four minutes and twenty-five seconds, I reset that target to a full five minutes.

Challenges of this kind helped me to wrestle back some semblance of independence. I'd always understood that Harry Potter's character arc was a story of light triumphing over dark. Mine was now the same. But while that was a great idea to cling on to, putting the concept into practice took some effort. As I settled into my new, post-pandemic life, there were some days when I could have been excused for staying in bed, flat on my back. But that was the easy way out. *And it brought in the dark.* So, when my body cried out for a lazy day, I made sure to sit upright where I could at least connect with the world. Doing something that would have seemed inconsequential as a younger, more able man felt like an achievement, and I experienced the same satisfaction when rooted to the bottom of my swimming pool because I was growing.

I was bringing in the light.

15

THE ARTIST'S WAY

Two pivotal events showed me that a new life was possible, and both took place in Guggenheim museums – one in New York City, the other in Bilbao. The first happened while visiting Manhattan in 2011. The Guggenheim building there is a construction masterpiece created by Frank Lloyd Wright, a designer the American Institute of Architects considers to be one of the greatest of all time. Much of this acclaim is due to a circular ramp that curls upwards at the heart of the building. Reaching towards a domed skylight in the ceiling, its offramps dispatch visitors to different floors, where they are then able to admire the art pieces curving around them. As I sat on the ground floor and stared upwards, the structure looked dizzying and overwhelming. But it was also a brilliant sight for anyone wanting to ride the slopes on wheels. Having admired the artwork, I skidded down the ramp, traversing left and right in much the same way that a skier might carve down a blue run on a mountain. As the art pieces blurred past in my peripheral vision, I experienced the exhibition in a unique way. Nobody else was having a moment like mine. In an environment dedicated to beautiful art, I had created a statement all my own. *A form of poetry in motion.*

I'd been a wheelchair user for several years. At that point, I was using a manual chair and I'd developed a love-hate relationship with my mode of transport. The most disabling thing about being in a wheelchair is the environment a person deals with. Sometimes

I even felt imprisoned because so many environments weren't designed to cater for people like me, and my limited mobility often made me feel like a second-class citizen. Pubs: a danger zone. Gigs: a nightmare. Five-star dining experiences: a logistical headfuck. Public buildings and their staircases, narrow doorways and high countertops were a painful reminder that I lived in a different world to most, but in the Guggenheim, my position as a wheelchair user felt like a gift.

This vibe was repeated in 2016 when I visited the Guggenheim in Bilbao, Spain – another building considered to be an architectural masterpiece. Its exterior was a jumble of random-looking glass, titanium and limestone curves, and set outside was *Tulips*, one of a series of sculptures made by the American artist Jeff Koons in his *Celebration* series. Constructed from brightly coloured reflective metal and designed to resemble a bouquet of oversized balloon flowers, Koons' *Celebrations* collection also features a series of oversized balloon dogs, the type made by kids' entertainers during the 1980s.

As I stared at one of its many iterations with Tommy, I noticed our curved, distorted silhouettes were reflected in the metal tulip blooms.

'Tom, look,' I said, pointing. 'How cool is that?'

'What do you mean?' he said, confused.

I laughed. '*It's us.* We're reflected. Do you know what that is?'

Tommy shrugged. 'Two bellends staring at two bellends?'

'No! *We're* in the sculpture. *We're* participating. That piece will never look the same ever again. It's a unique moment.'

Tommy laughed. *Whatever.* But as we moved away, I couldn't stop thinking about the Koons *Tulips.* The image lingered for days and I wondered if I'd experienced an epiphany, or a 'Call to Adventure' – an event described by the writer Joseph Campbell in his storytelling bible, *The Hero's Journey.* This, wrote Campbell, was 'a moment that signifies that destiny has summoned the hero and transferred his spiritual centre of gravity from within the pale of his society to a zone unknown'. In the Wizarding World narrative, Harry Potter's 'Call to Adventure' happened when the truth about his magic-wielding parents was revealed. By staring at the surface of a Koons balloon dog, had I stepped into a zone unknown too? Certainly, I felt as if my truth had changed. Life was art, art was life, and I should treat every day as a canvas or storyboard on which to tell my story or build something inspirational.

This wasn't exactly an unexpected realisation. As a stunt actor, my whole life had been expressive in some way. I'd created thought-provoking moments or explosive peaks in the cinematic narrative by risking my body in front of a camera. I suppose, with hindsight, it wasn't too dissimilar to a ballet dancer who evoked emotion by pirouetting across the stage, because in many ways everything I did on Harry Potter had been an artistic statement. When performing a reaction fall, I decided how much movement to generate through the air, and whether to make a hit look harder, acrobatic, or survivable. When arcing through the water in the Leavesden tank, I'd worked hard to perfect the same swimming stroke that a whale or dolphin might use, by flicking my legs gracefully.

But as a young stuntman, the thought that my movements were artistic statements rather than physical endeavours hadn't been so obvious. Yeah, I'd explored the studio's creative outposts during my breaks. There had been some incredible creators in the wardrobe, special effects and make-up departments and I'd soaked up their knowledge like a sponge. Their enthusiasm rubbed off on me. I wanted my stunts to be viewed in much the same way as an incredible special effect, or a beautifully designed costume. Whenever I delivered a gag, I'd run back to Video Village to check the frame, wanting to improve the work, but I'd considered my job to be athletic and risky, like an extreme sport, rather than art. After the *Tulips*, the sense that every move I made could be interpreted artistically felt game-changing.

After 2016, during my more reflective moments (and there were plenty of them), I made sure to dig into my emotions. In doing so, I realised that every part of my life, past and present, had the potential to be an artistic statement, and I only had to see it as such. The way I backlit my plants: *art*. The music I played during a beautiful sunset: *art*. The way I moved across the concentric circular ramps of a New York gallery, or appeared on the surface of a multi-million-dollar sculpture: *also art*. I'd grown up on film sets and been surrounded by some of the most brilliant minds in movie-making history. I'd also witnessed some incredible creative moments, whether that was Gary Oldman, David Thewlis and Sir Alan Rickman throwing down an acting masterclass, or through the directing magic of Chris Columbus, Alfonso Cuarón, Mike Newell and David Yates. This idea had been bubbling up for years, I just hadn't realised it.

Suddenly, that had all changed. Having been trapped in my wheelchair for over ten years, I understood that the idea of being a creator had always been inside me, even during those blurry few years in the aftermath of my accident. My drug-fuelled parties in Ibiza and Amsterdam weren't just debauched trips abroad. I'd been working as a curator, imagining up a different world for my friends to enjoy. When I'd ordered every cocktail on the list for the people alongside me in a bar, or paid for VIP treatment in an exclusive nightclub, I hadn't been showing off. I'd been creating experiences. I even reimagined past events as artistic happenings. Like the time a herd of elephants had approached my swimming pool at the Sabi Sabi Earth Lodge. Moments like that were living portraits, something beyond any photo or painting, and I would take the images to my death bed. I now saw it as my calling to make new ones.

★

Perception was truth and I embraced my role as a re-energised creative. What I found most interesting was the idea that I was able to make art from a unique perspective, especially once I'd lost the muscle strength to write freehand or hold a paintbrush. I loved taking photos because they captured a split second in life. Every image in the frame was suspended, motionless, and it weirdly reminded me of my dives when training for the British Stunt Register. Back then, I'd launched myself from the high board and, for the briefest of moments, I experienced a sense of weightlessness and make-believe, where the possibility of flight felt truly possible. Then gravity kicked in again. I arced down into the water, my body piercing the surface like a dagger. Photography gave me that same buzz. Whenever I saw a moment, something I wanted to freeze for ever – a flower in the garden, a bird fluttering around a feeder, one of my mates, or their kids playing in the pool – I'd hold a touch screen device with my working hand (thank God for technology). Then I'd click the shutter by pushing my nose against the screen.

Like all artists, it was down to me to figure out what type of emotions I wanted to evoke in others. Yeah, it seemed important to inspire people. But like a lot of creatives, I wanted to challenge people's thoughts, ideas and perceptions on what a disabled person could do. I suppose this was something of a throwback to my stunt days when I liked to prove people wrong, especially those performers or directors who might have doubted me because of my age, height or stature. My attitude on the Harry Potter set: *I'm a small man but I'm a brave motherfucker. Let me show you.* My attitude in a wheelchair: *I'm disabled, but it ain't going to stop me.* The reality was that my new creative position had been forced upon me and I had a choice – I could either resent it or embrace it, so I chose the latter and rethought everything about my world, from the way I presented myself to the way people viewed me. One step in this journey involved the angles that photographers used when taking my portrait. Rather than allowing them to shoot me from above, where the viewer's perspective was much higher, I asked them to crouch down and shoot me at hip height. I didn't want anyone looking down on me because of disability.

In many ways, this creative streak acted as a form of therapy. It certainly softened some of the sharper edges of real life, and it helped me to live in a bubble of joy, love and laughter, rather than merely existing in a shitstorm of resentment and anger. I started a podcast called *Cunning Stunts* where I interviewed my mates from the film business about their careers. This work was advanced when I made a short film of my own in 2019. Entitled *Keep on Rolling* and coming in at just over fourteen minutes, my film-making debut featured behind-the-scenes footage, an in-depth look at my accident, and the life of the stunt performer. I was staring down the barrel of a complicated surgical procedure at the time – the failed attempt to prevent the decline in my muscles – and I wanted the world to know about my work, my story and my art.

The filmmaker Dan Hartley saw something in my rudimentary work and suggested we expand my online short into something more substantial. He was an old colleague of mine and a successful documentary director. Meanwhile, Dan Radcliffe was also keen to get involved. I'd brought him on to *Cunning Stunts* once or twice because I needed a 'normie' for comedic balance, someone who didn't possess the mindset of a fall guy, and at that point his career had gone stratospheric. He'd appeared in *Swiss Army Man* (2016) with Paul Dano, which was written and directed by the two Daniels – Scheinert and Kwan. (They would later create the Oscar-winning *Everything Everywhere All at Once*.) There was also *Kill Your Darlings* (2013) and *Escape from Pretoria* (2020). It was good to have him interject, or express disbelief, when one of us casually mentioned being hit by a car, or the time someone had sky-dived from an exploding plane. His incredulity was bloody funny.

Whenever I mixed with them, both Dans tried to turn the camera on me. If ever I left the room, Radcliffe would interview my old teammates for anecdotes. This was his attempt at making a documentary about my life.

'We can tell your story in a better way than *Keep on Rolling*,' he said eventually.

I reluctantly agreed. Though I'd made my mini doc during the build-up to what could have been a fatal surgical procedure, my intention hadn't been to release the full story of my life. That had now changed, and between us – with help from the producers: Amy Stares plus Simon Chinn from the Oscar-winning production company Lightbox (*Man on Wire, Searching for Sugar Man*) – we stitched together a treatment that focused on our working relationship during the making of the Harry Potter films and the friendship that built throughout. Our pitch was snapped up by HBO studios. This work would later become a full-length documentary, entitled *The Boy Who Lived*.

The filming was cathartic. My former work colleagues and mates, like Dan and Marc Mailley, delivered emotional interviews for the film, as did my Hollywood dad, Greg Powell, who was particularly broken up by what had happened to me.

'I hate seeing him like that,' he said on the final cut. 'In the nicest way, I wish I'd never met him, when I see him like that. Because it wouldn't be like that if he never met me. I was the last one to touch him when he could actually walk, and I was the first one to touch him when he couldn't walk. And that's an awful feeling . . . I still blame myself because I was there.'

It was tough to hear that Greg was beating himself up over my accident. When I heard how he'd been talking, I burst into tears. Some people might have assumed that I would see him as being partially responsible for my injuries, but that honestly wasn't the case. Yeah, Greg was the stunt coordinator, and he oversaw the stunt department. But he was not at fault when it came to my accident. I can categorically say, hand on heart, that Greg always put the safety of his stunt crew first. He also nurtured me as a young performer; he cared for me and loved me. So, no: I didn't blame him at all. In fact, my feelings for him were full of love – they always will be. At a young age, Greg gifted me an opportunity in an industry that was full of nepotism and entitlement. He taught me how to be a man, and he pushed me to become one of the best stuntmen in the world. As I progressed, he felt incredibly proud.

When I listened to his interview during the making of *The Boy Who Lived*, I saw the pain in his eyes; the regret of what happened to me was sitting heavily in his heart, and it was clear he'd been carrying the weight and responsibility of my accident. But I didn't want him to have that hurt because *it wasn't his fault*. As a stunt performer, I'd accepted that my job was stacked with dangers and that every gag carried a risk. Greg's legacy shouldn't be attached to my injuries. Instead, he should be praised for being a working-class champion within the stunt industry. People should talk about him as being responsible for some of the most amazing cinematic stunt work of the past forty years. Regardless of what happened to me, I'll always love and respect the man, and I consider him as a part of my extended family. When Greg fed me lunch in the studio canteen that day, the only thing that had changed between us was the fact that I was finding a new form of independence. If Greg reads this book, he might feel one or two pangs of hurt and regret. But the truth is that I feel incredibly grateful to have him in my life. I will always call him a friend, and there will always be a seat at my table for him.

But the filming process for *The Boy Who Lived* was rough on everyone, given the subject matter. Over a ten-day shoot, we filmed Daniel and me talking about old times as I showed the world my new life. As my family and friends shared their stories, and I shared mine, a series of old wounds were reopened. That wasn't surprising given I had to reflect upon a brutal, life-changing event, all while trying to put on a sugary Hollywood gloss as I spoke.

Things might be different now, but at the time of writing this book, I hadn't yet watched *The Boy Who Lived,* mainly for self-care reasons. Psychologically, I couldn't put myself through it. As the months progressed after its release in 2023, I lost more and more function in my arm. I really didn't want to look back at myself from 2008 while thinking, *I wish I could do that now.* And I certainly didn't want to look back at me in 2012, 2015, 2018, and so on, with the same thoughts. Doctors have since put my life expectancy at around the sixty-five-years-old mark. At some point, I'm going to be unable to do anything for myself, so maybe I'll watch it then. For now, I have too much optimism and positivity in my life to go through it.

The Boy Who Lived was later nominated for the 2024 BAFTAs in the 'Single Documentary' category. I attended the ceremony, but like every pub, restaurant and cinema I've ever been to, the venue wasn't set up for people like me. For a quadriplegic without temperature control, the room was too cold to sit in. After three awards there was a dance ceremony, and I felt my body trembling with the chill. I looked across at Dan Hartley in the seat next to mine. 'Sorry, I'm out,' I said, moving backstage, where I had a nice evening chatting to the riggers and caterers working behind the scenes. I also felt a little aggrieved that, like the Oscars, these awards didn't give a toss about the hard work done by stunt performers. Among the 23 Academy Awards there are categories for costume design, and make-up and hair styling. It was then announced that from 2026 there would be an award for best casting. *What an absolute piss-take.* When people went to see *Mission: Impossible – Dead Reckoning Part One,* it was to see Tom Cruise fire himself off the edge of a cliff on a motorbike, not to look at Simon Pegg's haircut, or marvel at Rebecca Ferguson's outfits. Stunt performers, men and women who put their lives on the line to make movie magic, have been overlooked for too long.

The Paralympian Ellie Simmonds won the Single Documentary category for her brilliant *Finding My Secret Family*. Had our positions been swapped, and I'd been given the chance to use the BAFTA platform to further the cause, it had been my intention to raise awareness of the stunt performer's work during a prepared speech:

I obviously want to thank my best mate, Daniel. I know he's gutted he can't be here today, but you lot have got to watch him grow up on screen and I got to watch him grow as a man, and that's one of the greatest gifts you can have as a friend. I also want to say that it shouldn't take me to break my neck and share my pain, and my loved ones' pain, in a documentary to get a stuntman up on stage at the BAFTAs. Lastly, I want to remind everyone in this room that disability will affect you all, whether you like it or not, and we need representation in government, infrastructure and society, and ultimately policymakers, and a society that is inclusive for all people.

From what I've heard, a lot of people found comfort and hope in *The Boy Who Lived*, which was always my aim. I also received positive messages on Instagram nearly every day. This feeling was confirmed when my phone rang while I was travelling in Barcelona at the beginning of 2024. When I took the call, it was the actor Warwick Davis, who played Professor Filius Flitwick in the Harry Potter films, as well as Wicket the Ewok in *Return of the Jedi* and Willow Ufgood in *Willow*. Warwick, who was a child actor from the age of twelve, had been born with dwarfism, due to a condition called spondyloepiphyseal dysplasia congenita; his wife, Samantha, had achondroplasia, which resulted in the same physical stature. Sadly, she had passed away that year. After working together for many years I'm confident I could call Warwick a friend, and Sam was a champion for little people with their charity, Little People UK. When I heard the news, my heart broke for him.

I answered my phone and we spoke for a little while. 'I'm so sorry,' I said, over and over.

Then Warwick thanked me. 'I cannot tell you how much comfort your documentary brought me and Sam when we watched it together.'

Oh, mate.

'We were going through a tough time as a family, with Sam navigating medical issues,' he said. 'We watched your documentary, and it really helped us. I wanted to say thank you.'

I was overcome with emotion. The fact that my experience had brought Sam comfort ahead of her surgery brought me some peace after such a devastating loss.

★

I love visiting movie sets, just so I can reconnect with the art of cinematic storytelling. While I struggle to watch the Harry Potter films, I love losing myself in a film, especially as I've had a purpose-built movie room put into my house. Going behind the scenes and seeing how the magic is made always gives me a buzz, and in 2022 I was lucky enough to be invited on to the Leavesden Studios set of *Barbie*, which starred Ryan Gosling and Margot Robbie and was being directed by the brilliant Greta Gerwig.

The studio crackled with a powerful energy. The set was a blitz of pink and Technicolor. As I moved through the studio, as the guest of former Harry Potter producer David Heyman, I spotted the oversized *Barbie* playhouse and the *Barbie* car. It was like walking into a toy shop from another generation, except everything was bigger and bolder, and *pinker*. At the heart of it all was Margot Robbie – the film's lead. She seemed to be vibrating at a different frequency to everyone around her, and it was incredible to see such an amazing star at work. It reminded me of Dan Radcliffe once he had grown into his role in J.K. Rowling's Wizarding World.

It's rare that I feel nervous around another person. While being introduced to Margot, I'm sure my butterflies were down to the fact that I was terrified another episode of priapism might be around the corner. But she took the time to talk. There was plenty for us to chat about because her brother was working as a stunt performer on *Furiosa: A Mad Max Saga*, and it was incredible to speak to an actor who was at the peak of her powers. The entire set seemed to gravitate towards her presence.

★

Despite my optimistic bias and creative intent, there are still bad days. I'm not bulletproof, and on occasions my circumstances can get me down. All it takes sometimes is a thought, like a flashback from my past life, or an outbreak of FOMO while watching something on TV, like an event I can't attend because of my injuries. The BBC's coverage of Glastonbury is always a conflicting experience for me. Both beautiful and devastating, I love seeing the gorgeousness of humanity coming together to celebrate an amazing band or artist. The pain that follows afterwards is unavoidable though. I know I'll never get to experience that swirling sea of emotion for myself. Even if it were possible to get onsite, it's unlikely I'd be able to feel present at any point, because there are too many life-threatening factors for me to stress about.

How am I going to get back to my tent on wheels, in the mud?

How do I look after my skin and avoid sunburn, or sores?

How am I going to take a piss and change my catheter without getting an infection?

This is arguably one of the most challenging aspects of being disabled. I'm constantly having to consider the tiniest details just to get through the day – things I wouldn't have considered before 2009. It only takes one lapse in concentration for me to be in a world of pain. I recently put on a decent pair of trainers for a TV appearance because, like most people appearing on national telly, I wanted to look good. Before long, an old pressure sore had returned on my toe, but I didn't realise because everything below my point of injury is numb to any sensation. But this was the tip of a very big iceberg. Every now and then, someone will ask me a very innocent, human question: *What would you give to walk again?* My answer: *There are plenty of other things I'd like to bring back before walking.* Having two working arms, rather than one, would be a great start. A useful follow-up would be fingers and thumbs that grip, and I'd love for my body to be able to regulate my blood pressure properly, to stop me from having a stroke in the future.

Some sensation in my dick. Oh my God: *that would be amazing.* I'd also like to sweat again, weirdly, because that hasn't happened since my accident. Bowel and bladder control would be wonderful too, because having a bag strapped to the side of my leg isn't much fun. And what I'd give for an independent trip outside the house, one where I didn't have to worry about uneven pavements, or loose cobblestones, or anything that might flip me out of my chair. There's so much more: The ability to get my heart rate up through exercise. Bringing a kid into the world without feeling guilty. To be able to hold a loved one, stroke the dog, or hold a girlfriend's hair back while she's being sick after a big night out, the pair of us laughing and groaning.

Everyone sees a paralysed person – or a paraplegic, tetraplegic or quadriplegic – and assumes their dream is to walk again. *But fuck walking.* I'd take a long list of things before agreeing to stepping on my own two feet again. (Though, don't get me wrong: walking again would be *incredible*.)

It's for this reason that I've often pushed back on the disabled club and lived in my own way. I've never wanted to be a spokesperson for the community. Instead, I've wanted to run my own club, with my own rules. Partly, that's involved me reaching out to newly injured people on the spinal ward at Stanmore, so I can give them the information they might not have received elsewhere – like Vish did for me during my first round of rehabilitation. Every time I visit the ward for an appointment, I ask if there are any *new ones*. The nurse checks the latest arrivals, and I'll head over to their bay for a chat. I tell them my story and detail my recovery, before pointing out the approaching pitfalls and hurdles on their journey. Then I give them my number. If they want to ring me at any point, they can. I also believe in giving back through actions. I donate iPads to kids that can't afford them, table tennis equipment to community centres, and money to the Stanmore spinal ward through various charity drives, such as the Harry Potter Cricket Cup. Since 2009, an annual match featuring former Harry Potter cast and crew members has raised over £100,000. I see it as my duty to support the NHS after everything they've done for me.

I also make a point of helping my mates whenever they're having a rough time of it. During another trip to New York in 2023, for the premiere of *The Boy Who Lived*, we were driving through Manhattan on a crisp autumnal day. Brilliant blades of sunshine pierced the gaps between skyscrapers. Central Park was smothered in a carpet of burnt orange, yellow and brown leaves. As the car speakers played Ella Fitzgerald's 'Autumn in New York', we drove past the Dakota building where John Lennon had lived (and died). I sat up front, Tommy was behind me, and the music seemed to amplify the moment, like the soundtrack to a Martin Scorsese movie. The memories in my head always appear in a 16mm frame, as they did on a film camera, and for a moment, as we whizzed past the yellow cabs and human traffic, I felt as if my own biopic was playing out in front of me.

I called out to Tommy. 'This is beautiful,' I said. 'Let's be here now. Take in the moment—'

But Tommy seemed to be somewhere else entirely. He didn't respond.

'Mate, are you all right?' I said.

'I'm struggling to enjoy it,' he said sadly. 'Like, I now know that all this can be taken away.'

Throughout the pandemic, he'd experienced a terrible time. His dad had passed away in 2021. Then, a couple of months before our New York trip, his nan had passed away. I suspected both losses had taken a toll on him.

'And it *will* be taken away. I want to call my dad and tell him about being here. In New York. But I can't . . .'

Tommy had been my rock for the last ten years. He'd propped me up in some of my darkest moments, acting as my arms and legs, sometimes literally. I loved him like a brother and seeing him in such a bad way stirred up a wave of sadness, but I knew it was important we talked through his pain, even if we were on an American adventure. A cloud had been hanging over him for months and I suspected he'd probably wanted to chat about his grief before, but he'd held back. Though he was a best mate, Tommy was also my personal assistant, and it was his job to care for me daily. My welfare was his responsibility, and he might have feared that an emotional conversation would affect me negatively. But really, I was the person best placed for him to talk through the subject of loss. I lived in a body that was fading by the day, and I existed in a constant state of managed grief, where the only way to survive was to deal with my emotions honestly (rather than bottling them away) and productively (through positive action).

In the car, I gained a new perspective on Tommy's bereavement, and what he had been going through. And though I can't remember much of what was said at the time, I was there for him in a moment when he'd needed me most. I could never assist Tommy physically. I certainly couldn't lift him with my arms. But I was able to hold him emotionally. Knowing I could be there for him, when he had been there for me on so many occasions, gave me more pride than the film premiere and the positive responses to it. Tommy was more like a brother than a friend, and he was committed to sharing his life with me.

'Try and see the view while you can,' I said. 'Even though you can't share the story with the people that have gone, they'd be happy for you to be here, opening your eyes to the beauty of life instead of focusing on loss.'

But helping others helps me. It puts a positive spin on my day when things are turning to shit. As has challenging the expectations of what people think I can and can't do. In 2024, I posed for a portrait by James Eckersley – a photographer with several pictures hanging in the National Portrait Gallery in London. James contacted me with a pitch. Having watched *The Boy Who Lived*, he wanted to take a picture of me and, all being well, submit the results for an exhibition.

'If you have any ideas of how you want to be shot, let me know,' he added.

Yeah, I've got a fucking idea. 'How about I sit naked in my shower chair,* and I'll set my head on fire?' I said.

James laughed, probably out of shock at first. But the creative outline appealed to him. With a few phone calls, one of which was to Marc Mailley, who was now working as a stunt coordinator, we were able to find someone who could competently mix fire gel, a

---

* These were the wheels I used when taking a shower. Drenching a £20,000 electric wheelchair is never a good idea.

wallpaper-paste-thick substance made with KY jelly, with a glue paraffin on top. I'd only ever been set on fire once, during the filming of *The Lost Legion*, and only briefly. My arm and leg were set ablaze for a single shot, and it had been over in a matter of seconds. What I was planning to do in the photo was a lot scarier, but the rewards far outweighed the risks. When it came to posing for James's portrait, I didn't want to be seen as a man in a wheelchair, because I was so much more than that. I wanted people to see me as someone who took risks for art's sake. The best creatives challenge people's perceptions by putting their bodies, reputations and legacies on the line. I wanted to do the same.

James had already shot a background, a wintry woodland scene, where the trees had been stripped bare by the freezing temperatures. Beneath them, a carpet of leaves blanketed the floor. I hadn't fancied sitting in such an environment, the cold would have killed me. Instead, I sat in front of a backdrop featuring James's woodland image that had been set up outside my kitchen doors. Marc applied the gel to my skull in thick, gloopy dollops, and then set my head on fire. There were no nerves. I felt no fear. When I imagined the type of conversations my portrait might inspire, I thrummed with excitement. I wanted James's audience to see a different side of disability. I wanted their opinions to be challenged. I wanted observers to see a more intimate side of me. With *The Boy Who Lived* I'd bared my soul, but with the photograph I wanted to bare my body with all its deformities on display. In the final shot, my shoulders stooped slightly, my belly was distended because of the weight of my internal organs, and a piss bag was strapped to the side of my leg. Nothing was hidden away.

True story: I don't have many mirrors in the house, because I don't like looking at myself. But when James showed me the final shot, I didn't feel shame or regret. *I couldn't stop looking at it.* His photo was all of me, unfiltered, without smoke or mirrors. When I looked into the eyes of the person in the chair, I saw the real me: the man that for so long had lived as a boy. My journey started in Mum and Dad's back garden, where I'd jumped from my upstairs window and onto a trampoline positioned on the lawn some 20 feet below. It had ended with a job in which I'd risked life and limb to help tell an inspirational story. In doing so, I'd been at the heart of one of the biggest movie franchises in Hollywood history. I'd racked up more broomstick miles than any other performer in the Wizarding World; I'd battled trolls and dark-hearted wizards while evading fire-breathing beasts and Whomping Willows.

The first half of my life was an adventure. The second half remains full of dark uncertainty, and there's a lot of scary stuff for me to tackle, head on, but I refuse to live without hope. In many ways, I hold the spirit of Harry Potter close. I can't reread the books. I can't watch the films either. The experience, like thinking about Glaston-bury, is too painful. Instead, I take the character with me wherever I go by living with love and empathy, because after all those years of wearing his cape and glasses, Harry's story has left a permanent mark on me – like the lightning-bolt scar on his forehead.

For long periods of my life, I was more like Peter Pan, *the boy who didn't grow up*, than Harry Potter, *the boy who lived*, and I operated without accountability. But just as Harry was forced to mature and face some uncomfortable truths, so have I. The more I looked at my naked portrait and all its vulnerabilities, the more I realised the undeniable truth.

Breaking my neck had made a man of me.

THE BOY WHO LIVED
EPISODE 16: BE HERE NOW

CREATED BY DAVID HOLMES
WRITTEN BY DAVID HOLMES

RIPPLE PRODUCTIONS//

EPILOGUE

OPEN ON:

1701 DAVID'S HOUSE, ESSEX, ENGLAND

July 2024: DAVID is at home in his three-storey Essex home. The house is beautiful. Backlit plants make trippy shadows on the wall. A digital Matisse painting plays on a widescreen TV. Through the patio doors we see a smouldering pit fire and the swimming pool where David does his water therapy and hardcore breathing sessions.

But today is not a day for relaxation. At one end of the living room is a video camera on a tripod. A small team of creatives are gathered around it; one of them is a DIRECTOR, another a CAMERA OPERATOR. A third person holds a boom mic above David's head and takes care to remain out-of-shot. They are here to film David's TED talk — a presentation he had hoped to deliver live at a conference in Covent Garden, London. Because of a serious bout of food poisoning, he was unable to attend.

This absence has caused some serious FOMO. David had taken weeks to write the script, before committing it to memory. At one point, he even employed an acting coach to assist with his delivery. The work, though unused at the conference, has since paid dividends. As he talks to camera, David brims with confidence. The director reads along to his script and nods happily. This is going well . . .

DAVID:

. . . As a stuntman I had to be flexible, able to manage my fears, handle pressure. I had to be willing to face challenge and constantly improve myself. Turns out that this was the perfect rehearsal for becoming a quadriplegic. My new 'job' takes even more stamina, determination and mental agility. And it's 24/7.

So if you walk away from this talk, lucky you. If you walk out with a new perspective on life, then lucky me. So here goes: Some lessons from my own 'School of Hard Knocks'.

Number 1: ALWAYS LIVE IN THE PRESENT. So right now, I'm living in a body that's on a journey of neurological decline. Each day I'm having to let go of the remaining function of this one side. This reality comes with pain and frustration and requires huge tolerance. After my accident, I spent several years chasing my old life. But it really was gone for ever. Learning to love my new life took time. And, honestly, it's a work in progress. And it's always changing.

In the future, there's a chance independent breathing, speech and my ability to swallow might deteriorate, and I'll have to adjust again. What this means is that, in moments of clarity, I remind myself to be here now. To take a breath and be thankful I can still do that by myself. I enjoy it while I can . . .

David takes a beat and looks into the camera. No kidding. Those acting lessons have really paid off.

DAVID:
I'd like to ask you all now to wiggle your toes.

He sees the director looking at his feet. He's wiggling his toes.

DAVID:
You felt it? That means nerve signals are travelling from your brain to your toes at over 200mph. Trust me; that's a gift. Don't waste it.
    And that leads me on to my second point.
    ALWAYS LOOK FOR THE LIGHT.
The story of Harry Potter is about the triumph of light over dark and that's a great motto to live by. But it really does take work. Real work. We will all find ourselves in a tough place at one time or another

but it's up to us whether we actively seek out the light in these situations or settle for sitting in the dark.

I learned early on that sitting in the dark only brings more darkness. But, luckily, the same is true for the light; if you look for it, it will find you. Every day I wake up in a body that says to me, 'Just stay in bed, take the easy route, avoid the pain'; but of the past fifteen years, I've spent at least one of them in bed and I'm bored of it. There's only so many ceilings you can stare at. So I choose the pain and the fight of sitting upright.

He takes a deep breath. This speech has been months in the making. No way is he going to screw it up now.

DAVID:
So now on to my third piece of advice: BE A SURVIVOR, NOT A VICTIM.

After my accident I spent seven months in the spinal unit at Stanmore Royal Orthopaedic Hospital and, shit as I felt, I quickly realised I wasn't a victim. I'd always been a thrill-seeker and I'd chosen a job with known risks. I have to accept that reality.

In my time in the disabled community, I've met plenty of people whose disabilities are no fault of their own. A stunt accident led to my paralysis, and I decided early on that if I rebuilt my life with hate and blame as the foundation, the person that suffers the most would be me. I didn't want those things – or my accident – to define me.

In hospital I soon learned that negativity took up energy. Sometimes there was a place for anger – it could be helpful in physio. But otherwise, it was wasted. So instead, I learned to take control of the things within my control and let go of the things that fell outside it.

It's a lesson I still live by today. As I mentioned earlier, my breathing may eventually deteriorate but rather than sit and wait, I've started a breathwork course. After working with a free dive expert, my breath hold record is now four minutes twenty-five seconds. My Everest is actually five minutes. I'm controlling what I can.

So that brings me to my final point:
LAUGHTER IS ALWAYS THE BEST MEDICINE.

You only have to spend time in palliative care or on a spinal ward to know that joy is often one of the last things to leave us. In my darkest moments, being able to laugh at myself never failed to soften the blow. Not just for me but for my loved ones. Like the north star, humour is the light I look for whenever I feel lost and is easily the best chance of finding my way home.

In the background, the director smiles broadly. He looks at David and nods reassuringly. This is going great.

DAVID:
So, that's it; the end of the talk. You might have come today thinking you had nothing in common with a forty-year-old quadriplegic, but I hope I've shown you we're not so very different.

We both have the same choice about the way we view and live our lives. If you look at me and feel pity and wish you could do something to help, do this: don't let these lessons go to waste. Go away and do your best to incorporate what I've told you into all parts of your life. Don't be afraid to feel. Don't wait to make plans. Your decisions won't always be the right ones, but they'll probably make great stories for you to recount around the dinner table.

Take it from The Boy Who Lived: when you get the chance, always choose life.

David waits a moment, his eyes looking straight down the barrel of the camera. He's smiling. Ahead of him, the director gives a thumbs up.

DIRECTOR:
David, that was—

DAVID:
Some story, right?

DIRECTOR:
Well . . .

Yeah.

Thanks for sharing. You OK?

Must be . . . tough talking through that.

DAVID:
Yeah. But what are you gonna do? Truth is, I <u>am</u> a victim, but I just refuse to see myself through that lens. You'll go fucking crazy otherwise. I just live in the now. The other day, I sat by my back gate, overlooking the park. I watched the sunset and listened to a country singer called Zach Bryan.

Really nice. I made the most of that moment. I could independently go outside and open the gate. I could breathe on my own. I could sit there on my own and have that space on my own. Yeah. I don't know how long

I'm gonna have that for, so it's important I make it
feel precious.

*The camera crew are wrapping up. It looks like filming is
over for the day.*

DAVID:
[SHOUTING OUT] You get it?

CAMERA OPERATOR:
Great. Yeah.

DIRECTOR:
Yeah, we got it. I mean. It was fantastic.

DAVID:
[SIGHING HAPPILY] Thank fuck for that. Telling my
story . . . It's *a lot*.

ACKNOWLEDGEMENTS

To my family: my Mum, Susan, and Dad, Andy, thank you for raising me with love, teaching me gratitude and humility, and for progressing me into life with faith and the knowledge that through love even the hardest of things can be endured. To my older brother Paul, my sister Suzanne and my nephews Sebastian and Callum, I hope life will always be kind to you and even when it's not, never forget to look for the light. To my youngest brother Adam, thank you for always being someone I can rely on and for loving me, despite how hard it is for you to share my pain.

To all my dear friends. I'm very fortunate to be able to say I cannot list you all. Thank you for always being there for me; I am humbled to receive the love and support from so many people, and I'll thank a few of them now.

Tommy, there are not enough pages in this book for me to express my gratitude on your continued commitment to helping me live my life. I'm pretty sure I've been in your arms as much as your own children. You have literally been my arms and legs, you've carried me up mountains, across beaches and through some of the hardest parts of my journey as a disabled man, and I couldn't love you more. You are a true example of what a best friend is.

Daniel Radcliffe, the whole world got to watch you grow up on the screen and I have got to watch you grow as a man. I consider it one of the greatest privileges to share life with you. I love you mate, keep smashing it as you always have.

Malgorzata, thank you for being my friend, caregiver and for putting up with me. Tom Di Cap, thank you for helping me see the world, for all the giggles from the inappropriate jokes that are behind us, and for the many more that will be in front of us. Jon Stevens, you are a kind, gentle soul who brings many gifts to my life as a friend and a work colleague, I look forward to many more bedtimes with you belting out ballads. Luke Smith, thank you for being another man I can rely on. I'm grateful for your friendship, your care and your kindness.

Marc Mailley, I'm so incredibly proud of all your achievements in life as a husband, a father and a professional, and I am honoured to call you one of my best friends. The sky is your limit so keep flying. Danny Lawrence, since we were twelve years old, we have been best friends. I am proud of the man you are, the man you have been and the man you will always be. Molly Lamb, thank you for being my sister, my friend, and someone I have been able to share the best and worst parts of life with. Love you, Mol. Amy Stares, thank you for helping me help others, producing my story and for sharing life with me. You are a great friend, an amazing mother and a talented creator. Never stop looking for stories to tell. Will Pike, thank you for being my candle in the darkest of places and for continuing to make me jealous of your exceptionally good hair. Sophie Barrington, thanks for your soft touch and warm heart.

There are a few people in my work life who have helped me in my career: my gymnastics coaches Nick Inns and Jeff Hewitt Davies, thank you for your life lessons and being my role models when I was growing up. Greg Powell, thank you for giving me the opportunity to fly, and for welcoming me into your family and they will always be a seat at my table for you. Thank you to Chris Columbus for all the fun and bringing Harry from the page to the screen. To J.K. Rowling for giving the world, the gift of magic.

To the worldwide stunt community, members of the British Stunt register and my film family, never underestimate the importance of good stories and great art.

ACKNOWLEDGEMENTS

Dan Hartley, thank you for sharing my story with the world. I'm so incredibly lucky to have had my documentary directed by a friend and you should be incredibly proud of all the good it is doing in the world.

Matt Allen, thank you for taking this journey with me in writing, our book now belongs to the world.

I would like to thank the NHS for saving my life, you are the parent every British citizen takes for granted. You have been there for us since the moment we were born, and you will be there for us until the very end. Thank you to all who work for the institution and all the caregivers in society who dedicate their lives to helping others live theirs.

To every human being in the world. We are all on this rock together, so let's try and look after this magnificent planet, forgive and be kind to one to another, protect the most vulnerable humans, plants and animals and pass on a better world to the children of tomorrow.

And finally, to all people across the disabled community: never accept the limitations society wrongly sets for us. Keep striving for change and, in the spirit of Harry Potter, never give up on hope.